MAY 09 2012

The Teaching for Social Justice Series

William Ayers—Series Editor
Therese Quinn—Associate Series Editor

The Assault on Public Education:
Confronting the Politics of
Corporate School Reform
WILLIAM H. WATKINS, EDITOR

Pedagogy of the Poor:
Building the Movement to End Poverty
WILLIE BAPTIST & JAN REHMANN

Grow Your Own Teachers:
Grassroots Change for Teacher Education
ELIZABETH A. SKINNER, MARIA TERESA
GARRETÓN, & BRIAN D. SCHULTZ, EDITORS

Girl Time: Literacy, Justice,
and the School-to-Prison Pipeline
MAISHA T. WINN

Holler If You Hear Me: The Education of a
Teacher and His Students, Second Edition
GREGORY MICHIE

Controversies in the Classroom:
A Radical Teacher Reader
JOSEPH ENTIN, ROBERT C. ROSEN,
& LEONARD VOGT, EDITORS

Spectacular Things Happen Along the Way:
Lessons from an Urban Classroom
BRIAN D. SCHULTZ

The Seduction of Common Sense:
How the Right Has Framed the Debate on
America's Schools
KEVIN K. KUMASHIRO

Teach Freedom: Education for Liberation
in the African-American Tradition
CHARLES M. PAYNE & CAROL SILLS
STRICKLAND, EDITORS

Social Studies for Social Justice:
Teaching Strategies for the Elementary
Classroom
RAHIMA C. WADE

Pledging Allegiance:
The Politics of Patriotism in America's Sc
JOEL WESTHEIMER, EDITOR

See You When We Get There:
Teaching for Change in Urban Schools
GREGORY MICHIE

Echoes of Brown:
Youth Documenting and Performing the Legacy
of *Brown v. Board of Education*
MICHELLE FINE

Writing in the Asylum:
Student Poets in City Schools
JENNIFER MCCORMICK

Teaching the Personal and the Political:
Essays on Hope and Justice
WILLIAM AYERS

Teaching Science for Social Justice
ANGELA CALABRESE BARTON, WITH
JASON L. ERMER, TANAHIA A. BURKETT,
& MARGERY D. OSBORNE

Putting the Children First:
The Changing Face of Newark's Public Schools
JONATHAN G. SILIN & CAROL LIPPMAN, EDITORS

Refusing Racism:
White Allies and the Struggle for Civil Rights
CYNTHIA STOKES BROWN

A School of Our Own: Parents, Power, and
Community at the East Harlem Block Schools
TOM RODERICK

The White Architects of Black Education:
Ideology and Power in America, 1865–1954
WILLIAM WATKINS

The Public Assault on America's Children:
Poverty, Violence, and Juvenile Injustice
VALERIE POLAKOW, EDITOR

Construction Sites: Excavating Race, Class, and
Gender Among Urban Youths
LOIS WEIS & MICHELLE FINE, EDITORS

Walking the Color Line:
The Art and Pr⸺⸻ ⸺acist Teaching

Schools
LONSKY, &
ITORS

stice:
⸺⸺ocracy and Education Reader
WILLIAM AYERS, JEAN ANN HUNT,
& THERESE QUINN

The Assault on Public Education

CONFRONTING THE POLITICS OF CORPORATE SCHOOL REFORM

EDITED BY

William H. Watkins

Foreword by Michael W. Apple

TEACHERS COLLEGE PRESS

Teachers College, Columbia University
New York and London

Published by Teachers College Press, 1234 Amsterdam Avenue, New York, NY 10027

Library of Congress Cataloging-in-Publication Data

The assault on public education : confronting the politics of corporate school reform / edited by William H. Watkins ; foreword by Michael W. Apple.
    p. cm. — (The teaching for social justice series)
    Includes bibliographical references and index.
    ISBN 978-0-8077-5254-8 (pbk. : alk. paper)
    1. Business and education—United States. 2. Education—Economic aspects—United States. 3. Education and state—United States. 4. Education—Aims and objectives—United States. 5. Public schools—United States. 6. Educational change—United States. I. Watkins, William H. (William Henry), 1946–
    LC1085.2.A78 2011
    371.010973—dc23   2011025500

ISBN 978-0-8077-5254-8 (paper)

Printed on acid-free paper
Manufactured in the United States of America

19 18 17 16 15 14 13 12   8 7 6 5 4 3 2 1

To the lasting memory of
Nana Baffour Amankwatia, II,
the "generous one" known to many as
Professor Asa Grant Hilliard, III,
and all that have and continue to give their lives
that we all learn and live in peace and justice.

Contents

Foreword *by Michael W. Apple*   ix

Acknowledgments   xv

Introduction   1
    William H. Watkins

1. **The New Social Order:**
   An Educator Looks at Economics, Politics, and Race   7
       William H. Watkins

2. **Neoliberal Urbanism, Race, and Urban School Reform**   33
       Pauline Lipman

3. **The Rise of Venture Philanthropy and the**
   Ongoing Neoliberal Assault on Public Education:
   The Eli and Edythe Broad Foundation   55
       Kenneth Saltman

4. **Test Today, Privatize Tomorrow:**
   Using Accountability to "Reform"
   Public Schools to Death   79
       Alfie Kohn

5. **The Neoliberal Agenda and the**
   Response of Teachers Unions   97
       Jack Gerson

6. **The Role of the Religious Right
    in Restructuring Education**   125

    Malila N. Robinson and Catherine A. Lugg

7. **Resuscitating Bad Science:
    Eugenics Past and Present**   143

    Ann G. Winfield

8. **"It's All About the Dollars":
    Charter Schools, Educational Policy,
    and the Racial Market in New Orleans**   160

    Kristen L. Buras

9. **Re-Imagining Public Education**   189

    William H. Watkins

About the Editor and the Contributors   193

Index   196

Foreword

One of the many tasks in which committed critical scholar/activists in education must engage is to "bear witness" to what is happening; to uncover what dominant groups wish to hide (Apple, 2010). If this task isn't taken as seriously as it deserves, what we see, and just as crucially what we *do not* see, will be determined by groups whose agendas often are expressly opposed to an education that is worthy of its name. This is especially the case now when we constantly are being told that so much that is wrong with this society can be laid at the feet of our public education system and the people who labor under such difficult conditions in it. The task of bearing witness is something that *The Assault on Public Education* does indeed take seriously.

Across the political spectrum, it is widely recognized that there is a crisis in education. Nearly everyone agrees that something must be done to make it more responsive and more effective. Of course, a key set of questions is: Responsive to what and to whom? Effective at what? And whose voices will be heard in asking and answering these questions? These are among the most crucial questions one can ask about education today, and they are among the questions that guide the book you are about to read.

Let us be honest. The educational crisis is real—especially for the poor and oppressed. But, as usual, dominant groups have used such "crisis talk" to shift the discussion onto their own terrain. Those of us who lived through the years of No Child Left Behind, and its damaging effects on education, hoped there would be a major shift in educational policies. The threat of privatization would no longer hang over schools. Curricula would no longer be made up simply of low-level facts to be mastered for seemingly mindless tests. Teachers would no longer have to spend weeks doing nothing but test preparation with their students. Poor children of color would no longer be so over-represented in special education classes, shunted there as an excuse for not dealing with the realities of racism in the larger society. Schools finally would get the resources they needed to try to compensate for the loss of jobs, ever-increasing impoverishment, lack of health care, massive rates of incarceration, and loss of hope in the communities that they served. A richer and more vital vision of education would replace the eviscerated vision of education that reigned supreme.

Ah yes, all would change. And even if all did not change, we would see very different approaches to education than those that had dominated the previous years. Some things have changed. But much still remains the same.

One of the major reasons for the continuation of dominant discourse and policies is that the very nature of our common sense about education is constantly being altered. This is largely the result of the power of particular groups who understand that if they can change the basic ways we think about our society and its institutions—and especially about our place in these institutions—they can create a set of policies that will profoundly benefit themselves more than anyone else. Dominant groups have actively engaged in a vast social/pedagogical process, one in which what counts as a good school, good knowledge, good teaching, and good learning is being radically transformed.

Let me say more about this process. In a large number of countries, a complex alliance and power bloc have been formed that have increasing influence in education and all things social. The power bloc, what I have called *conservative modernization*, combines four major groups (Apple, 2006). The first and the strongest one includes multiple factions of capital who are committed to neoliberal marketized solutions to educational problems. For them, private is necessarily good and public is necessarily bad. Democracy—a key word in how we think about our institutions and our place in them (Foner, 1998)—is reduced to consumption practices. The world becomes a vast supermarket, one in which those with economic and cultural capital are advantaged in nearly every sector of society. Choice in a market replaces more collective and more political actions. *Thin* democracy replaces *thick* democracy. This demobilizes crucial progressive social movements that have been the driving force behind nearly all of the democratic changes in this society and in our schools.

In education, this position is grounded in the belief that the more we marketize, the more we bring corporate models into education; and the more we can hold schools', administrators', and teachers' feet to the fire of competition, the better they will be. There actually is very little evidence to support this contention—and a good deal of evidence that it increases inequality (see Apple, 2006; Lipman, 2011). But neoliberalism continues to act as something like a religion in that it seems to be impervious to empirical evidence, even as the crisis that it has created in the economy and in communities constantly documents its failures in every moment of our collective and individual lives.

The second most powerful group in this alliance is neoconservatives who want a "return" to higher standards and a "common culture." In the face of diasporic populations who are making the United States a vast and impressive experiment in continual cultural creation, they are committed to a conservative culturally restorative project, pressing for a return to an imposed sense of nation and tradition that is based on a fear of "pollution" from the culture and the body of those whom they consider the "Others." That there is a crucial and partly hidden (at least to some people) dynamic of race at work here is not unimportant, to say the least (Gillborn, 2008; Leonardo, 2009; Lipman, 2011). Neoconservatives assume something that isn't there, a consensus on what should be "official" knowledge. They thereby evacuate one of the most significant questions that should be asked in our schools: What and whose knowledge should we teach? In their certainty over what a common culture is supposed to be, they ignore a key element in this supposed commonness. What is common is that we disagree. Indeed, what needs to be "the common" is the constant democratic and deliberative process of asking the question of what is common (Williams, 1989).

A third key element in conservative modernization is composed of authoritarian populist religious conservatives who are deeply worried about secularity and the preservation of their own traditions. They too wish to impose a "common." For them, "the people" must decide. But there are anointed people and those who are not. Only when a particular reading of Christianity is put back in its rightful place as the guiding project of all of our institutions and interactions will we be able to once again claim that this is "God's country." In the process, they inaccurately construct themselves as the "new oppressed," as people whose identities and cultures are ignored by or attacked in schools and the media. It is not an accident that one of the fastest growing educational movements right now is home schooling (Apple, 2006; Apple & Buras, 2006). While the home schooling movement is varied, these decisions are often driven by conservative attacks on public schools and once again by fear of the "Other."

Finally, a crucial part of this ideological umbrella is a particular fraction of the professionally and managerially oriented new middle class. This group is made up of people who are committed to the ideology and techniques of accountability, measurement, and the "new managerialism," to what has been called "audit culture" (Apple, 2006; Leys, 2003). If I may be permitted to speak a bit too cutely perhaps; for them, if it moves in classrooms, measure it. And if it hasn't moved yet, measure it anyway in case it moves tomorrow. They too are true believers, ones who believe that in installing such procedures and rules, they are "helping." For them, more evidence on schools', teachers', and students' performance—usually based simply on the limited data generated by test scores—will solve our problems, even though once again there is just as much evidence that this too can create as many problems as it supposedly solves (Gillborn & Youdell, 2000; Valenzuela, 2005). Demonstrating that one is "acting correctly" according to externally imposed criteria is the norm. "Perform or die" almost seems to be their motto.

While there are clear tensions and conflicts within this alliance, in general its overall aims are to provide the educational conditions believed necessary both for increasing international competitiveness, profit, and discipline, and for returning us to a romanticized past of the "ideal" home, family, and school.

This new alliance has integrated education into a wider set of ideological commitments. The objectives in education are the same as those that guide its economic and social welfare goals. They include the dramatic expansion of that eloquent fiction, the free market; the drastic reduction of government responsibility for social needs; the reinforcement of intensely competitive structures of mobility, both inside and outside the school; the lowering of people's expectations for economic security; the "disciplining" of culture and the body; and the popularization of what is clearly a form of social Darwinist thinking. All of these tendencies and more are visible in the chapters included in this book.

The seemingly contradictory discourse of competition, markets, and choice on the one hand, and accountability, performance objectives, standards, national testing, and national curriculum on the other, has created a situation in which it is hard to hear anything else. Even though these seem to embody different tendencies, actually they oddly reinforce one another and help cement conservative educational positions into our daily lives. The results are not pretty.

Before I became a university professor I was an elementary and secondary school teacher and the president of a teachers union. Thus, like many of the people included in this book, part of my commitment has always been to work at the intersections of theory, policy, and practice and to expand the sphere of critical educational efforts at each of these levels. I mention this because in my work with schools, teachers, social movements, and community activists, I have been deeply impressed with the courage of committed educators, community activists, and students in these schools and communities. Such courage is even more important today.

As *The Assault on Public Education* makes so very clear, throughout the United States—and in many other nations as well—we are witnessing the growth of a destructive set of policies in education and the larger society. Neoliberal policies of privatization and marketization, and the attacks on labor that so often accompany them—in combination with neoconservative cultural policies that involve a return to elitist and anti-democratic knowledge—are having truly damaging effects. In the face of such movements and tendencies, educators and social activists in countries throughout the world have had to mobilize to stop the spread of such tendencies.

Why is this important? Perhaps because the effects of conservative modernization are increasingly visible in education. As I and many others have shown, neoliberal and neoconservative policies in particular, in concert with new managerial impulses, do not interrupt the stratification of education, except for a very limited group of students. Instead, as study after study has made clear, and as this book so clearly demonstrates, the ultimate results do not reflect the rhetoric so widely circulated by dominant groups. Poor and working-class children and many children of color, and their knowledge and histories, are even more marginalized. The vast majority of these same children either gain no benefits whatsoever or they and their schools are left in even worse condition than before.

Yet, this is not all. It is also clear that there are some very damaging effects on teachers and administrators. Neoliberal and neoconservative policies create worse, not better, conditions in terms of workload, pressure, and lack of resources for the educators who work in the schools that are now suffering from unremitting attacks. This is powerfully visible in another volume recently published by Teachers College Press, *Pedagogy, Policy, and the Privatized City* (Buras et al., 2010), which takes New Orleans as a case in point of the destructive effects of such policies.

But this is still not all. Such policies also reinstall a vision of curriculum that perhaps is best described using Bourdieu's (1986) concept of "symbolic violence." In the curricular policies that emanate from these conservative movements, neither the subaltern nor teachers have a significant voice (Apple & Buras, 2006).

The issue of teachers is significant. Those who favor the odd combination of marketization on the one hand and even tighter control of the curriculum and testing on the other hand employ the language of democracy and responsiveness. Yet, hidden beneath this fine-sounding, and often cynical, rhetoric is an attack on teachers and on teachers unions. Underneath their language is a powerful antipathy to public employees. This should be deeply distressing to all of us, since any institution that acts in dismissive and undemocratic ways toward the employees who work in it every day cannot be considered democratic.

Committed educators must stand together to fight against the antidemocratic restructuring that we are witnessing. Together, nationally and internationally, we can and must build a collective movement that supports an education that is respectful both of our teachers and of all of our students and the communities from where they come—and that denies neoliberals and neoconservatives the right to change our societies in ways that increase the advantage of those who already have economic, social, and cultural capital. As my and others' experiences in this nation and in so many other ones have so powerfully shown, there is great risk right now. Yet these experiences also have shown that even in the face of organized attacks, the long struggle to build and defend an education that is worthy of its name continues (Apple, 2010; Apple et al., 2003).

Thus, we should take the position of being "an optimist with no illusions." These are difficult times, but these are also times when it is equally visible that a large number of educators and cultural and political activists in the United States and elsewhere are deeply committed to both defending and building policies and practices in curriculum, pedagogy, and evaluation that expand the sphere of democratic and critical dialogue and keep emancipatory educational possibilities alive. *The Assault on Public Education* provides us with a set of articulate analyses of what the future likely will hold if we do not engage in the hard and committed labor of countering these dangerous tendencies today.

—Michael W. Apple
John Bascom Professor of Curriculum and Instruction and
Educational Policy Studies, University of Wisconsin, Madison

REFERENCES

Apple, M. W. (2006). *Educating the "right" way: Markets, standards, God, and inequality* (2nd ed.). New York: Routledge.

Apple, M. W. (Ed.). (2010). *Global crises, social justice, and education*. New York: Routledge.

Apple, M. W., Aasen, P., Cho, M. K., Ganden, L. A., Oliver, A., Sung, Y. K., Tavares, H., & Wong, T-H. (2003). *The state and the politics of knowledge*. New York: Routledge.

Apple, M. W., & Buras, K. L. (Eds.). (2006). *The subaltern speak: Curriculum, power, and educational struggles*. New York: Routledge.

Bourdieu, P. (1986). *Distinction*. Cambridge, MA: Harvard University Press.

Buras, K. L., Randels, J., Salaam, K. Y., & Students at the Center. (Eds.). (2010). *Pedagogy, policy, and the privatized city: Stories of dispossession and defiance from New Orleans*. New York: Teachers College Press.

Foner, E. (1998). *The story of American freedom*. New York: Norton.

Gillborn, D. (2008). *Racism and education: Coincidence or conspiracy?* New York: Routledge.

Gillborn, D., & Youdell, D. (2000). *Rationing education: Policy, practice, reform, and equity*. Philadelphia: Open University Press.

Leonardo, Z. (2009). *Race, whiteness, and education*. New York: Routledge.

Leys, C. (2003). *Market-driven politics: Neoliberal democracy and the public interest*. New York: Verso.

Lipman, P. (2011). *The new political economy of urban education: Neoliberalism, race, and the right to the city*. New York: Routledge.

Valenzuela, A. (Ed.). (2005). *Leaving children behind*. Albany: State University of New York Press.

Williams, R. (1989). *Resources of hope*. New York: Verso.

Acknowledgments

The battle to save universal, free, and tax-supported public education is well underway. Powerful corporate forces once again tell us that what is good for business, is good for all of us. The lives and futures of millions are at stake. We acknowledge the courageous teachers, parents, and students who soldier on in the cause of just and equitable education for all.

Thanks go to *Workplace: A Journal for Academic Labor* for permission to reprint Professor Saltman's article and to Alfie Kohn for permission to reprint "Test Today, Privatize Tomorrow." Additional gratitude to Christine Olson, University of Illinois at Chicago, for computer support.

Introduction

William H. Watkins

OUR CHANGING WORLD

Dramatic changes are underway in America and the world. The physical and ideological landscape of the nation is being reconfigured. Bedrock institutions and the traditions of yesteryear have disappeared or have been transformed. New and more intense financial accumulation is at the heart of major, even monumental, restructuring. Changes in technology, political philosophy, and the distribution of wealth and power now reorganize government, cities, work, laws, schools, opportunities, rights, and the fabric of our democracy.

The changes are confusing to many people, if not most. In addition to the economic and political changes already underway, the more recent and un-anticipated "Great Recession" has turned into the great obsession. Confusion has turned to fear as ordinary people are faced with ongoing financial crises, decline, and uncertain futures. The economic crisis is inextricably connected to social crises. Confounded and impatient Americans now question the belief that our society is self-correcting.

The computer chip has brought us to the precipice of the unseen. Millions are displaced as commodities can now be produced with far fewer workers. For the first time in human history, the obsolescence of human labor is foreseeable. The nature of work, its organization, and the labor market are forever altered.

The combined triumph of market economics, neoliberalism, and privatization has re-engineered banking, lending, regulation, and the "safety net." We are now under the supreme protection of the "hidden hand" and "magic" of the market.

The wealth gap in America and the world has never been greater. While a handful accumulate unimaginable riches, others have moved from relative to absolute poverty. Pauperization has emerged as a key theme in American life.

"FIXING" THE SCHOOLS

Public education is one of those institutions being altered in the new social order. Public education exists within, not outside, this context. Schooling is undergoing major reform and transformation. Powerful hegemonic forces have appropriated the legitimate concerns of those underserved and unhappy with schools. "Fixing" the nation's schools is high on the corporate agenda as corporations fund major educational initiatives. Corporate education "reformer" Bill Gates can now commit more discretionary money annually to education than the United States Department of Education. Barons of wealth, in effect, now make public policy.

With little public input, corporations and foundations now guide school reorganization. They are fashioning a new America to conform to their economic and political ideology. School "reform" is a major target in the scheme. Employing the language of democracy and distress, corporate reformers mask tyrannical political actions. The proposed sweeping changes inevitably disrupt the long-cherished concept of the neighborhood school. Great concern is now expressed about the social consequences of this enterprise.

A thorough understanding of their plan is required.

Corporate ideology influences the writing of new federal legislation, the creation of nontraditional schools, the lambasting of colleges of education, and the advocacy of curriculum change without engaged democratic debate. The mugging of public education is engineered by "reformers" deeply committed to the market vision. School reform is inextricably connected to the reconfiguration of the labor market, urban gentrification, and the new social order.

Nested within sociopolitical and economic lenses, this book is about school, power, race, society, justice, and the future. The consequences of school reform are earthshaking. The restructuring of public schools will likely dismantle universal public education as we know it and "de-school" significant populations of Black, Brown, and poor people. School closings and reconfigurations are now a fact of life in major American cities. This book provides a deep critical examination of the attack on universal, open, and free education now called school "reform."

EMBRACING THE "CRITICAL" TRADITION

Conceptually, this book is driven by the critical tradition. Many trees have been destroyed explicating the tenets and relevance of critical theory and its broader applications, which I prefer to call *critical studies*. Critical studies have opened academic disciplines, most often within the social sciences and humanities, to further pursue issues of race, class, power, gender, and exclusion. "Counter-stories" often result from critical inquiry. In the broadest terms, the field of education and its subfield, curriculum study, recognize critical studies as originating in early 20th-century populist, progressive, Frankfort School, Marxian, neo-Marxian, feminist, revisionist, anti-canonical, and iconoclastic discourses. Perhaps there is consensus that critical studies respond to the applications of (capitalist) hegemony, totalitarianism, colonialism, racism, paternalism, and domination.

Leonardo (2009) has surveyed critical social thought, its origins, definitions, denominations, contributors, and promise. He writes: "Critical social theory [henceforth CST] is a multidisciplinary framework with the implicit goal of advancing the emancipatory function of knowledge" (p. 13). He goes on to argue that CST is tied to both theory and practice. It is wedded to notions of equity, social justice, and freedom.

Confronting the master narrative and the hegemonic canon, the critical tradition has informed us about politics, race, gender, and so on. Critical studies fuel gender studies, ethnic studies, cultural studies, revisionist historiography, and more. The use of political economy as part of the "critical" tradition is indispensable to understanding school dynamics.

Political economy is widely employed as an analytical tool in this volume. Often overlooked or linked exclusively to the Marxian tradition, political economy turns our attention to the organization and distribution of wealth, the labor market, the impact of technology, and exploitation. Critical political economy points to the wielding of wealth as power to influence public policy.

This book is designed to both inform and serve as an organizing tool for teachers, parents, students, and citizens committed to genuine public education. The text is candid and strident. We name names and speak truth to power. It is our hope that this work will contribute to an informed conversation and debate on the future of schooling in America.

ORGANIZATION AND THEMES FOR THIS BOOK

The organizing thesis of this volume holds that the congealing of neoliberalism, techno-globalism, authoritarian plutocracy, and crisis is reconfiguring public education and other institutions. Public education, as we know it, is under threat. This book explores the ideas, institutional forces, and people reshaping our world and our schools.

The chapter authors address several questions. How are our world, our country, and our schools changing? Who benefits? Who loses? What philosophies

are involved? What people and institutions are involved? How can public education be not only saved but re-imagined?

This authoritative and interdisciplinary book relies on data and analysis
from university professors, teachers, researchers, and "ordinary" people. The
text explores and critiques salient issues in corporate school reform. The authors, experts in their field, look to unearth both actors and actions. The powerful forces behind school "reform" are shown to be driven by partisan politics
and vested interests. The perpetuation of inequity, racism, and privilege is the
inevitable outcome of the project of corporate school reform.

In Chapter 1, I, a book editor and professor, set the tone for the book. In accessible language, I draw from sociopolitical and economic discourses to address
foundational questions. This chapter offers scope and context for the volume. It
defines the new social order. Utilizing supporting data, it focuses on de-industrialization, changes in production, the new role of financial speculation, displacement, new wealth, new power arrangements, new racial politics, and new poverty.
The sociopolitical context for proposed school "reform" is presented.

In Chapter 2, noted urban education scholar Pauline Lipman argues that
current urban school reforms are integrally linked to neoliberal economic and
political processes that are redefining U.S. cities. In this highly racialized process, gentrification, tourism, downtown development, and leisure zones for
the affluent are built over and against working-class communities of color. She
holds that the neoliberal city is economically, socially, and spatially unequal.
Consumption-based development, alongside shifts from public investment in
social welfare to private development projects, displaces working-class people
and communities of color, which often are contained in ghettoized communities. Using Chicago as a case study, she concludes that the marketization of
urban schools through "choice" and privatization and the regulation of students
of color through high-stakes testing, standardized knowledge, regimented instruction, military schools, and basic skills schools all contribute to corporate
domination of the city and the regulation of people of color, particularly youth.

Kenneth Saltman in Chapter 3 explores "venture philanthropy," the project
of monied individuals and corporations shaping "new" educational organizations and policy. The Broad family, profiled here, is among the leaders in this
effort. The prospect of an entirely new and profitable industry, combined with
neoliberal economic and political philosophy, has lured corporate people into
the business of schools. The chapter illustrates how a policy strategy modeled
on corporate hedge funds uses private money to steer public policy toward new
"theories" of learning and leadership. The vision of Broad, Gates, and the other venture philanthropists is to replace public schools, teacher education, and
educational leadership with privatized models run by corporate and military

leaders. Central to this project is an effort to reduce the value of teaching and learning to that which can be numerically quantified, tested, and replicated. This poses a threat to the possibility of public schools functioning as critical and intellectual sites for the expansion of egalitarian social relations. These projects encourage a form of teaching that is de-skilled and de-professionalized. The corporate educational reforms of the venture philanthropists create a new two-tiered system, with short-term profits for investors made possible by skimming public tax money that could be going back into public schooling. At stake in these reforms are the questions of how the public is subsidizing the abdication of control over public school governance and practice, and what kinds of oppositional action can set the stage for radically democratizing public school finance, governance, and pedagogy.

Alfie Kohn has dedicated a lifetime of scholarship to the criticism of testing and the standards movement. Chapter 4, his reprised article, offers a no holds barred critique of No Child Left Behind and mandatory standardized testing, noting the consequences for urban and marginalized students. Kohn describes how the corporate privatizers appropriate the rhetoric of freedom and construct a narrative of failure to justify their plan for "reform." The strident attack on teacher training is included in their rhetoric. He dramatizes the wedding of "accountability" to privatization. Of great importance, Kohn connects the standards and testing "movement" to recent attacks on colleges of education.

Working people in America fought and died for the right to form unions and bargain collectively. Although sometimes compromised, unions generally have tried to protect the rights of workers. Corporate neoliberalism wages all-out war on unions in general and teachers unions in particular. Chapter 5 is written by Jack Gerson, an Oakland high school teacher and union activist. With great depth of understanding, he examines the impact of neoliberal corporate school "reform" on teachers unions. This threat has draconian consequences for teachers, one of our nation's most valuable assets, but also among the most undervalued and de-professionalized professionals in American society.

Chapters 6 and 7 offer two looks at powerful social ideology employed in the assault on public education. In this political climate, the religious right has gathered momentum and extensive resources. Religion has always been a political and cultural football in America, and it has been central in social, political, and educational debates dating to colonial days. Religious opportunists denounced Elvis Presley and Rock & Roll as the devil's music. The killing of women's choice activists has been "justified" on religious grounds. Even wars are waged in the name of God. In Chapter 6, Malila Robinson and Catherine Lugg examine how religion has been appropriated by the hard "right" in its condemnation of prevailing "secular" education. The right's interest in morality and family is joined to its vision of schooling. The chapter offers thoughtful insights into the social and political agenda of the "religious right" in reshaping public education.

No discussion of education in America is complete without reference to race. Race has been a barometer of privilege and position since the early 1600s. America's racial concerns remain a complicated phenomenon, especially in a society undergoing re-engineering. Scientific racism and eugenics, past and present, have been used to endorse progressive pedagogical and disciplinary practices that, in practice, operate to define and enforce access in society. The racial discourse has monumental consequences. It shapes the debate on who should live and die, equitable access to social resources, reproductive technology (including cloning), the application of civil rights, and perhaps most obviously, the current frenetic compulsion to measure, test, and hold students "accountable." In Chapter 7 eugenics scholar Ann Winfield reveals deep-seated foundational ideology influencing societal and educational structuring.

The destruction of public education, as we know it, has already begun. Following Hurricane Katrina, the entire New Orleans public school system was reconstituted. New governance, charter schools, and a diminished teachers union are featured in the new system. Accountant Paul Vallas, former CEO of Philadelphia and Chicago school systems, was brought in to create the school system of the future. In Chapter 8, Kristen Buras offers an insider's view of the New Orleans debacle. She exposes the racial politics and "free" market ideology driving that city's charter school movement.

Finally, I sum up what is at stake. Simply stated, the bounty of the earth, and who controls it, provides the theatre and context of all human history. The battle between the haves and have-nots, the propertied and propertyless, the owners and workers, and the powerful and powerless continues to dominate human history. The battle for public education has apocalyptic consequences. Will education become a "reconstructionist," liberatory, and ethical force that fosters social equity, enlightenment, and individual self-realization, or will the corporate vision prevail? What propositions and ideas might lead to a more just system of public education? The fight for truly public education might join the labor, women's, and civil rights movements as one of the great social movements in America.

REFERENCE

Leonardo, Z. (2009). *Race, whiteness, and education*. New York: Routledge.

CHAPTER 1

The New Social Order

An Educator Looks at Economics, Politics, and Race

William H. Watkins

I am a knowledge worker and political activist. My research and writings focus on questions of power, race, and education. More narrowly, I am interested in the connections of the sociopolitical, economic, and racial arrangements of society to the shaping of ideology, knowledge, and culture. In this chapter, I say little directly about education but rather seek to explore the changing political environment and the new social order.

I propose this chapter as a kind of "state of the union" discussion. While our politicians usually tell us the union is strong but we still have work to do, the story is far more complicated. Our country and the world are in the throes of monumental economic, political, social, and cultural changes. A page of history has been turned. As one concerned with schooling and knowledge selection, I want to understand how the new social order might impact public education.

Major surgery is proposed for public education. While other examinations explore "crisis," "school failure," the "achievement gap," racist practices, funding inequities, teacher preparation, leadership, and organizational issues, this project turns to the broad sociopolitical, economic, and ideological factors reshaping society and public education.

My argument is straightforward. The political economy of our country has changed once again. Human society, property relations, wealth distribution, power, and especially the labor market were reorganized around hand tools and reorganized again around the steam engine. We are now being organized around digital technology. We have moved into a new era of techno-globalism where the political ideology of neoliberalism prevails. Powerful economic forces, a plutocracy, now restructure social and institutional life in America. Those same powerful forces seek to destroy old institutions incapable of realizing their desires. In the process American "democracy" has become a performance where the public are spectators.

Universal public education, as we have known it, is under threat. The plutocrats want a new educational system that creates a technocratic elite, presumably allowing the United States to better compete and continue to dominate the globalized world economy. This chapter will try to explain in understandable language what is going on. Several questions will be addressed: How is America changing? Why is America changing? Who is making these changes? How will public education be impacted?

AMERICA IN TRANSITION:
A FRIGHTENING OVERVIEW

This nation is being jolted as millions are physically and psychologically displaced. What appeared a short time ago to be calm, stability, predictability, and prosperity has turned into a "ball of confusion." Our sacred cows are now shattered. Yesterday's corporate vice president may be today's grocery store bagboy. Parts of the Constitution and its Bill of Rights are challenged by the Patriot Act. The "war on terror" hysteria and detention issues at Guantanamo, for example, have reopened legal discussions on the jailing of citizens without the rights to habeas corpus and counsel. A handful of greedy corporations and banks bogart the nation's wealth and cause immeasurable suffering. Good-paying jobs in manufacturing are replaced by low-paying service sector positions. Our pensions and savings, once considered untouchable, are now vanishing into thin air. Political elections, once thought fair, now are routinely tainted by "smart" machines, crookery, financial irregularities, and uncertainty. Our neighborhood schools, which served generations of families, are mysteriously closing. Automated telephone messages now "answer" our pleas for help and information. Even the sanctity and protections of home ownership are disrupted as high courts declare that private property can now be legally and forcibly "purchased" by Wal-Mart. Surgically inserted computer chips soon might monitor every move of every person born in this country. Millions go hungry, homeless, and sick in a society of great affluence and resources. Peace and tranquility are threatened by the specter of crises and "permanent war" (Bacevich, 2010). America has moved into a new social order.

The social order is the representation of politics, economics, culture, racial/ ethnic relations, and morality, among other things. In America the social order is especially complex owing to the nation's history, diversity, dynamism, and ever-changing social structure. The dominant mode of production most often shapes the social order. New methods of production help create a new order as they require the destruction of the old order and old basis for society.

Farm life created agrarianism. The machine age created industrialization. The tools of production help name the social order as the economy helps define social and institutional life. While the economy is not the sole determinant of social life, it describes how the wealth is organized and how people earn a living, and it helps forge institutional and attitudinal behavior. Today, some own but don't work; others work but don't own. Owners and workers inevitably see the world differently.

In capitalist America, for example, capitalism dominates the occupational, governmental, cultural, religious, and intellectual institutions of society. Capitalism has undergone many changes. Early capitalism involved small-scale production, trade, and competition. Small-scale production turned into its opposite, large-scale production, that is, monopoly replaced competition (Magdoff, 1978). The early 20th century ushered in the merging of industrial capital with banking to create large-scale corporate finance capitalism (Lenin, 1916/1939). By the end of the 20th century, de-industrialization occurred. Speculative capitalism grew as huge fortunes were made in stocks, futures, hedge funds, derivatives, credit swaps, and other creative schemes. The capitalist class accumulates wealth on the basis of the labor of the world's people, speculates on and profits from debt, manipulates the world's currencies, and now privatizes public assets.

The ethos of competition, accumulation, consumerism, privilege, and ethnic antagonism accompanies all the stages of capitalism. While opposition and social movements exist, the capitalists "rule the roost" because they control the state. The state is defined as the military, the prisons, the courts, the police, the schools, the corporate media, and the means of people management, punishment, and control.

What is happening in the 21st century? How can we make sense of this crazy world where even the top economists and theorists don't agree. Again we turn to the changing economy for clues.

TECHNO-GLOBALIZATION: REORDERING THE WORLD

The Computer Chip: A New Techno-Economic Paradigm

Historians one day might see circa 1980 as the watershed of a new economic and political world order. Several dramatic events occurred. First, the technological revolution became firmly established. The computer chip, introduced in the 1970s, forever altered human labor and human relations. The "chip," which could activate machinery, meant that for the first time production, the basis of all economies, could occur without human labor. Traditional concepts of employment, wages, and value were scrapped as millions were and are soon to be displaced. Chip technology accompanies robotics, fiber-optics, lasers, and magnets in the creation of a new world.

Second, the marketplace profoundly affected globalization. Expanded productive capacity created fierce competition and reliance on high-tech methods. Industrial production, once concentrated in the West, has been dispersed and compartmentalized throughout the world. The only rule is that production moves to its cheapest source. "Third world" children now manufacture many of our daily commodities for pennies per day. There no longer exists a logical or balanced relationship between production and consumption. Often those who manufacture goods can never buy those goods.

Money, Money, Money

The highly regarded United Nations report *The World Distribution of Household Wealth* (Davies, Sandstrom, & Shorrocks, 2006), alongside many supporting studies, reports that the richest 1% of adults own 40% of the world's assets, the richest 2% of adults own 50% of the world's assets, and the richest 10% of adults own 85% of the world's assets.

Concentrated wealth is at the heart of the new social and economic order. One hundred fifty plus years of corporate profit accumulation have created an extreme pyramid. The data from United Nations research studies (UNU-WIDER, 2010) mathematically demonstrate that Bill Gates, the Walton family, and Warren Buffett possess more wealth than the combined countries of Afghanistan, Angola, Bangladesh, Benin, Bhutan, Burkina Faso, Burundi, Cambodia, Cape Verde, Central African Republic, Chad, Comoros, Republic of Congo, Djibouti, Equatorial Guinea, Eritrea, Ethiopia, Gambia, Guinea, Guinea-Bissau, Haiti, Kiribati, Laos, Lesotho, Madagascar, Malawi, Maldives, Mali, Mauritius, Mozambique, Myanmar (Burma), Nepal, Niger, Rwanda, Samoa, Sierra Leone,

Solomon Islands, Somalia, Sudan, Tanzania, Togo, Tuvalu, Uganda, Yemen, and Zimbabwe.

Wolff (2000) informs us that the net worth of the top 1% of wage earners in the United States comes to $10,204,000. The average net worth of the bottom 40% is $1,900. Mishel, Bernstein, and Allegretto (2007) report that the wealthiest 10% of the U.S. population now own nine-tenths of all stocks.

Another indicator of the new plutocracy is the dramatic rise in the salaries of CEOs. Far outstripping the salary increases of production workers, they have skyrocketed into the stratosphere even though some companies are in or near bankruptcy proceedings. Equilar, Inc., an executive compensation research firm based in Redwood Shores, CA, provided data to the *Chicago Tribune* (2010) on the annual cash and stock option compensation of leading corporate CEOs in Chicago. Included are Miles D. White, Abbott Laboratories, $26.2 million; W. James McNerney, Jr., Boeing, $19.4 million; Irene Rosenfeld, Kraft Foods, $26.3 million; James A. Skinner, McDonald's, $17.6 million; Thomas J. Wilson, Allstate Insurance, $10.4 million; Patricia A. Woertz, Archer Daniels Midland, $15 million; and Brenda C. Barnes, Sara Lee, $12.5 million. *Forbes* (2005) reported that United Healthcare CEO William W. McGuire earned $124.8 million in 2005. *Forbes* (2005) stated:

> The heads of America's 500 biggest companies received an aggregate 54% pay raise last year. As a group, their total compensation amounted to $5.1 billion, versus $3.3 billion in fiscal 2003. (p. 1)

Anyone exposed to the 2000 census data might not believe they were describing the United States. One-fifth of all children now live below the poverty level. The median wage of former welfare recipients is $6.61 per hour. Ninety percent of former welfare recipients do not own a vehicle. Median annual income for individuals with less than a 9th-grade education is $17,261. For those with 9–12 years of education (no diploma), the figure is $21,737. Approximately 22 million White people live below the poverty level. Nearly 8.5 million African Americans live in poverty. The startling figures go on and on. Census data from 2010 will likely reveal increased pauperization. The economic recession of 2008 has elevated the misery. Currently national unemployment exceeds 9.5%, alongside the uncounted who have given up on obtaining employment or simply live for years with family money earners.

The emergence of speculative capitalism has significantly altered world commerce. Banks and the "banksters" have become all-powerful in the 21st century. Financial speculation in stocks, bonds, futures, derivatives, credit swaps, and other ventures have reorganized the distribution of wealth. Nearly one and one-half trillion dollars pass through clearinghouses every day. Financial "ventures" have become the source of great profit and sometimes great disappointment. A redistribution of the wealth is underway whereby the top 1% of the population in the United States now controls nearly half of the nation's wealth. Similar accumulations occur in the global environment. What drives globalization? What does it mean? Who benefits from it? Who loses? How did we get to this place?

Technology, Displacement, Globalism, and Change

The new labor-replacing methods of production lower the rate of profit and expel workers from the economy. As digitization replaces whole categories of work, it is shaping the world economy around mobile capital, cheap labor, debt, and speculation.

Technology displaces workers, making labor cheap. The immense surplus value circulating globally is produced off the backs of a smaller and smaller percentage of workers who are unable to purchase the commodities they produce because they are paid wages that keep them and their families living in poverty. One half of the world's children live in poverty. Some 3 billion people—nearly half the world—live on less than $2 per day. In addition, electronic technology replaces workers in production. With fewer and fewer workers earning sufficient income to allow them to purchase commodities, the economic foundations of the capitalist system are cracking.

Debt is exploding. Credit makes up the difference between what is earned and what is needed. This goes for governments as well as for individual workers.

Financial speculation is expanding. The thirst for investment is unquenchable. Financial and speculative capitalists thrive on our debt more than on our ability to work. The growing predominance of speculative capital is beginning to shape social and political life.

Credit creation, consumer debt, and fictitious or assumed wealth temporarily prop up the economy, but this is a false and fragile foundation. As the value of labor power continues toward zero, every advance of speculative capital or debt increases the gap between wealth and poverty both at home and around the world.

Capital from everywhere forces open markets anywhere. Although the world's capital is increasingly mobile, the United States continues its drive for political domination. The drive for national domination over globally integrated capital and the geopolitical battle for control of strategic resources like oil accelerate political instability and the danger of war. Nuclear weapons raise the stakes of that danger.

While the capitalists of the world battle over who will dominate the world economy and how, they are united around the need to maintain their economic and political supremacy over the growing global class of poor.

The global economy stands on a fragile foundation. The political struggle for control and domination is intensifying and spreading instability. War, human displacement, and destruction are spreading and escalating with horrifying consequences for the peoples of the world. Neither the American economy nor the American worker is immune. The social and political results could take some time to mature, or events could move very quickly. Let us look a little deeper into the changing dynamics of work in America.

From Fordism to Flexible Production

Reaching a high level of refinement and efficiency, the Fordist assembly line paradigm had shortcomings. All parts had to be made to fit together before assembly. The line involved continuous, uninterrupted perfected production. A centralized venue imposed a rigidity to the process of production. In effect, the assembly line became almost too efficient, producing far more than the market demanded. Market economists refer to this as a problem of economies of scale. Marxists call it the crisis of overproduction.

Flexible production, introduced in the early 1980s, provides an integrated world economy. It joins design, production, and management with telecommunications. Five basic changes occur in the productive process: computer-assisted design, computer numerical control, use of industrial robots, automated transfer systems, and process control systems. Flexible production allows for decentralization of both ownership and production. A new car, for example, may have the engine block made in Japan, the tires made in Akron, the body stamped in Mexico, the electrical lines made in Taiwan, and then may be assembled by giant robots in Tennessee. Flexible production fragments and casualizes labor. Significant work is now being done by part-time employees, while large numbers of people work from home or satellite operations. Capitalists no longer have to pay for armies of laborers. The aggregate manufacturing system is now shedding 400,000 workers per year in the United States alone (Hoogvelt, 1997).

The decentralization and automation of commodity production are accompanied by expanded financial speculation. Money investment is now more profitable than manufacturing. All of the world's financial markets are now deregulated and somewhat integrated. The old trade wars involving goods are now replaced by investment wars. In a globalized world economy, money is mobile as never before. Billions of dollars may be invested in the Hong Kong stock market on Monday and moved by a keystroke on the computer to the London stock exchange by Wednesday. The International Monetary Fund and World Bank are now the lenders and regulators of the world's wealth. It is understandable why Paul Wolfowitz, a central architect of globalized U.S. foreign policy, was placed as head of the World Bank during the spring of 2005.

Defining Globalization as Social Architecture

Globalization is more than the sum of its parts. It is more than economic change. It is more than political change. It is more than cultural evolution. It is more than public policy. It is the new "social architecture" (Hoogvelt, 1997) for the world. It represents the restructuring of our nation's and the world's economic, political, legal, cultural, and spatial framework. New forms of production are undertaken. The transfer of wealth from the poor to the billionaires provides the foundation for other institutional changes. Privatization is an especially noteworthy theme. This new economic structure is accompanied by a new philosophy of governance, neoliberalism.

NEOLIBERALISM AND RESTRUCTURING

Politics is the concentrated expression of economics. Dramatic economic changes always are accompanied by changes in the power structure and political framework. Neoliberalism has emerged as the prevailing theory of governance (Harvey, 2005; Lipman, 2004, 2011). Fundamental distinctions between political parties disappear in the neoliberal state. The global neoliberal state requires the government to withdraw from much of its social service or "safety net" activity. The emergent task of the national government is to protect the new pyramided economic structure, protect private property, and control inflation, seen as the killer of an economy where financial speculation flourishes.

The political expression of neoliberalism was evidenced in changing world leadership and ideology. The 1980s represented an end to traditional politics in the United States as the liberal democratic state was ill suited for the new globalized world order. The emergence of Reagan, Thatcher, Gorbachev, and Pope John Paul II, the so-called "conservative restoration," altered world history. Neoliberalism demands that the government abandon social welfarism in favor of privatization. Neoliberalism wages war on the state-sponsored safety net. It demands that the priorities of the political state are to protect property rights and maintain an arm of force. It also demands ideological universalism cloaked by sham democracy and theatrical elections. One-body rule is masked by the multi-party state. In the United States, the traditional division between liberal and conservative is now a dead issue as the major political parties have become indistinguishable one from the other. Well-publicized partisanship and bickering mask the fact that neither speaks for the downtrodden and dispossessed.

Neoliberalism is undergirded by the end of bipolarity and the emergence of the United States as the sole superpower. Small "nonaligned" countries can no longer play one superpower against another. Humanitarianism is giving way rapidly to a new greed that victimizes those least able to help themselves.

Authoritarianism undergirds the neoliberal state in the globalized world. In the United States, presidents, governors, mayors, and elected representatives engage in unilateral decision making, flaunt emergency powers, and regularly step beyond traditional boundaries. Many big-city mayors have taken over governance of the school district. Chicago's mayor recently gave himself permission to bulldoze an active airport. Heightened reliance on police powers is inescapable.

Economic and political restructuring inevitably impact the legal system. Centuries of legal convention and protections are being scrapped. Legal oversight of industry is now a joke. The energy industry basically regulates itself. Representatives of Goldman Sachs regulate the financial instruments market. The healthcare industry filters new legislation, guaranteeing continued profits as it nixes single-payer healthcare. No objective body protects the consumer from price gouging and defiling the environment. The goat now "guards" the cabbage.

The politics of exclusion has replaced the protection of the public and the individual. Examples of exclusion are everywhere, as over 2 million people are now incarcerated; pending new legislation, 50 to 80 million people exist without health insurance; pension plan abandonment has thrust the elderly into a state of uncertainty; and Congress actually *debated* an extension of the voting rights bill. Laws and plans to expel and exclude "undocumented" people have reached the level of hysteria. Perhaps the greatest assault is that no one is policing the police.

Neoliberal globalization has impacted the sociology of space. Anthony Giddens (2002) has written that globalization reconstitutes the world as a single space where advanced communications allow local events and culture to be shaped by influences on the other side of the world. There appears to be a world order forging social control, creating standards of normative behavior, and whipping us into conformity.

Modernization theorists in the 1970s held out hope for development and international economic progress. Today's neoliberal globalists offer no such promise or apologia. Today's world is all about profit and wealth accumulation at any cost. The pyramiding of wealth means some will experience great adversity in the new world order. While the peasantry and dispossessed of many countries suffer, Sub-Saharan Africa, drowning in debt and disease, is now the venue of the great human apocalypse.

WAR, MILITARISM, AND THE NEW SOCIAL ORDER

History is replete with powerful forces carving and re-carving the world between them. The Berlin conference (1885–1886) found the imperial nations of Western Europe partitioning Africa. The conclusion of the Spanish-American War (1898) found the United States taking possession of Spain's former colonies. The collapse of the Ottoman Empire at the end of World War I was accompanied by the Sykes-Picot Agreement (1916) allowing England and France to partition the Middle East.

Early in the 21st century, the leaders of the world frantically meet in G-7, G-9, G-20, and so on, summits trying to avert crises and maintain the current hegemonic structure of Western superiority. Like gangsters and drug lords have always done, they must make rules and territorial arrangements allowing them to function in détente. Absent democratic deliberation inside their nations, leaders now enact military treaties, trade agreements, environmental accommodations, immigration quotas, intellectual property laws, and lending arrangements.

Superpower Status: Blessing or Curse?

After World War II, the "military industrial complex" became a fixture in the United States. It employs millions and devours over 60% of federal tax dollars. The baseline congressionally approved military budget for 2009 was:

$653 billion—Department of Defense
$150 billion—other federal departments
$162 billion—supplemental funds

This accounts for 47% of the world's total military spending. It is seven times larger than the arms budget of China, the number 2 spender. It is larger than the next 14 countries' spending combined. The United States spends over 4% of its gross national product on the military (War Resisters League, 2010).

Noted economist James Cypher (1987) coined "the iron triangle of milex" to dramatize spending in the new period. The triangle's sides are government, civilian, and the military. Approximately 90,000 companies enjoy military contracts (Dowd, 2006); however, the largest consortia, such as the Carlyle Group and the Halliburton interlocking companies, receive the lion's share. Dowd (2006) estimates that 25 companies receive 50% of the defense business.

Tales of waste and corruption are now well known. Hearings in the House Committee on Armed Services in 1984 revealed that the defense industry was paying $750 per toilet seat and $1,150 for a $4.88 wrench. That committee reported that the military paid $10,168 on merchandise worth $92.44 at retail hardware stores. Projects such as the Stealth bomber, the B-2 fighter jet, the LHD-7 amphibious assault ship, the Star Wars system, and many others wasted billions of dollars. Dowd (2006) reports that official military expenditures from 1990 to 2002 were $4 trillion plus a 2/3 multiplier effect.

These figures, as shocking as they are, represent a tiny fraction of milex, as regular "supplementary" congressional appropriations now feed the war machine. Other funds are hidden away in the budgets of foreign aid, the space program, the CIA, and miscellaneous subterranean pockets. The CIA budget alone is estimated at over $40 billion (Dowd, 2006). Another $4 billion is believed to be hidden in the Department of Energy's budget. As of November 2006, the total figure for milex was estimated to be in excess of $900 billion.

Human Costs

Militarization is killing people at home and abroad. As of this writing, over 1,000,000 civilian casualties are reported in Iraq alone. War cost estimates are $1,128,000,000,000. At today's market prices, that same expenditure could have funded 45,000,000 children to attend 1 year of Head Start; 16,000,000 4-year college scholarships; 3,000,000 new units of public housing; or the hiring of 6,000,000 public school teachers for 1 year (National Priorities Project, 2010).

Beyond death, destruction, and waste, a psychology of militarization is salient in the culture. The mass media saturates the airwaves with gratuitous violence. Gun toting in public has re-emerged reminiscent of the wild west. Of great importance, the military now moves aggressively into public education. Chicago, for example, has a number of military schools and plans to increase ROTC-type programs.

Permanent War?

The rise of techno-globalism and neoliberalism was accompanied by changes in the world's balance of power. The fracturing of the Soviet Union/ Eastern Block, an anemic European Union, and its own powerful military have left the United States as the sole superpower in the world. Militarily unchallenged on a global scale, the United States is faced with a seemingly insoluble Middle East problem and an unending series of prickly skirmishes and revolutionary movements in Latin America and elsewhere.

After 9/11, the "War on Terror" and "Bush Doctrine" of preemptory actions became the risky new military policy. They involve overthrowing governments that might harbor enemies or present potential threats. The rapid overthrow of governments in Iraq, Afghanistan, and Haiti stunned the world. The United States is now committed to decades of military action in the Middle East. The oil wars threaten to lead to "permanent war" (Bacevich, 2010).

ISSUES TO PONDER

The issues raised in this chapter require extensive inquiry. There are immediate concerns about the relationship between the governing political state and the people's welfare. Also, what about the wealth gap, now the largest in human history?

The Changing State

The consolidation of corporate power raises theoretical and practical questions about the continuing nature and function of the state. Is the nation-state obsolete in the global order?

As technology and the new order alter the arrangements between employers and workers, they also reorganize institutional and human relationships. The political state is contested. Capital formerly needed the state to help guarantee a reliable domestic workforce and market. Today capital demands that such functions be removed.

As the machinery of force and political power of one class over another, the state is being reconstructed to serve the needs of capital under today's conditions. In the United States, the state, the corporations, the banks, and speculators are merging to play this role and enforce the political power of those who own the means of accumulating wealth based on a system of exploitation. Private corporations now set public policy, including educational policy. Public assets and functions are privatized—transferring property from public to private ownership. Public debt owed to private investors opens the state to manipulation of policy. The sovereignty of private property creates a tyranny that undermines human rights and civil society.

Capital simply doesn't need the U.S. working class in the same way it did through the stages of early capitalism, maturing capitalism, and even imperialism. This is the basis for the demolition of the social contract that guaranteed economic security for a large section of the population and a safety net for those at subsistence. This is the basis for the attacks on our constitutional rights and universal education.

The state does not transform all at once. We are witnessing the attempts and steps to adjust to the new situation. But the direction is clear. The U.S. state is undergoing a profound shift from a nation-state, in the sense of protecting the market and the social relations within one country, to that of expanding the market and protecting the sanctity of private property globally, while abandoning responsibility for society nationally. The economic imperatives of market and employment no longer can hold the economy and society together. The political imperatives of laws, force, intimidation, and violence increasingly come into operation—all to the detriment of society as a whole.

Expanding the Gap in Wealth

While the owners of capital always got richer off the backs of the poor, the social safety net provided some relief. The possibilities and hopes of young people rising above the level of their parents are now questioned. Today, the combination of labor-replacing technology wedded to private ownership of the means of production threatens the livelihood of every worker. Lives are shattered, with the splinters flying apart in different directions—immigrant workers with no rights, auto workers with no jobs, the prospect of cities with no libraries, water wars, service workers with no benefits, education and the environment at the mercy of the corporations.

Today it is not only the inevitable unraveling of the economy, but also the deliberate actions of the state that are deforming our lives and ushering in a new political climate. Workers throughout the country are facing conditions long endured in rural Mississippi. As these changes in capital and the state enrich those with property and destroy the economic middle ground in American society, they also are bringing into being and shaping a new stratum that gets nothing from the capitalist system. This class is not a static category of people.

The ultra-rich can afford privatized services; the poor are forced into desperate struggles for survival; those in the middle are becoming poor. As society polarizes between wealth and poverty, we see the destruction of a way of life enjoyed by a large section of the U.S. working class.

Expelled from the economy and abandoned by the government, this growing class is drawn from all walks of life. An increasing number of displaced, abandoned, and dispossessed people cannot get what they need to sustain life.

Creation of a New Class

Karl Marx (1848) wrote of a proletariat or working class created with the rise of capitalism. He acknowledged that many workers were not working. He referred to the unemployed as the reserve army of labor. He also wrote of a "lumpen" or ragged proletariat, that is, hustlers, thieves, swindlers, brothel keepers, drug dealers, and so on. Today's new class is not accounted for in Marx's work. Rooted in the technological revolution and accompanying decline of demand for human labor, poverty now extends far beyond traditional victims. Davis, Hirschl, and Stack (1997) argue this new class is created by the destruction of industrialization. One feature of this group is its multiracial composition. The rigid racial stratification of the past is being reshaped.

THE POLITICAL ECONOMY OF RACE: SOME OBSERVATIONS

This author has dedicated a lifetime to researching Black education and especially the racialized curriculum (see, e.g., Watkins, 1993, 2001, 2003, 2005, 2010; Watkins, Lewis, & Chou, 2001). I do not wish to restate my work here; rather I wish to briefly call attention to a few salient issues impacting race, politics, and schooling. Although the focus here is on African Americans, other groups will be mentioned. First, data indicate the racial and wealth gap persists between African Americans and Whites. Second, the "new Black middle class" and its porous status must be acknowledged in any racial overview. Third, the changing demographics and developing politics of Latinos are mentioned. Finally, speculation is offered on unfolding race alignments in the new social order.

The Racial Wealth Gap Continues

Since 1968, the year Martin Luther King, Jr., was assassinated, the income gap between Blacks and Whites has narrowed by just 3 cents on the dollar. In

2005 the median per capita income in the United States stood at $16,629 for Blacks and $28,946 for Whites (Applied Research Center, 2009). At this slow rate of progress, income equality will not be achieved for 537 years.

African American families in the United States have a median net worth of $20,600, only 14.6% of the $140,700 median White net worth. The median net worth for Latino families is $18,600, only 13.2% of median White net worth. Between 1983 and 2004, median Black and Latino wealth inched up from 7% to 10% of median White wealth (Applied Research Center, 2009). At this rate, wealth equality for Blacks and Latinos collectively will not be attained for 634 years.

In 2004, for every dollar of wealth held by the typical White family, Black families held only 40 cents. In 2007, the national median family income for Blacks was $40,259, or 59% of the median family income for Whites. Data from the Applied Research Center suggest the gap on this national measure has widened during this decade, with Black families earning a high of 62% of the median family income of Whites in 2001, and a low of 58% in 2004 and 2005 (Applied Research Center, 2009).

The Bush-era recession has affected the racial wealth gap. The racial gap widened by 2004 as a result of the recession and joblessness. In 1995, the median income of African American families was 60.9% of that of White families (in 2004 dollars: $31,966 versus $52,492). By 2000, when the unemployment rate fell to 4.0%, the ratio was 63.5% (still a very large income gap: $36,939 versus $58,167 in 2004 dollars), the highest level on record, going back to 1947. That data translates to an income loss for the typical Black family of over $1,000 in 2004 alone. This finding suggests that unless the very favorable labor market conditions of the latter 1990s return and are maintained, racial income gaps are likely to widen further. The Black home ownership rate, for instance, sits at 47% and the Latino at 49.7%, compared with 75% for Whites (data from Applied Research Center, 2009).

These and other disparities remain significant and especially evident when we examine the polarization of assets and wealth. Despite slow collective gains, a new Black middle class has emerged since the late 20th century.

The Black Middle Class: A Status Report

The Black middle class in America has its roots in the "slave aristocracy" (Bullock, 1967). That group was offered the privileges of favor, housework, supervision, literacy, and other benefits. Over time the Black middle class remained relatively small but constant. Land acquisition, especially in the rural south, provided a base. Segregation created the conditions for an entrepreneur-ial class of Black service providers to prosper.

In the early 20th century, newly educated Blacks set themselves apart in Greek letter societies, Jack and Jill clubs, and other exclusive social circles. By World War II a distinct "Black bourgeoisie" was salient. Frazier (1957) causti-cally describes this group:

> Since the black bourgeoisie live largely in a world of make-believe, the masks which they wear to play their sorry roles conceal the feelings of inferiority and of insecurity and the frustrations that haunt their inner lives. Despite their attempt to escape from real identification with the masses of Negroes, they can not escape the mark of oppres-sion any more than their less favored kinsmen. In attempting to escape identification with the black masses, they have developed a self-hatred that reveals itself in their de-preciation of the physical and social characteristics of Negroes. Likewise their feelings of inferiority and insecurity are revealed in their pathological struggle for status within the isolated Negro world and craving for recognition in the white world. (p. 213)

In the decades following World War II, a powerful and strident civil rights movement, contextualized by national prosperity, combined with the politics of expediency to expand the Black (and Latino) middle class. The end of American apartheid quelled strident social protests, found affluent Blacks abandoning ur-ban ghettos, created new racial arrangements, and witnessed new Black popu-lations presenting themselves in public life. Blacks now exist at every level of the government, military, higher education, corporate organization, mass me-dia, and the worlds of sport and entertainment. Lacy (2007), Gatewood (2000), Patillo-McCoy (1999), and Landry 1987) expand the inquiry into the lives of the Black middle class.

From Reconstruction to the New Deal, the Black population tended to iden-tify as Republican, as they, particularly in the southern United States, were seen as more racially liberal than the Dixiecrats. Blacks shifted in significant num-bers to the Democrats with the election of Franklin Roosevelt, whose New Deal particularly benefited economically disadvantaged minority communities and helped forge the coalition that dominated American politics for the next 30 years.

The increased economic prosperity of the top one-third of the African American population in the late 20th century coincided with the emergence of techno-globalism and neoliberalism. Those increases were accompanied by ide-ological shifts. Numbers of Blacks identified as Republican, and attitude surveys note shifts toward political conservatism. Black conservatives often embrace the self-empowerment and personal accomplishment messages of the Bible, Booker T. Washington, and Frederick Douglass. Influential Blacks, for example,

Clarence Thomas, Colin Powell, and Condoleezza Rice, were showcased at the highest levels of governance.

The Bush recession has weakened the economic gains of the Black middle class. The Institute for Assets and Social Policy (http://iasp.brandeis.edu/) reports that one-third of the Black middle class are threatened with falling incomes. Those incomes declined by 3% between 2000 and 2007. Despite the downturn, many Blacks remain economically and ideologically conservative.

According to a Pew Research Center (2003) study, 13.7% of Blacks identified as "conservative" or "extremely conservative," with another 14.4% identifying as slightly conservative. However, the same study indicated that less than 10% identified as Republican or Republican-leaning in any fashion. Likewise, ongoing Pew Research Center surveys showed that nearly 20% of Blacks identify as religious right. The 2003 Pew study indicated that only 7% of Blacks identify as Republican.

In October 2004, a Joint Center for Political and Economic Studies (JCPES; http://www.jointcenter.org/) poll reported that 18% of Blacks surveyed said they intended to vote for GOP incumbent George W. Bush. It turned out that Bush didn't need a lot of Black support to get re-elected. He got 11% support from Blacks, according to CNN.com, not a lot, but enough to win a close contest against Democrat John Kerry and distant third-party candidate Ralph Nader.

More recent polls by the JCPES report a 60% decline in Black identification with the Republican Party. BlackAmericaWeb.com reported on the record number of GOP delegates of color in attendance at the 2004 Republican National Convention in New York City—167 or nearly 7% of all delegates, double the representation at the 2000 convention.

In summary, the Black bourgeoisie may be wobbly; however, it is a fixture in the social and political life of the nation. The shifting status of emergent "minorities" and newly de-classed people must be reconsidered in the state of the union. While the hierarchy of race remains in place, the economic and political landscape of the country quakes. The concept of a cohesive African American people is cloudy. This characterization was more accurate when the pressure of segregation isolated African Americans from the rest of society. Such isolation allowed for the creation of a common identification and a common political agenda that are now fractured.

The Browning of America

The "Browning" of America is noteworthy, as Latino populations have numerically outstripped African Americans. Within the new economic order, the demand for immigrant and migrant labor has declined, leading to a new public policy. As of this writing, a wall, some of it electronic, is being constructed, at great cost to the U.S. taxpayers, along the border between Mexico and the United States. Apparently, our lawmakers have not learned the lessons of history at Berlin and Gaza that the consequences of walling people in and out of a place and space are dire. Even the walls of Jericho came tumbling down.

Politicizing Race in the New Social Order

Systemic White chauvinism/racism originated in the practices of colonialism, domination, and privilege, not psychological deviance. American capitalists skillfully seized upon differences in race, gender, religion, ability, and other areas to create a hierarchical structure that exploits the many for the profit of the few. Ignoring political economy and the impact of neoliberalism, racial, especially education, theorists too often rely on the formulas of the past. Many locate the spine of racism in attitudes, institutions, the law, and social practices. While racism certainly manifests in the above venues, we cannot ignore that racism is historically and politically constructed, not biologically transmitted and permanent.

Affluent White people have benefited greatly from their protected position in North America. Throughout the 20th century, a White "labor aristocracy" was maintained by industrial, skilled, high-paying union jobs. Recent de-industrialization and the dynamics of speculative capitalism diminish that capacity. Today's speculative capitalists are *not* re-investing in industry in North America. They are pocketing the profits from financial investments. A disappearing entrepreneurial middle class, service sector jobs, and declining wages characterize today's labor market. Large sections of the previously comfortable White middle class employed in basic industry, for example, auto and steel, are being jettisoned. Millions upon million of people are now displaced from labor, some permanently. The ability to provide racial bribery and racial rewards is diminished.

We are left with these realities. By all measures of income, unemployment rates, education attainment, incarceration, and other indicators within the misery index, people of color continue to occupy the lowest socioeconomic status rankings in the nation. In the economic recession of 2008 to the present, people of color have been disproportionately targeted for usurious subprime mortgage loans alongside other abuses. America's version of ethnic cleansing now witnesses the redistribution and reassignment of urban populations through gentrification, the destruction of public housing, and other assorted programs of social engineering. Black and Latino communities in cities like Los Angeles,

Chicago, and New York, notably Harlem, are unrecognizable from 30 years ago. Racial hostility and hierarchy remain intact, yet the prerequisites for White privilege are eroding.

The notion of the post-racial society is absolute fiction. Racism persists in both attitude and institution. The financial rewards attached to racism are threatened. The race to the bottom has included people of all colors. It must be concluded that economic class distinctions have increased in significance.

ASSESSING PUBLIC EDUCATION:
NEW CONDITIONS, NEW INQUIRIES

This chapter has attempted to explicate the sea change in the American economic and sociopolitical environment. This is not a quantitative change. This is not a hiccup. There is no going back to normalcy because there is no more normal. The ABCs of our existence are being reordered. This is a qualitative and major change in the labor market, politics, and culture of basic life in this nation. Public education, as we know it, likely will not survive. Because we are in the midst of the restructuring, we cannot predict with certainty where it will go.

Vested economic power has directly asserted itself into education policymaking. It has been argued here that the study of political economy provides a much needed and additional weapon in the arsenal of inquiry. Education theorists, practitioners, and citizens must understand the politics of schooling. Political economy helps us interrogate emergent interventions of corporate power.

The Corporate Intrusion

The triumph of techno-global neoliberalism finds corporations and corporate wealth interjecting themselves into the policymaking processes as never before. Disregarding public input, corporate forces now possess extensive, near monopolistic powers in re-imagining, reforming, and restructuring public education. Stealthily removed from the political and public deliberative process, educational reform is now erected by think tanks, wealthy foundations, and shadowy "workforce" commissions little known by the general public or professional educators. In Chicago, for example, the draconian Renaissance 2010 educational plan was the product of the Commercial Club of that city. Such forces promote market "solutions" as a panacea for an "ailing" institution.

At the national level, many foundations and sponsored groups, such as Heritage, Gates, Broad, and Annenberg, involve themselves in education "innovation." One such group, the National Center on Education and the Economy (NCEE), has quietly emerged. Funded by Gates, Rockefeller, Ford, Carnegie, Kodak, Walton, Boeing, Xerox, Pew, Gannett, and MacArthur foundation money, this commission is conceiving a new and different kind of public education. NCEE's New Commission on the Skills of the American Workforce convened in 2005, producing a report, *Tough Choices or Tough Times* (2007).

Tough Choices or Tough Times

Tough Choices is a follow-up to NCEE's first significant report issued in 1990, *America's Choice: High Skills or Low Wages*. That report posited that the world labor market was dividing along the lines of high skill versus low wage. Manufacturers in the global economy had a choice of engaging either of these two distinct markets. The developed world offered high skills, while the underdeveloped world offered low wages. The United States was viewed to be a part of the high-skill market.

Upon reassessment, NCEE found that analysis shortsighted. It failed to understand that in some developing nations a highly skilled workforce was evolving simultaneously alongside cheap labor. China and India were prime examples. These new players could offer the best of both worlds, thus attracting a substantial portion of the producing market.

NCEE ascertained that the United States was the leader in vertical integration, that is, in moving products from raw materials to market. It would take other nations some time to catch the United States in this area. The United States had to seize upon this competitive advantage and further upgrade its commitment to highly skilled labor, as low-skill labor was in demand decline. NCEE analyses posited that the algorithms for low-skill labor allowed it to be more easily automated. Future competitiveness and profitability resided in the cultivation of skilled labor. In short, the United States should pursue the high-skill option; however, to do so required a more skilled labor force.

The inescapable conclusion for NCEE was that America's educational system was not prepared for this new competitive environment. The current educational structure was conceived for an earlier era. The transition from an agricultural to an industrial society required some rudimentary skills, but they fell far short of the demands of the new technological era. An upgraded and transformed educational system was required. The new labor force requires "new literacies." The highly skilled workers of the future, NCEE asserts, will have to understand abstractions, be able to synthesize and innovate, be disciplined, and, most of all, be well organized.

Upon providing that rationale, *Tough Choices* surveys the current "problems" with America's educational system. Highlighted problems include:

- Teachers are recruited from the less able.
- We tolerate enormous amounts of waste.
- Academic gains are not keeping pace with per-pupil expenditure; gains of the past are leveling off.
- There is growing inequality in family income, contributing to widening the achievement gap.
- Unlike some other nations, we have failed to motivate our students to work hard.
- Teacher compensation is related to time in service, not quality of output.
- Our testing system rewards students who excel in routine work, ignoring higher order thinking, creativity, and innovation.
- School bureaucracies have become stultifying.
- The people we are counting on to change America are already in the workforce and unable to affect change.
- It is difficult or impossible for adults in the workforce to obtain continuing education or improve their skills.

The report concluded that we need a qualitatively new kind of educational system. The old system cannot be patched. There is not enough money to transform the existing education structure and curriculum. The heart of the document is the ten recommendations or "steps" for a new system of public education.

Step One: Assume that we will do the job right the first time.
Step Two: Make more efficient use of available resources.
Step Three: Recruit teachers from the top third of high school and college bound students.
Step Four: Develop standards and assessments to meet the needs of tomorrow.
Step Five: Create high-performance schools and school districts.
Step Six: Initiate high-quality universal early childhood education.
Step Seven: Provide strong remedial support to disadvantaged students.
Step Eight: Enable every member of the adult workforce to obtain new literacy skills.
Step Nine: Create personal competitive accounts for all students.
Step Ten: Create regional competitiveness authorities. (p. 9)

Testing is central to the NCEE's vision of the new public school. The commission proposes a mandatory universal exam be administered to all high school students at 16 years of age. This exam is to be a rigorous one normed on international standards. Students not passing the exam could not proceed to higher education. Their recourse would be to retake the exam until satisfactory scores were achieved.

Critics can argue that this plan creates another barrier for underachieving students. This exam would likely be the end of the dream for many youngsters. On the other side, it would help identify those capable of participation in the new technocracy. A new technocracy capable of competing in the world market provides the recurring theme in this group's plan for educational reform. Economic competitiveness appears as the driving theme in educational reform. It can be seen once again that education is inextricably wedded to political economy.

NCEE boasts that its proposals and concepts are gaining support from state legislators, businesspeople, and professional educators. Their fetish with market economics trumps any notions of civil society, human tolerance, participatory democracy, or self-actualization.

CONCLUSION: THE SOCIAL ORDER, POLITICAL ECONOMY, AND EDUCATION IN POST-DEMOCRATIC AMERICA

Employing political economics to explain the changing social order has been the focus of this chapter. The movement from one social order to another often happens quickly and without rehearsal or script. Arnove (1980) explains that the reorganization of society at the beginning of the 20th century occurred without accompanying explanation. Financial gatekeepers and vested economic interests feared the labor unrest plaguing Europe would spread to America. Hegemonists quickly found rationale and apologia to explain the new politics, wealth inequities, and societal arrangements. The academic community offered, for example, Spencer's (1861) Social Darwinism and Edward Thorndike's (1911) work on "individuality" as explanations for ability and wealth difference. Other constructed notions of meritocracy, such as the Horatio Alger fables, were advanced to defend the new narrowing of wealth and power.

Similarly, the currently evolving new techno-global social order unfolds without rehearsal. Even the plutocrats find themselves aboard a runaway train. Theorists, neoconservatives, spin doctors, culture makers (Takaki, 2000), and agents of ideation are again hard at work. Francis Fukuyama (1992), for example, offered that the big problems of society have been resolved and we need only to maintain liberal democracy. The construction and distribution of "explanation" in this new period are pending. Political ideology is far too important to be left to chance.

Ideological management and knowledge selection (Apple, 1979, 1983; Spring, 2010), long a part of public education and curriculum making, have taken on increased importance. The globalized economy and neoliberal politics have made new demands on education, thinking, and practice. As the venue of policymaking shifts from education "experts" to corporate people, we can expect the objectives of the new technocracy to play a crucial part in the "new" educational system. The study of politics and the economy becomes more urgent.

The Oxford Dictionary defines *political economy* as:

> that branch of the art of government concerned with the systematic inquiry into the nature and causes of the wealth of nations, although it is now often used loosely to describe political aspects of economic policy-making. Since the seventeenth century the meaning of the term has fluctuated widely. It is possible nevertheless to identify three broad traditions of political economy which currently influence political science. These are, first, the tradition of classical political economy; secondly, the Marxian tradition; and finally, the tradition of political economics which uses statistical and modelling techniques to test hypotheses about the relationship between government and the economy. (http://www.highbeam.com/doc/1O86-politicaleconomy.html)

The study of political economy has become a part of the *endangered* curriculum in American education. Examination of the Marxian tradition has disappeared at all levels. Why, we might ask, is this the case? The answer is obvious. Americans have chosen democracy, not plutocracy. The plutocrats disdain exposure. Their deeds and misdeeds are hidden from public scrutiny. Their manipulation of the wealth-producing processes, the tax system, the curriculum, and the apparatus of governance would not likely find public approval.

The new political order, the plutocracy, operates within a dialectic of openness and secrecy. On one hand, technology has opened up communication and access to information as never before. C-SPAN now televises the daily deliberations of lawmaking bodies. Indefatigable bloggers relentlessly drudge for every piece of minutia. John and Jane Q. Citizen now have cameras and recording equipment in the palm of their hands. Everyone has a song to sing.

On the other hand, the plutocrats now proceed without fear of oversight, countervailing forces, or public outcry. All pretenses of participatory democracy have been abandoned. The corporate media is on lockdown. Free inquiry in the classroom is harnessed by the demands of standardized tests. Social criticism is controlled. Wars, the expansion of police powers, further concentrations of wealth, energy policy, and designs on public education proceed without any public input. Position begets opposition. Hegemonists proceed at their own peril!!!

REFERENCES

Apple, M. (1979). *Ideology and curriculum*. London: Routledge & Kegan Paul.

Apple, M. (1983). *Education and power*. Boston: Ark Paperbacks.

Applied Research Center. (2009). *Racial income gap chronic problem even before the meltdown* [Check the color line 2009—Income report]. Available at http://colorlines.com/archives/2009/02/report_racial_income_gap_chron.html

Arnove, R. (Ed.). (1980). *Philanthropy and cultural imperialism: The foundations at home and abroad*. Bloomington: Indiana University Press.

Bacevich, A. (2010). *Washington rules: America's path to permanent war* [American Empire Project]. New York: Henry Holt & Co.

Bullock, H. (1967). *A history of Negro education in the south: From 1619 to present*. Cambridge, MA: Harvard University Press.

Chicago Tribune. (2010, May 23). p. 8 [Business section].

Cypher, J. (1987, March). Military spending, technical change and economic growth. *Journal of Economic Issues, 21*(1), 33–59.

Davies, J. B., Sandstrom, S., & Shorrocks, A. (2006). *The world distribution of household wealth*. (World Institute for Development Economics Research, United Nations University), & Wolff, E. N. (NYU).

Davis, J., Hirschl, T. A., & Stack, M. (Eds.). (1997). *Cutting edge: Technology, information capitalism and social revolution*. London: Verso.

Dowd, D. (2006, Winter). US military expenditures: Beneficial or harmful? Or, who benefits and who pays? Available at http://www.stateofnature.org/milex.html

Forbes. (2005, May 9). Forbes CEO compensation (S. De Carlo, Ed.). Available at http://www.forbes.com/2005/04/20/05ceoland.html

Frazier, E. F. (1957). *Black bourgeoisie*. New York: Free Press.

Fukuyama, F. (1992). *The end of history and the last man*. New York: Free Press.

Gatewood, W. (2000). *Aristocrats of color: The black elite, 1820–1920*. Fayetteville: University of Arkansas Press.

Giddens, A. (2002). *Runaway world: How globalization is reshaping our lives*. London: Profile.

Harvey, D. (2005). *A brief history of neoliberalism.* New York: Oxford University Press.

Hoogvelt, A. M. M. (1997). *Globalization and the post colonial world: The new political economy of development.* Baltimore, MD: Johns Hopkins University Press.

Lacy, K. R. (2007). *Blue-chip black: Race, class, and status in the new black middle class.* Berkeley: University of California Press.

Landry, B. (1987). *The new black middle class.* Berkeley: University of California Press.

Lenin, V. I. (1939). *Imperialism: The highest stage of capitalism.* New York: International Publishers. (Original work published 1916)

Lipman, P. (2004). *High stakes education: Inequality, globalization, and urban school reform.* New York: Routledge Falmer.

Lipman, P. (2011). *The new political economy of urban education: Neoliberalism, race, and the right to the city.* New York: Routledge.

Magdoff, H. (1978). *Imperialism: From the colonial age to the present.* New York: Monthly Review Press.

Marx, K. (1848). *The Communist manifesto.* Petrograd: Martin Lawrence Ltd.

Marx, K. (1967). *Das kapital: A critique of political economy.* Chicago: Henry Regnery Co. (Original work published 1867)

Mishel, L., Bernstein, J., & Allegretto, L. (2007). *The state of working America 2006/07.* Ithaca, NY: Economic Policy Institute, Cornell University Press.

National Center on Education and the Economy (NCEE). (2007). *Tough choices or tough times.* San Francisco: Jossey-Boss. Available at http://www.ncee.org

National Priorities Project. (2010). Cost of war. Available at http://www.nationalpriorities.org/costofwar_home

Patillo-McCoy, M. (1999). *Black picket fences: Privilege and perils among the black middle class.* Chicago: University of Chicago Press.

Pew Research Center. (2003, November 5). *The 2004 political landscape.* Washington, DC: Author.

Spencer, H. (1861). *Social statics.* New York: Appleton.

Spring, J. (2010). *The American school: A global context from the Puritans to the Obama era.* New York: McGraw Hill.

Takaki, R. (2000). *Iron cages: Race and culture in nineteenth century America.* New York: Oxford University Press.

Thorndike, E. (1911). *Individuality.* Boston: Houghton Mifflin.

United Nations University–World Institute for Development Economics Research of the United Nations University (UNU-WIDER). (2010, 2009, 2008). Helsinki, Finland: United Nations.

War Resisters League. (2010). Where your income tax money really goes. Available at www.warresisters.org/pages/piechart.htm

Watkins, W. H. (1993, Fall). Black curriculum orientations: A preliminary inquiry. *Harvard Educational Review, 63*(3), 321–338.

Watkins, W. H. (2001). *The white architects of black education: Power and ideology in America, 1865–1954.* New York: Teachers College Press.

Watkins, W. H. (2003). Curriculum, culture, and power: Reshaping the education of African Americans. In C. Yeakey & R. Henderson (Eds.), *Surmounting all odds: Education, opportunity and society in the new millennium* (pp. 31–50). Greenwich, CT: Information Age.

Watkins, W. H. (Ed.). (2005). *Black protest thought and education.* New York: Peter Lang.

Watkins, W. H. (2010). Education of blacks in the south. In C. Kridel (Ed.), *Encyclopedia of curriculum studies* (pp. 321–322). Thousand Oaks, CA: Sage.

Watkins, W. H., Lewis, J., & Chou, V. (Eds.). (2001). *Race and education: The roles of history and society in educating African American students.* Boston: Allyn & Bacon.

Wolff, E. N. (2000). Recent trends in wealth ownership, 1983–1998. Available at http://129.3.20.41/eps/mac/papers/0004/0004047.pdf

CHAPTER 2

Neoliberal Urbanism, Race, and Urban School Reform

Pauline Lipman

Chicago has long been a focus of national attention on urban education policy, and its plan to remake public education is no exception. In 2004, Chicago's mayor announced Renaissance 2010 (Ren2010), a plan to close 60–70 schools and reopen 100 new schools, at least two-thirds as charter or contract schools run by private organizations with greater autonomy than regular public schools. According to Chicago Public Schools (CPS) Ren2010 website, from 2002 to Fall 2009, CPS closed, phased out, consolidated, or turned over to private management 58 schools and opened 74 charter, 14 contract, and 31 performance[1] schools under Ren2010. Although 2010 has passed, the policies continue. Renaissance 2010 is an experiment to reinvent the third largest U.S. public school system as an education market. Part of the agenda is to create schools to serve mixed-income communities developed on the sites of demolished public housing.

In 2000, Chicago launched the Plan for Transformation (PFT), one of the most extensive revamps of public housing in the United States. The plan has nearly completed demolition of 22,000 units, including "family" units of three, four, or five bedrooms. Under the federal HOPE VI public housing redevelopment plan, the PFT calls for severely distressed (decayed) public housing complexes to be renovated or replaced, many as mixed-income developments (Bennett, Smith, & Wright, 2006). HOPE VI is a neoliberal housing policy that shifts public housing to the market, with a focus on vouchers in the private housing market, private management of public housing, and mixed-income developments. This significantly reduces state provision of affordable low-income public housing. Chicago researchers estimate that less than 20% of former residents will return to the new developments (Venkatesh, Celimli, Miller, Murphy, & Turner, 2004; Wilen & Nayak, 2006).

Viewed through the lens of neoliberal urbanism, the PFT is part of a development agenda that merges local, national, and transnational capital, in partnership with city government, to make Chicago a first-tier global city (Lipman, 2004). The heart of that agenda is downtown development, tourism, and gentrification of large sections of working-class and low-income Chicago, particularly communities of color (see Demissie, 2006), marketization of public services and public goods, and corporate–state governance partnerships. The city's aggressive support for capital accumulation and corporate involvement in city decision making extends to incentives to developers and corporate and financial interests, public–private partnerships, the city's bid for the 2016 Olympics, cuts in funding for public welfare, weakening labor unions, and privatization of public assets from the Chicago Skyway Bridge to parking meters to schools.

Although neoliberalism as a process unfolds differently in different contexts, Chicago is a particularly sharp instance of the interrelationship of neoliberal urban restructuring, the politics of race, and U.S. urban school reform. Ren2010 is a market-based plan centered in a high-level partnership of the school district, the mayor, and the most powerful financial and corporate interests in the city. In this chapter I argue that education policy is integrally linked with the neoliberal agenda of city officials and the financial and corporate elite (see also Lipman, 2008a, 2011; Lipman & Haines, 2007). I also examine the cultural politics of education policy, how it "makes sense" on the ground and how neoliberalism is materialized through the actions of social movements and social actors. I focus specifically on (1) the discourse of racial pathology underpinning mixed-income schools/housing, and (2) rearticulation of discourses of equity and self-determination to the market and individual choice through charter schools. I am especially interested in how the "good sense" in these policies connects with people's lived experiences to further a hegemonic neoliberal urban agenda and the implications for constructing a counter-hegemonic movement.

I want to clarify at the outset that I am not claiming a simple correspondence or determinist relationship between neoliberal urban development and education. The process is dialectical and contested, and there are local histories, specific relations of social forces, micropolitics, and ideological complexities. Moreover, there is a certain amount of what Stephen Ball (1994) calls "ad hockery" in the creation of education policy at all levels. Nevertheless, education policy works to materially and ideologically consolidate neoliberal urban development. I use Chicago as a case study to advance this broad argument grounded in the assumption that we cannot analyze education policy outside this larger framework, while also accounting for variation and local specificity.

I take a multidisciplinary approach to urban political economy and education, drawing from critical urban sociology, critical geography, urban policy and planning, and sociology of education. For this discussion I find particularly helpful Gramsci's (1971) elaboration of the role of ideology and culture in the construction of hegemony. I refer to the processes through which dominant social forces bring under their leadership sectors of other classes and social groups by constructing a common sense that resonates with lived experiences and by disarticulating elements of liberatory social ideologies to their agendas. Subaltern groups also exercise agency in this process, tactically aligning themselves with aspects of dominant agendas in an effort to "make do" within the constraints of the present situation (Pedroni, 2007). My analysis draws on public archival data, data produced by community organizations, and interview and participant observation data collected from 2004 to 2010 at numerous community and school board meetings, community forums, activist coalition meetings, public events sponsored by Chicago Public Schools, press conferences, and meetings with CPS officials. The interviews and field notes from this research inform a larger study of Chicago education policy, race, and neoliberal urbanism (Lipman, 2011). Interviews with parents, teachers, administrators, school staff, and students for a study on the effects of school closings in the Midsouth area of Chicago (Lipman, Person, & Kenwood Oakland Community Organization, 2007) also inform my analysis. I begin with a summary of neoliberal urbanism and Chicago's Ren2010 education policy. From there I move on to discuss cultural politics of this policy. Finally, I suggest how this analysis might help frame a counter-neoliberal education agenda.

NEOLIBERAL URBANISM

Brenner and Theodore (2002) argue that "cities have become strategically crucial geographic arenas in which a variety of neoliberal initiatives . . . have been articulated" (p. 351). Despite neoliberal theory of reduced government, Harvey (2005), Brenner and Theodore (2002), Peck and Tickell (2002), and others contend that "actually existing neoliberalism" involves the active intervention of the state on the side of capital, first to destroy existing institutional arrangements, and then to create a new infrastructure for capital accumulation by intensifying exploitation of labor and privatizing social infrastructure and institutions. Peck and Tickell describe the two phases as "roll back" and "roll out" neoliberalism. Roll back neoliberalism involves destruction of Keynesian artifacts (e.g., public housing, fully funded public schools), policies (e.g., redistributive social welfare, labor protections), agreements (e.g., federal redistribution of revenue to cities), and institutions (e.g., Department of Housing and Urban Development) (see Hackworth, 2007). Roll out neoliberalism then creates new practices and institutions or reconstructs existing ones.

Beginning in the 1970s, roll back neoliberal policies reduced federal funding for cities, setting the stage for city governments to cut public services and disinvest in public institutions. Driven by market ideologies, the local state in the roll out phase replaced Keynesian welfare state arrangements with public–private ventures, municipal tax laws to subsidize development, and privatized public services as a way to make up for federal funding shortfalls. These policies tilt governance and ownership of public institutions toward private interests (Smith, 2002), undermine democratic institutions, and produce the "democratic deficits" that characterize neoliberal governance.

Neoliberalization of cities also was propelled by economic globalization and deregulation, which weakened the tight coupling of urban and national economies that characterized the industrial era. As cities compete directly in the global economy for international investment, tourism, highly skilled labor, and production facilities, including the producer services that drive globalization (Sassen, 2006), marketing cities and specifically their housing and schools has become a hallmark of urban entrepreneurship. Downtown luxury living and gentrified neighborhoods, as well as new "innovative" schools in gentrified communities and choice within the public school system, are located in this inter-city competition (Lipman, 2004).

Facilitated by municipal government, gentrification has become a pivotal sector in neoliberal urban economies (Fainstein, 2001; Hackworth, 2007; Smith, 2002) and a critical element in the production of spatial inequality, displacement, homelessness, and racial containment. "Gentrification as a global urban strategy is a consummate expression of neo-liberal urbanism. It mobilizes individual property claims via a market lubricated by state donations and often buried as regeneration" (Smith, 2002, p. 446). Cuts in federal funding have opened up municipal policy to greater reliance on property tax revenues, and cities have become more dependent on, and subsidizers of, the real estate market through public giveaways of land and subsidies that funnel public tax dollars to developers. Real estate development is also a key speculative activity, with properties operating as financial instruments. Speculation, in turn, drives up property values and property taxes, forcing out lower income renters and homeowners. This cycle of redevelopment and displacement is located in what Harvey (2001) calls the "spatial fix": "Capitalism perpetually strives, therefore, to create a social and physical landscape in its own image and requisite to its own needs at a particular point in time, only just as certainly to undermine, disrupt and even destroy that landscape at a later point in time" (p. 333).

Within this urban dynamic, Hackworth (2007) argues that the "inner city" is a site of extreme transition and "soft spot" for neoliberal experimentation. An icon of vilified Keynesian welfare state policies (e.g., subsidized public housing, public health clinics, and public hospitals), the inner city is now a focus of "high profile real estate investment, neoliberal policy experiments, and governance changes" (p. 13). Areas that were home to low-income communities of color are foci of public–private partnerships, gentrification complexes, privatization, and de-democratization through mayoral takeovers of public institutions and corporate-led governance bodies. This context defines the stakes involved in closing schools in urban core areas and creating new schools to market new mixed-income developments to the middle class.

Neoliberal development involves new kinds of connections among public and private institutions and new financing tools. A key tool is tax increment financing (TIF). The city declares an area "blighted" and unlikely to be developed without the diversion of tax revenues to support development. Once an area is declared a TIF, property tax revenues for schools, libraries, parks, and other public works are frozen for 23 years, and all growth in revenues above this level are put in a TIF fund. TIF funds subsidize developers directly and pay for infrastructure improvement costs (e.g., new sewer systems and street grids). As of Fall 2009, Chicago had about 159 TIFs, many in the most developed sections of downtown and areas already undergoing real estate development (Smith, 2006, p. 291). TIFs facilitate a transfer of public funds to banks, realtors, and major contractors, and create conditions for multimillion dollar profits in real estate sales and speculation, while siphoning off funds that could be used for schools, libraries, and so on.[2] Once declared a TIF zone, the city also can force owners to sell homes and businesses under the right of eminent domain, clearing the way for development.[3]

The entrepreneurial university also has become a key actor in the acquisition and development of land, partnering with the city and private investors to redevelop "inner-city areas." In Chicago, the University of Illinois–Chicago is a central partner in the redevelopment of a nearby African American West Side community into the multimillion dollar University Village gentrification complex of town homes, condominiums, retail outlets, and restaurants that have displaced public housing residents, low-income rental units, and public schools and are encroaching on the Mexican immigrant community of Pilsen. The University of Chicago's expansion into the African American South Side Woodlawn neighborhood and the Illinois Institute of Technology's central role in the massive Midsouth development project on the site of several miles of now-demolished public housing high-rises are other examples. In each case, the university is an anchor for real estate development and the rebranding of the community. As I argue below, it is also implicated in education markets.

Structural and ideological racism is central to neoliberal urban development. Andrew Barlow (2003) notes, "In the United States, the 400-year legacy of highly organized, state-sponsored systems of racism have great significance for the ways in which the 'grid' of globalized relationships come into being" (p. 9). Post-World War II suburbanization policies, followed by massive deindustrialization in urban areas in the 1970s and 1980s, produced White flight, disinvestment in urban public infrastructure (including public housing and schools), and physical decay of the built environment as well as unemployment and the elimination of social services and decline of community institutions (Lipsitz, 1998). These policies reduced real estate values in the urban core, creating conditions for gentrification, and provided grounds to demolish public housing and transfer public schools to the market. The cultural politics of racial pathology, fueled by a moral panic over "inner-city" crime, "intergenerational poverty," and high-profile police occupation of African American and some Latino communities, provided the ideological soil for a racially coded neoliberal ideology of individual responsibility and reduction of "dependency" on the state (Wacquant, 2001). This was the ideological ground to restructure or eliminate government-funded social programs and institutions.

EDUCATION AND SPATIAL RESTRUCTURING OF THE CITY

The process of closing public schools and reopening them as quasi-market public–private ventures is integral to the neoliberal urban project. The idea for Ren2010 was proposed by the Commercial Club of Chicago (CCC), an organization of the city's most powerful corporate, financial, and civic leaders (*Left Behind*, 2003). The CCC created the Renaissance Schools Fund, a high-level partnership with CPS, to select, evaluate, and partly fund Ren2010 schools. The national significance of Chicago's market-driven school agenda is reflected in the comments of Andrew J. McKenna, Chair of the Civic Committee of the CCC: "Chicago is taking the lead across the nation in remaking urban education. No other major city has launched such an ambitious public school choice agenda" (Clowes, 2004). Discursively, Ren2010 rearticulates the purpose of public institutions to managerialism, citing inefficient use of space and accountability measures as the rationale for closing schools without regard for what actually is happening there, how school buildings actually are used, and what kinds of educational programs are offered (see Greenlee, Hudspeth, Lipman, Smith, & Smith, 2008). The very serious decision to close neighborhood schools in working-class communities of color is reduced to cost–benefit analyses, furthering this discourse in relation to public institutions.

Ren2010 epitomizes the democratic deficits of neoliberal policy generally, as decisions about public transportation, housing, development, and infrastructure are made by mayor-appointed boards, public–private entities, and experts, with public participation relegated to appointed advisory committees. Ren2010 eliminates elected Local School Councils (LSCs) comprised primarily of parents and community members (mainly working-class people of color), with the power to hire the school principal and approve the budget and school improvement plan. The significance of LSCs extends beyond schools because they are one of the few grassroots, democratically elected bodies with decision-making power in public institutions in the city. In place of LSCs, charter and contract schools are governed by appointed boards with no required accountability to parents and communities. Thus the contest over Ren2010 is partly a contest over democracy and who should have a voice in public affairs. In this sense, when they are at their best, LSCs develop people's collective capacities to engage in democratic governance and control of community institutions. Michael Katz (1992) points out that by redistributing power to parents and community representatives, LSCs "asserted the capacity of ordinary citizens to reach intelligent decisions about educational policy" (p. 62). Charter and contract schools are also non-union, further disenfranchising people who work in the schools.

The process of closing schools instantiates the democratic deficits of neoliberal policy. Decisions are made by appointed public officials and corporate partners behind closed doors and validated by the *performance* of public hearings that parallel those held to legitimate the destruction of public housing (Bennett, Smith, & Wright, 2006). With no more than 1 month's notice that the Board of Education plans to close a school, a public hearing is set, generally at Board offices downtown, often during work hours when few parents can attend. Although purportedly data-gathering sessions, these public hearings—where parents, students, teachers, and community members mobilize each year to pour out their hearts in defense of their schools— seem to have little weight. The Board of Education admitted at its February 18, 2009 meeting, where it voted to close all the schools recommended by the CEO, that it had not even looked at the transcripts of these hearings. (Board members rarely attend the hearings; they're simply recorded by a Board-appointed hearing officer.) In the end, the mayor-appointed school board meets in private and rubber stamps whatever the mayor-appointed CEO of schools recommends.[4] Experiences of disregard for parents and community members run deep. A school staff support person in a Midsouth school reported on his school's closing: "Nobody down here was really taken into account when they were doing it [closing the school]. No one in this community was supposed to even know about it until it was time to slap it on us" (interview, December 2006).

Many of the school closings can be linked to gentrification and displacement of working-class people of color. Just as disinvestment produced decay and facilitated demolition of public housing, disinvestment in public schools in the same communities created conditions to close them. Our interviews with school staff in several Midsouth schools revealed a history of failure of CPS to respond to requests for building improvements and maintenance, cuts in essential staff, and lack of necessary resources in schools with histories of inequitable treatment (Lipman, Person, & Kenwood Oakland Community Organization, 2007). Having been "set up for failure," education accountability provided the tools to identify schools to be closed. All this is legitimated by the racialized discourses that construct African American and Latino urban schools and communities as deficient, derelict, and dysfunctional (Wilson, 2007).

The mayor and the CEO of CPS see schools as a cornerstone of the return of middle-class families (Olszewski & Sadovi, 2003), with the city marketing "innovative" schools as anchors in gentrified and gentrifying communities. Closing schools in low-income communities of color under Ren2010 and reopening them with new identities is part of rebranding these neighborhoods for a new clientele. For example, the University of Chicago operates several charter schools in a gentrifying area; CPS has opened Montessori schools to attract middle-class parents, and the latest rounds of school closings led to the replacement of several neighborhood schools serving working-class students of color with selective-enrollment, magnet schools. The MacArthur Foundation (2005) underscores the importance of schools in mixed-income developments: "The city has made a commitment to improving the local schools, without which the success of the new mixed-income communities would be at great risk."

Ren2010 was launched with the Midsouth Plan to close 20 of 22 schools in the Midsouth area in 2004. (The plan was defeated by concerted protest.) Under the Plan for Transformation, this area, which had been home to a vast track of high-rise public housing complexes, is being redeveloped into five mixed-income communities with 8,000 new homes—one-third of them reserved for public housing, although research suggests far fewer residents actually will be relocated to these developments (Venkatesh et al., 2004; Wilen & Nayak, 2006). When the Midsouth Plan was proposed, the area was one of the most intensely gentrifying areas of the city based on percent change in housing prices and housing units sold (Lipman & Haines, 2007). Schools are centers of community, and closing them facilitates dispersal of existing residents and further destabilizes communities faced with loss of public housing. The new schools, with new identities, are then part of rebranding the area. In Midsouth community meetings, the link between school closings and gentrification was a dominant theme (Lipman & Haines, 2007). The same charge has been repeated in other parts of the city where schools to be closed are located in attractive locations in areas in various stages of gentrification.

The correlation between gentrification and school closings is supported by Figure 2.1, which shows the location of closed schools in relation to a key indicator of gentrification, percent change in median house prices, 2002–2004 and 2004–2006. The figure shows that school closings are in areas in early stages of gentrification as well as in areas with intense gentrification. One interpretation is that closing schools that serve low-income students of color and reopening them as new schools is part of the infrastructure to attract investors to develop an area and in turn to market the area to new home buyers (Varady & Raffel, 1995).

Figure 2.1. Schools Closed, 2001–2007: Percent Change in Median House Prices

Source: Greenlee et al., 2008, pp. 19–20

I argue then that school policy is integral to the racialized socio-spatial restructuring of the city through displacement, gentrification, and exclusion of working-class and low-income people of color. Although cast as a positive strategy for urban decay and the achievement of social stability, gentrification is driven by local, national, and global finance capital and is a means for the middle and upper-middle classes to claim control of the city—materially and culturally (Fainstein, 2001; Hackworth, 2007; N. Smith, 1996). The class and racial nature of this process is, as Neil Smith (1996) points out, hidden in the language of "mixed-income communities," "regeneration," and "renaissance." A global city driven by neoliberal economic and social logics simply has no room for public housing as devised in the 1950s and 1960s or for low-income African Americans who are, from the standpoint of capital, largely superfluous in the new economy, "threatening" to corporate and tourist culture, and sitting on what has become extremely valuable land. This defines the stakes involved in closing schools and creating new ones marketed to the middle class and to mixed-income developments.

Although I do not have space to discuss the resistance to these policies, it is important to note that there has been fierce opposition in the communities affected since 2004, including several citywide coalitions that included community organizations, unions, school reform groups, an organization for the homeless, and progressive teacher organizations (see Brown, Gutstein, & Lipman, 2009; Lipman & Haines, 2007). But what I want to turn to here is how these policies win adherents among the public, including some who stand ultimately to lose by neoliberal development.

CULTURAL POLITICS OF RENAISSANCE 2010

In this section I focus on the cultural politics of neoliberal education policy. My analysis attends to the power of discourses and ideologies to reframe issues and generate consent for hegemonic policies. It also points to the central role of ideology in developing a counter-hegemonic social movement. Challenges to neoliberal policies in favor of more liberatory ones must include a "conscious collective attempt to name the world differently" (Apple, 1996, p. 21). I consider two aspects: (1) ways in which neoliberal policies call up and resonate with embedded ideologies, with a focus on the culture of poverty as a racist ideological underpinning of policies for mixed-income schools and housing; and (2) the "good sense" (following Gramsci, 1971) of neoliberal policies, specifically charter schools, and ways in which they resonate with lived experiences and social realities. I turn first to the discourse of the "culture of poverty" as an ideological underpinning for mixed-income schools and housing. Then I propose an initial analysis of the cultural politics of charter schools, particularly ways in which they resonate with challenges of negotiating the failure of public schools to serve people of color and with historical struggles for self-determination.

Mixed-Income Schools, the Culture of Poverty, and Displacement

The central premise of HOPE VI is that high concentrations of very low-income people produce social pathologies that are at the root of an intergenerational cycle of poverty (Popkin, 2006). Proponents of the "deconcentration thesis" assume that eliminating large public housing projects, dispersing residents, and relocating them to mixed-income areas will lead to improvements in behavior, workforce participation, and, ultimately, self-sufficiency and a higher standard of living. Middle-class homeowners are expected to provide the role models and social capital that low-income people need to work themselves out of poverty (Brophy & Smith, 1997), as well as the political clout to ensure better public services, including schools. The argument for relocating low-income children to mixed-income schools is based on similar assumptions. Drawing on correlations between social class and school achievement, Richard Kahlenberg (2001) argues for the positive influence of middle-class students and parents on low-income students and parents. Kahlenberg points to the benefits to low-income children of being with middle-class children, who he claims exhibit superior language skills, motivation, and behaviors. This "common sense" is echoed in the HOPE VI literature: "Lower-income children benefit from having middle-income children in the classroom" (Raffel, Denson, Varady, & Sweeney, 2003, p. 75). In Chicago, new schools in HOPE VI mixed-income developments are expected to be one of the benefits of the demolition of public housing.

However, the many problems with the Plan for Transformation are well documented, for example, displacement, the low percentage of tenants returning to mixed-income developments, lack of one-to-one replacement, exclusionary screening policies and rules, and failure to adequately track residents (Bennett, Smith, & Wright, 2006). It is also questionable that mixed-income developments will benefit the majority of low-income displaced families or that income mixing is a solution for students (Lipman, 2008a). Rather, plans to link mixed-income housing and schools make it clear that marketing to middle-class families is the priority (Raffel et al., 2003). The one-third of units in mixed-income developments set aside for public-housing–eligible tenants do not necessarily go to former residents. In fact, work requirements, drug testing, housekeeping checks, background checks, and other exclusionary regulations ensure that many former public housing residents will not be able to return to their old neighborhoods to live in new mixed-income developments. The supposed opportunity to move to better performing schools conceals the reality of displacement and exclusion. Most displaced public housing students have been relocated to schools academically and demographically similar to those they left, with 84% attending schools with below-average district test scores and 44% in schools on probation (Catalyst Chicago, 2007). Concerns that mixed-income schools are not really for low-income families run through community meetings, public hearings, press conferences, and rallies opposing Ren2010. These concerns are validated by research on the displacement of public housing children and their lack of access to mixed-income schools in HOPE VI projects in other cities (Raffel et al., 2003; Varady, Raffel, Sweeney, & Denson, 2005).

But these realities are obscured by the ideological force of a discourse of race, poverty, morality, and behavior that resonates with the persistent racialized narrative in U.S. history of the "undeserving poor" (Katz, 1989). Although the "culture of poverty" was temporarily discredited in public policy discourse in the 1970s, the pathologization of poverty was revived with sociologist William Julius Wilson's influential underclass theory[5] and became the driving theory for the HOPE VI deconcentration consensus (Imbroscio, 2008). Bruce Katz, Vice President and Director of the Metropolitan Policy Program of the Brookings Institution, and major proponent of HOPE VI, cites public housing as "the most egregious example of how spatial concentration of poverty leads to welfare dependency, sexual promiscuity, and crime" (in Bennett, Hudspeth, & Wright, 2006, p. 194). Cultural deficit theories have remained a potent force in education, and the "culture of poverty" narrative has been reinvigorated, popularized, and legitimated for a new generation of teachers by the education entrepreneur Ruby Payne (Ng & Rury, 2006). In 2005, the CEO of CPS (now U.S. Secretary of Education) proposed closing an African American high school in a very low-income community because it exhibited "a culture of failure." Although framed in the language of class, the subtext is race. The low-income students at the center of these reforms are primarily students of color, and their supposed behavioral and attitudinal deficiencies fit the stereotypes of racialized cultural deficit theories. In this color-blind sleight of hand, race is present by implication, yet absent in the mixed-income discourse in which culture is a signifier for race (Bonilla-Silva, 2003).

Poverty as social pathology is linked to the supposedly restorative and disciplining effects of the market to encourage individual responsibility and initiative, self-discipline, and regeneration of decaying public institutions. According to this neoliberal logic, while public housing and public schools breed dysfunction and failure, private management, the market, and public–private partnerships foster excellence through entrepreneurship, competition, and choice. Neoliberal doctrine is braided to White supremacist discourses—"public" and "private" are raced metaphors, with the private associated with what is "good" and "White," and the public associated with what is "bad" and "Black" (Haymes, 1995, p. 20). The logics of capital and race intertwine as ideological grounds to eliminate public housing and close schools in Black communities.

Discursively, the policies shift public policy from economic redistribution to behavior modification, obligating the state to do nothing about root causes of poverty, racism, substandard and scarce affordable housing, and failing schools. They mask the nexus of political and investment decisions, state and capital logics, through the neoliberal era of the past 30 years that drove de-industrialization and disinvestment in inner cities as capital moved to speculative markets and sought cheap labor elsewhere. Thus they obscure the root causes of unemployment and the degradation of the built environment and deterioration of education and public housing in low-income urban neighborhoods, laying the groundwork for a new round of investment.

At the same time, "mixed-income" solutions appropriate the discourse of democracy and struggles for racial inclusion (Kahlenberg, 2001). At a forum on Ren2010 and the PFT to promote mixed-income developments, Arne Duncan, CEO of CPS, decried race and class segregation in schools (despite overseeing the institution of new magnet schools that reproduce this segregation), and he lauded the "social learning" from mixed-income schools (field notes, Renaissance Schools forum, November 17, 2005). This discourse makes displacement and gentrification permissible, even progressive. Rachel Weber (2002) notes that the neoliberal state grapples with two contradictory imperatives: creating conditions for capital accumulation and managing potential political resistance. Mixed-income policies speak to this contradiction. They facilitate the expropriation of public goods (public schools and housing) and further gentrification and the real estate market, while the democratic and inclusive discourse of mixed-income communities and schools, coupled with discourses of racial pathology, legitimate expropriation.

Cultural Politics of Charter Schools and Choice

The failures of public schools to meet test score benchmarks and parents' frustration with public schools have opened the door to the rapid growth in charter schools. The proliferation of charter schools opens public education to the market through private management of publicly funded schools and a system of consumer choice. School authority is invested in appointed boards, which may be local community organizations or groups of teachers, but increasingly charter school boards contract with for-profit Educational Management Organizations (EMOs) that are paid a fee to run multiple franchises (Ford, 2005). These large charter school ventures are another arena of capital accumulation facilitated by the cycle of disinvestment, devaluation, and reinvestment in urban areas and public institutions.

That said, we need to ask why charter schools have support beyond corporate boardrooms. In fact, why do some attract progressive teachers, recruit students of color, and develop liberatory educational models? What do we make of the complex politics of charter schools?

The New Schools Expo, held in February 2008, gives us an example of the complicated cultural politics of choice and charter schools. The expo was held at Williams Multiplex (a precursor to Ren2010 schools) and was sponsored by CPS, Parents for School Choice (http://www.parentsforschoolchoice.org/), and the Illinois Network of Charter Schools.

The expo to market charter schools to prospective students and their parents was, according to the *Chicago Defender* newspaper, attended by over 700 parents and students, mostly African American. The school parking lot was jammed with school buses that provided free transportation from the South and West Sides (African American communities). The packet of registration materials contained two glossy brochures on Ren2010, leaving no doubt that Ren2010 was central to the promotion of charter schools and that Ren2010 was the sole face of CPS at this event. Tracy Hayes, Communications Director of the Commercial Club's Renaissance Schools Fund, told the *Chicago Defender*: "We are very pleased with this event and plan to make it an annual affair" (Hutson, 2008). Bankrolled by the Illinois Network of Charter Schools, the expo was organized by Parents for School Choice, comprising dozens of African American women in red tee shirts emblazoned with the slogan: "My Choice: Great Schools. Our children's education in OUR hands. Parents for School Choice." (The group's second expo, in 2009, was attended by 4,000 people and funded by the CCC's Renaissance Schools Fund and the Gates Foundation.)

At a workshop titled "Your Child, Your Choice—New Schools from a Parent's Perspective," led by Parents for School Choice, a panel of parents and students talked about their negative experiences in public schools and the virtues of choice and charter schools. During the question and answer session, a parent in the audience from Miles Davis elementary school addressed the panelists and audience. (Parents at Miles Davis had fought since 1992 for a new building to replace their dilapidated facility. Now that the new building was almost completed, CPS planned, under the latest round of Ren2010 school closings, to turn it into a selective-enrollment magnet school. Neighborhood students would have to compete for limited enrollment slots in the new school. She appealed for support in the community's struggle to keep Miles Davis a neighborhood school. "I want the choice to send my kids to the new Miles Davis. The Board [of Education] is taking that away with Ren2010 and turning Miles Davis into a magnet school. We have a right to the school. That's our choice." She went on, "Since you all are for choice, I hope you will support us."

As the issues surrounding the new Miles Davis school exemplify, choice and charter schools are complex and highly political matters. Gramsci (1971) argued that the construction of hegemony entails ruling groups winning over other social strata to their agenda to form a dominant social bloc and gaining leadership over it. Ideologically, this is accomplished through reshaping common sense by building on people's lived experiences and needs. This does not imply that people are social dupes. A fundamental condition is that working-class people, people of color, and others who are marginalized, oppressed, and exploited act in conditions not of our own making but within the terrain available to us. In a time of strong, progressive social movements, oppressed people ally to push for a liberatory agenda. Absent a strong social movement, in periods when the agenda of dominant classes and social groups is posed as the only alternative, options for action are more limited. People may make tactical decisions to "work the system," to find cracks within an overall retrograde system to address immediate needs (Pedroni, 2007). This is particularly the case when the dominant agenda rearticulates legitimate grievances and immediate needs to its program. I think the neoliberal agenda, and charter schools specifically, exemplify this dynamic.

This theory is helpful in considering how neoliberalism becomes a hegemonic economic, social, and ideological force in the city—how it is materialized on the ground and how it might be contested. Considered in this way, neoliberalism is a process that works its way into the discourses and practices of the city through the actions of local actors, not just elites, but also marginalized and oppressed people (see Pedroni, 2007). The origins and meanings of charter schools are contradictory, located in neoliberal ideology and the logic of capital, but also in aspirations for political and cultural self-determination and frustration with the failure of public schools to educate and be responsive to communities of color in particular. Because charter schools have greater autonomy than regular public schools, they also appeal to teachers' aspirations for professional independence, flexibility, and critical practice in the face of the coercive and reductionist policies of No Child Left Behind and big urban school districts like Chicago. In these cases, teachers and communities see charters as spaces for agency in an otherwise highly centralized and regimented regime (Lipman, 2008b).

Most charter schools in Chicago are corporate-style franchises, but a few are led by community organizations or groups of teachers and parents seeking an alternative to the dominant practices of public schools. Some educators and communities of color take advantage of the greater flexibility offered by charter schools to develop culturally relevant, community-centered, social-justice–oriented education, and some socially conscious teachers choose charter schools for their promise of greater flexibility and professional authority in the face of top-down accountability policies. Thus, paradoxically, although the proliferation of charter schools is a neoliberal initiative to marketize public education, it also opens a crack for some liberatory initiatives. However, the ability of these initiatives to sustain themselves and compete in the corporate charter school market environment may be another story (see Wells, Scott, Lopez, & Holme, 2005).

Chicago's charter schools are concentrated in African American and Latino areas of the city where public schools historically have been under-resourced and that bear scars of decades of racism and public and private disinvestment. Parents' support for alternatives to regular public schools is a reasonable response to the persistent failure of public schools to provide equitable education in communities of color. This theme is reflected on the website of Parents for School Choice. It notes, front and center, that "only 45% of Chicago Public School students graduate from high school, and only 3 of every 100 African-American and Latino males in Chicago Public Schools earn a college degree" (http://www.parentsforschoolchoice.org/). Concerns with safety in public schools, lack of academic and social support for the academic success of young Black men, lack of individual attention, and unresponsive administrators run through the group's materials.

Ideologically, the charter school movement resonates with struggles for self-determination in communities of color: the 1960s community control struggles in New York, Chicago, and elsewhere, and the long tradition of Black Independent Schools. This is clear in the framework of the Betty Shabazz charter schools, which come out of the Black Independent School tradition, are rooted in African values and collective development, and explicitly challenge the deficit theories that undermine the education and future of Black children, proclaiming: "Our children bring everything they need to school." This theme echoes in the slogan on the tee shirts worn by Parents for School Choice: "My Choice: Great Schools. Our children's education in OUR hands." In a context in which parents see few viable alternatives in neighborhood schools, and in the absence of a strong social movement to transform public education, the charter school movement provides a space for individual agency.

Yet, while community-centered schools like the Shabazz schools have a collective ethos, in the neoliberal context, the larger charter school agenda rearticulates self-determination to individual choice and agency to personal responsibility. In the face of a failed public system where the neighborhood school is no longer seen as a viable educational option, a good parent must be an informed education consumer and find a way to transport her/his child to a school out of the neighborhood if necessary. One mother on a panel at the expo said, "My old school was convenient, but sometimes you have to say forget about convenience. You have to take the bus. As parents we can't blame other people, we have to take charge ourselves."

Roger Dale (1989/1990) describes the process of introducing choice in one part of the British educational system to "facilitate a shift from collectivism to individualism, from a view that a common school is desirable to one that encourages parents/consumers to shop around and maximize their children's opportunities of enjoying an 'uncommon' education" (pp. 12–13). Progress is equated with neoliberal market solutions that offer equity through market choices and quality through competition. This discourse reshapes the discussion of public education and defines the range of possible actions. While it is a discourse crafted by elites, it also is materialized through the actions of people on the ground in the face of the urgent necessity to act in a space of few alternatives.

CONCLUSION

The plan to close 20 of the 22 schools in the Midsouth in 2004 was defeated by a coalition of community organizations, Local School Councils, unions, and progressive teachers, with African American community organizations and parents in the lead. Every round of Ren2010 school closings and conversions to magnet schools and charters has been met with resistance: pickets at the Board of Education, door-to-door organizing, demonstrations at schools, student walk-outs, press conferences, school and community meetings, and Black, Latino, and White alliances. There is much discussion about an elected school board and a percolating discussion about building a movement, like the one that elected Harold Washington mayor in the 1980s, to take back the city.[6] This conversation reflects the recognition that education is linked with an urban agenda that is producing increasing economic, social, and spatial inequality and exclusion along lines of race, ethnicity, and class. This represents an emergent ideological current with roots in the historical struggles for equitable housing, schools, and community economic development in Chicago. It is one ideological current at play in the contention over education policy. Yet the PFT marches on, slowed only by the economic crisis and the stall in the housing market. Ren2010 continues.

Ren2010 and the larger neoliberal urban agenda succeed in large measure in the absence of a clear viable alternative. Regardless of whom their funders are, the concerns articulated by Parents for School Choice are grounded in the historical and present reality of the failure of too many public schools to educate children of color and the lack of control families and communities have over their children's education. The underlying concerns are aligned with those of parents fighting school closings, who argue that public schools should serve the community and that the community should have a voice, and who propose fundamental changes and improvements in their schools. Further, some charter schools may provide models for what liberatory education in public schools should look like. Challenging the neoliberal agenda requires attention to the common sense that has been constructed around it and to the deeply felt concerns of families and communities and teachers to which it speaks.

At the same time, neoliberal plans to displace African American families and students and create schools that appeal to the middle class are legitimated by a racialized discourse of pathology. The construction of "easily discardable people and social life" (Wilson, Wouters, & Cremmenos, 2004, p. 1181) is central to generating broad public consensus around the logic of dismantling public housing and closing schools and dispersing residents. Every school that is closed for "failure" reproduces the "truth" of dysfunctional communities of color. This "truth" legitimates turning over schools in Black communities to corporate "turnaround" operators, disbanding Local School Councils, running schools through charter school companies, and top-down decisions by school officials about what kind of school a community should have.

The disenfranchisement, the striving for some measure of community control over schools and the work that goes on in schools, the goals of making schools serve their community's development—these are threads running through the contradictory politics of neoliberal educational reforms in Chicago. Neoliberalism is a process. It is fraught with contradictions and contention that play out in local contexts. These contradictions can be particularly instructive for those of us committed to working for the transformation of public education and a more just social order. If educators and communities are to challenge the neoliberal urban agenda with an alternative agenda, they will need to draw on not only the outrage at closing schools and closing down democratic participation, but also the ways in which these policies resonate with people's experiences and struggles.

NOTES

1. This includes three military academies. It also includes three small high schools fought for through a hunger strike by Mexican mothers and grandmothers. School founders publicly disavowed connection with Ren2010 although CPS continues to claim them on its website (http://www.ren2010.cps.k12.il.us/docs/Renaissance2010Schools.pdf)

2. As of this writing, Chicago's Mayor is sitting on a $1 billion TIF slush fund that he controls (Joravsky & Dumke, 2009).

3. For extensive coverage of Chicago TIFs, see *The Reader TIF Archive* at http://www.chicagoreader.com/tifarchive/

4. In 2008, an organization designated to manage five turn-around schools advertised 100 teaching positions in the schools and closed the application process 7 days before the board met to vote on closing the schools and turning them over.

5. Wilson argued that structural changes in the economy and the exodus of middle-class African Americans from inner-city communities breed an underclass culture that is a principal barrier to African American labor force participation.

6. Washington was Chicago's first and only Black mayor, elected through a mass movement coalition of African Americans, Latinos, and progressive whites.

REFERENCES

Apple, M. (1996). *Cultural politics and education.* New York: Teachers College Press.

Ball, S. J. (1994). *Education reform: A critical and post-structural approach.* Buckingham, UK: Open University Press.

Barlow, A. L. (2003). *Between fear and hope: Globalization and race in the United States.* Lanham, MD: Rowman & Littlefield.

Bennett, L., Hudspeth, N., & Wright, P. A. (2006). A critical analysis of the ABLA redevelopment plan. In L. Bennett, J. L. Smith, & P. A. Wright (Eds.), *Where are poor people to live? Transforming public housing communities* (pp. 185–215). Armonk, NY: M.E. Sharpe.

Bennett, L., Smith, J. L., & Wright, P. A. (Eds.). (2006). *Where are poor people to live? Transforming public housing communities.* Armonk, NY: M.E. Sharpe.

Bonilla-Silva, E. (2003). *Racism without racists.* Lanham, MD: Rowman & Littlefield.

Brenner, N., & Theodore, N. (2002). Cities and the geographies of "actually existing neoliberalism." *Antipode, 34*(3), 349–379.

Brophy, P. C., & Smith, R. N. (1997). Mixed income housing: Factors for success. *Cityscape: A Journal of Policy Development and Research, 3*(2), 3–31.

Brown, J., Gutstein, E., & Lipman, P. (2009). Arne Duncan and the Chicago success story: Myth or reality? *Rethinking Schools, 23*(3), 10–14.

Catalyst Chicago. (2007, February). Special report: School autonomy all over the map. Available at http://www.catalyst-chicago.org/news/index.php?item=2141&cat=23

Clowes, G. (2004). Competition and partnerships are keys to Chicago renaissance plan. *School Reform News.* Available at http://www.heartland.org/publications/school%20 reform/article/15701/Competition_and_Partnerships_Are_Keys_to_Chicago_ Renaissance_Plan.html

Dale, R. (1989/1990). The Thatcherite project in education: The case of the City Technology Colleges. *Critical Social Policy, 9*(27), 4–19.

Demissie, F. (2006). Globalization and the remaking of Chicago. In J. P. Koval, L. Bennett, M. I. J. Bennett, F. Demissie, R. Garner, & K. Kiljoong (Eds.), *The new Chicago: A social and cultural analysis* (pp. 19–31). Philadelphia, PA: Temple University Press.

Fainstein, S. (2001). *City builders: Property development in New York and London, 1980– 2000* (2nd ed.). Lawrence: University of Kansas Press.

Ford, B. (2005). The significance of charter schools and the privatization of standards: Holding the wolf by the ears. *Policy Futures in Education, 3*(1), 16–29.

Gramsci, A. (1971). *Selections from the prison notebooks* (Q. Hoare & G. Nowell Smith, Eds.). New York: International Publishers.

Greenlee, A., Hudspeth, N., Lipman, P., Smith, D. A., & Smith, J. (2008). *Examining CPS' plan to close, consolidate, turn-around 18 schools* (Data and Democracy Project: Investing in Neighborhoods, Research Paper Series, 1). Collaborative for Equity and Justice in Education and Nathalie P. Voorhees Center for Neighborhood and Community Improvement, University of Illinois-Chicago.

Hackworth, J. (2007). *The neoliberal city: Governance, ideology, and development in American Urbanism.* Ithaca, NY: Cornell University Press.

Harvey, D. (2001). *Spaces of capital: Towards a critical geography.* London: Routledge.

Harvey, D. (2005). *A brief history of neoliberalism.* Oxford: Oxford University Press.

Haymes, S. N. (1995). *Race, culture and the city.* Albany: State University of New York Press.

Hutson, W. (2008, February 13). Parents and students attend new schools expo. *Chicago Defender.* Available at http://www.chicagodefender.com/article-444-parents-and-students-attend-new-schools-expo.html

Imbroscio, D. (2008). "United and actuated by some common impulse of passion": Challenging the dispersal consensus in American housing policy research. *Journal of Urban Affairs, 30*(2), 111–130.

Joravsky, B., & Dumke, M. (2009, October 22). The shadow budget. *The Reader.* Available at http://www.chicagoreader.com/chicago/the-chicago-shadow-tif-budget/Content?oid =1218391

Kahlenberg, R. D. (2001). *All together now: The case for economic integration of the public schools.* Washington, DC: Brookings Institution Press.

Katz, M. (1989). *The undeserving poor: From the war on poverty to the war on welfare.* New York: Pantheon Books.

Katz, M. B. (1992). Chicago school reform as history. *Teachers College Record, 94*(1), 56–72.

Left Behind. (2003). A report of the Education Committee of the Civic Committee. Chicago: Commercial Club of Chicago.

Lipman, P. (2004). *High stakes education: Inequality, globalization, and urban school reform.* New York: Routledge.

Lipman, P. (2008a). Mixed-income schools and housing: Advancing the neoliberal urban agenda. *Journal of Education Policy, 23*(2), 119–134.

Lipman, P. (2008b). Paradoxes of teaching in neoliberal times. In S. Gewirtz, P. Mahony, I. Hextall, & A. Cribb (Eds.), *Changing teacher professionalism: International trends, challenges and ways forward* (pp. 67–80). London: Routledge.

Lipman, P. (2011). *The new political economy of urban education: Neoliberalism, race, and the right to the city.* New York: Routledge.

Lipman, P., & Haines, N. (2007). From education accountability to privatization and African American exclusion—Chicago public schools Renaissance 2010. *Educational Policy, 21*(3), 471–502.

Lipman, P., Person, A., & Kenwood Oakland Community Organization. (2007). *Students as collateral damage? A preliminary study of Renaissance 2010 school closings in the Midsouth.* Chicago: Kenwood Oakland Community Organization. Available at http://www.uic.edu/educ/ceje/index.html

Lipsitz, G. (1998). *Possessive investment in whiteness: How white people profit from identity politics.* Philadelphia: Temple University Press.

MacArthur Foundation. (2005, Spring). *Revitalizing Bronzeville: Mixed-income housing is key to community strength* [Newsletter]. Available at http://www.macfound.org/site/apps/nlnet/content2.aspx?c=lkLXJ8MQKrH&b=1075127&ct=1464617&notoc=1

Ng, J., & Rury, J. L. (2006). Poverty and education: A critical analysis of the Ruby Payne phenomenon. *Teachers College Record.* Available at http://www.tcrecord.org/Content.asp?contentid=12596

Olszewski, L., & Sadovi, C. (2003, December 19). Rebirth of schools set for South Side. *Chicago Tribune*, Sect. 1, p. 1.

Peck, J., & Tickell, A. (2002). Neoliberalizing space. In N. Brenner & N. Theodore (Eds.), *Spaces of neoliberalism: Urban restructuring in North America and Western Europe* (pp. 33–57). Oxford: Blackwell.

Pedroni, T. C. (2007). *Market movements: African American involvement in school voucher reform.* New York: Routledge.

Popkin, S. J. (2006). The HOPE VI program: What has happened to the residents? In L. Bennett, J. L. Smith, & P. A. Wright (Eds.), *Where are poor people to live? Transforming public housing communities* (pp. 68–92). Armonk, NY: M. E. Sharpe.

Raffel, J. A., Denson, L. R., Varady, D. P., & Sweeney, S. (2003). *Linking housing and public schools in the HOPE VI public housing revitalization program: A case study analysis of four developments in four cities.* Available at http://www.udel.edu/ccrs/pdf/LinkingHousing.pdf

Sassen, S. (2006). *Cities in a world economy* (3rd ed.). Thousand Oaks, CA: Pine Forge Press.

Smith, N. (1996). *The new urban frontier: Gentrification and the revanchist city.* New York: Routledge.

Smith, N. (2002). New globalism, new urbanism: Gentrification as global urban strategy. *Antipode, 34*(3), 427–450.

Smith, J. L. (2006). Mixed-income communities: Designing out poverty or pushing out the poor? In L. Bennett, J. L. Smith, & P. A. Wright (Eds.), *Where are poor people to live? Transforming public housing communities* (pp. 282–300). Armonk, NY: M. E. Sharpe.

Varady, D. P., & Raffel, J. A. (1995). *Selling cities: Attracting homebuyers through schools and housing programs.* Albany: State University of New York Press.

Varady, D., Raffel, J. A., Sweeney, S., & Denson, L. (2005). Attracting middle-income families in the HOPE VI public housing revitalization program. *Journal of Urban Affairs, 27*(2), 149–164.

Venkatesh, S. A., Celimli, I., Miller, D., Murphy, A., & Turner, B. (2004, February). *Chicago public housing transformation: A research report.* New York: Center for Urban Research and Policy, Columbia University.

Wacquant, L. (2001). The penalization of poverty and the rise of neo-liberalism. *European Journal of Criminal Policy and Research, 9*(4), 401–412.

Weber, R. (2002). Extracting value from the city: Neoliberalism and urban redevelopment. *Antipode, 34*(3), 519–540.

Wells, A. S., Scott, J. T., Lopez, A., & Holme, J. J. (2005). Charter school reform and the shifting meaning of educational equity: Greater voice and greater inequality? In J. Petrovich & A. S. Wells (Eds.), *Bringing equity back: Research for a new era in American educational policy* (pp. 219–243). New York: Teachers College Press.

Wilen, W. P., & Nayak, R. D. (2006). Relocating public housing residents have little hope of returning: Work requirements for mixed-income public housing developments. In L. Bennett, J. L. Smith, & P. A. Wright (Eds.), *Where are poor people to live? Transforming public housing communities* (pp. 239–258). Armonk, NY: M.E. Sharpe.

Wilson, D. (2007). *Cities and race: American's new black ghetto.* London: Routledge.

Wilson, D., Wouters, J., & Cremmenos, D. (2004). Successful protect-community discourse: Spatiality and politics in Chicago's Pilsner neighborhood. *Environment and Planning A, 36*, 1173–1190.

CHAPTER 3

The Rise of Venture Philanthropy and the Ongoing Neoliberal Assault on Public Education

The Eli and Edythe Broad Foundation

Kenneth Saltman

In the past decade educational policy and reform increasingly have come under the sway of a new form of philanthropy. Venture philanthropy is modeled on venture capital and the investments in the technology boom of the early 1990s. Venture philanthropy pushes privatization and deregulation, the most significant policy dictates of neoliberalism (Harvey, 2005),[1] by championing charter schools, voucher schemes, private scholarship tax credits, and corporate models of curriculum, administration, and teacher preparation and practice; in addition, it is also consistent with the steady expansion of neoliberal language and rationales in public education, including the increasing centrality of business terms to describe educational reforms and policies: *choice, competition, efficiency, accountability, monopoly, turnaround*, and *failure*. Venture philanthropy in education—whose leading proponents include the Bill and Melinda Gates Foundation, the Eli and Edythe Broad Foundation, and the Walton Family Foundation—departs radically from the age of "scientific" industrial philanthropy characterized by Carnegie, Rockefeller, and Ford. These traditional philanthropies, despite pursuing a largely conservative role of undermining radical social movements, nonetheless framed their projects in terms of the public good and sought to provide individuals with public information through schools, libraries, and museums.

The Assault on Public Education: Confronting the Politics of Corporate School Reform, edited by William H. Watkins. Copyright © 2012 by Teachers College, Columbia University. All rights reserved. Prior to photocopying items for classroom use, please contact the Copyright Clearance Center, Customer Service, 222 Rosewood Dr., Danvers, MA 01923, USA, tel. (978) 750-8400, www.copyright.com.

Venture philanthropy treats schooling as a private consumable service and promotes business remedies, reforms, and assumptions with regard to public schooling. Some of the most significant projects involve promoting charter schools to inject market competition and "choice" into the public sector, as well as using cash bonuses for teacher pay and to "incentivize" students.

Venture philanthropy treats giving to public schooling as a "social investment" that, like venture capital, must begin with a business plan, must involve quantitative measurement of efficacy, must be replicable to be "brought to scale," and ideally will "leverage" public spending in ways compatible with the strategic donor. In the parlance of venture philanthropy, grants are referred to as "investments," donors are called "investors," impact is renamed "social return," evaluation becomes "performance measurement," grant reviewing turns into "due diligence," the grant list is renamed an "investment portfolio," charter networks are referred to as "franchises"—to name but some of the recasting of giving on investment. Within the view of venture philanthropy, donors are framed as both entrepreneurs and consumers, while recipients are represented as investments. One of most significant aspects of this transformation in educational philanthropy involves the ways that the public and civic purposes of public schooling are redescribed by venture philanthropy in distinctly private ways. Such a view carries significant implications for a society theoretically dedicated to public democratic ideals. This is no small matter in terms of how the public and civic roles of public schooling have become nearly overtaken by the economistic neoliberal perspective that views public schooling as principally a matter of producing workers and consumers for the economy and for global economic competition.

Although educational philanthropy and venture philanthropy in particular represent a very small portion of the roughly $600 billion annual expenditure on education in the United States, venture philanthropy has a strategic aim of "leveraging" private money to influence public schooling in ways compatible with the longstanding privatization agendas of the political right; conservative think tanks such as the Heritage Foundation, the Hoover Institution, and the Fordham Foundation; corporate foundations such as ExxonMobil; and corporate organizations such as the Business Roundtable and the Commercial Club of Chicago. The central agenda is to transform public education in the United States into a market through for-profit and nonprofit charter schools, vouchers, and "scholarship" tax credits for private schooling, or "neovouchers." Venture philanthropies such as New Schools Venture Fund and the Charter School Growth Fund are being financed by the large givers and aim to create national networks of charter schools, charter management organizations, and Educational Management Organizations (EMOs). These organizations are explicit about their intent to radically transform public education in the United States through various strategies. Along these lines, the venture philanthropists also are working in conjunction with large urban school districts and business groups to orchestrate such plans as New York's New Visions for Public Schools, Chicago's Renaissance 2010, and similar mixed-income/mixed-finance schools and housing projects in Portland, OR, Boston, and elsewhere. These coordinate the privatizations of schooling and housing and gentrify coveted sections of cities. Venture philanthropy projects are aggressively seeking to re-imagine teacher education through online and onsite initiatives and educational leadership on the model of the MBA. The key players of venture philanthropy in education —including but not limited to such leaders as Gates, Walton, Fisher, and Broad—are able to exercise influence disproportionate to their size and spending power through strategic arrangements with charter- and voucher-promoting organizations, think tanks, universities, school districts, and schools. The seed money desperately sought by underfunded schools allows the venture philanthropists to "leverage" influence over educational policy and planning, curriculum and instructional practices, and the very idea of what it means to be an educated person. Although the implications for educational reform are vast, there has been scant scholarship on venture philanthropy in education.[2]

The Obama administration's approach to education shares the venture philanthropy perspective and agenda, imagining public schooling as a private market within which schools must compete for scarce resources. The neoliberal ideal of public–private partnership can be found at the center of this agenda, as charter schools are being aggressively supported as a means of injecting "competition" and "choice" into the public sector. In fact, the Obama administration has taken the cue from the largest venture philanthropy, the Gates Foundation. The central project of the Gates Foundation in the first decade of the new millennium has been charter school expansion. As soon as Obama was elected in the fall of 2008, Gates redirected the foundation's educational influence in the direction of graduation rates. Obama's announcement in the summer of 2009 of the Race to the Top competition among public school districts and states for a limited pool of money not only replicates the punitive educational doctrine of the Bush administration but also is informed by the Eli Broad prize, discussed below, which uses competition between locales for limited scholarship money in an attempt to steer educational policy. In what follows here I criticize the major Broad educational reform projects and by extension the Obama administration's embrace of the same policies and assumptions about education.

THE ELI AND EDYTHE BROAD FOUNDATION

A crucial part of venture philanthropy's aim to radically transform public schooling on the model of the market involves remaking administrator preparation on the corporate model. The Eli and Edythe Broad Education Foundation is the most active and aggressive venture philanthropy with this focus. Broad is funding educational leadership training projects to recruit corporate, military, and nonprofit leaders to public education. The Broad Foundation also is seeking to deregulate teacher and administrator preparation programs, which will take such programs away from the purview of universities and put them under the control of private nonprofit companies that largely embrace corporate ideology. Broad is funding scholarships for schools and students that pay out for "achievement gains." The Broad initiatives are unified in an emphasis on standardized test-based performance achievement tracking, a goal of creating test databases for long-term tracking of student test scores to direct educational policy and to determine the effectiveness of teacher and administrator preparation programs. The Broad Foundation also is working to expand privatization in the form of charter schools and to "franchise" charter management organizations. While on the surface these initiatives may not seem closely related, they share a common set of ideals and a cohesive vision for public schooling that can best be understood as an expression of neoliberal ideology applied to education.

In education, neoliberalism has taken hold with tremendous force, remaking educational common sense and pushing forward the privatization and deregulation agendas. The steady rise of business language and logic in pedagogy, policy, curriculum, and administrative doctrine suggests the sweeping extent to which neoliberal ideals have succeeded in taking over educational debates. Neoliberalism appears in the now commonsense framing of education exclusively through presumed ideals of upward individual economic mobility (the promise of cashing in knowledge for jobs) and the social ideals of global economic competition. The "TINA" thesis that has come to dominate politics throughout much of the world (There Is No Alternative to the Market) has infected educational thought, as the only questions on reform agendas appear to be how best to enforce knowledge and curriculum conducive to national economic interest and the expansion of a corporately managed model of globalization as perceived from the perspective of business. Despite the financial crisis and utter failure of unfettered deregulation of private markets in education, neoliberal assumptions continue to reign supreme as much of the market-based educational reform of the Bush administration is carried forward by Obama and the Democratic party. What is dangerously framed out within the neoliberal view is the role of democratic participation in societies ideally committed to democracy and the role of public schools in preparing public democratic citizens with the tools for meaningful and participatory self-governance. By reducing the politics of education to its economic roles, neoliberal educational reform has deeply authoritarian tendencies that are incompatible with democracy. As the only concern becomes one of the efficient enforcement of the "right" knowledge, critical engagement, investigation, and intellectual curiosity, not to mention cultural and class differences, appear as impediments to learning, as teachers are treated as deskilled deliverers of prepackaged curricula, prohibiting their potential as critical intellectuals.[3]

After earning billions in real estate and finance, Eli Broad created and runs the Broad Foundation. In retirement he has been working full-time on urban public school reform. Broad is one of the three largest venture philanthropies, along with the Bill and Melinda Gates Foundation and the Walton Family foundations. However, of the three, Broad has done by far the most to transform the running of public schools by seeking to influence administrator preparation, the meaning and value of teacher and administrator quality, and school boards.

Broad's educational activities derive from a few key assumptions about improving public schooling, including: (1) that the problems facing public schools are administrative problems caused by bad management practices—especially bad public school managers who lack the leadership skills of the private sector; (2) that public school improvement begins with top-down reform; (3) that educational quality can be understood principally through standardized test-derived achievement scores; and (4) that poor and minority students suffer from an "achievement gap" that can be remedied through better educational methods and management. On their own many of these assumptions are widely held rather than specific to Broad. However, taken together these assumptions are closely aligned with the neoliberal educational reform movement as championed by not only the venture philanthropists but also neoliberal think tanks like the Fordham Foundation, American Enterprise Institute, Hoover Institution, and leading right-wing policy wonks associated with them, especially Chester Finn and Frederick Hess, among others.

In what follows here I focus on three dimensions of Broad's educational projects to illustrate how what is represented in academic and public discourse as generosity, care, excellence, and improvement ought rather to be understood as an expression of particular values, visions, and political ideologies in education that are hostile to public forms of schooling, that celebrate and promote a corporate and private rather than public perspective on educational governance, and that have an anti-intellectual and anti-critical approach to knowledge and curriculum.

THE LEADERSHIP AGENDA

A central priority of the Eli Broad Foundation is to recruit and train superintendents and principals from outside the ranks of professional teachers and educational administrators and, related to this, to shift administrator preparation away from universities and state certification to the control of outside organizations that embrace corporate and military styles of management and that share the venture philanthropy agenda. These programs include, most notably, Broad, New Leaders for New Schools (NLNS), and KIPP's training program. At the core of these initiatives has been the neoliberal celebration of the private sector and denigration of all things public. In this view, educational leadership is imagined ideally as corporate management, and the legacy of public educational administration is devalued. Policy literature in the area of educational administration refers to what Broad spearheads for leadership as the "deregulation agenda."

Writing that the Broad Foundation is part of this movement to end certification and licensure in universities, BetsAnn Smith (2008) has done one of the most comprehensive examinations of the deregulation agenda and the effort to create outside deregulated educational institutions for leader preparation. Smith argues that not only is there no evidence justifying the deregulation movement that is being pushed by right-wing think tanks and corporate foundations, but that the turn to outside leaders relies heavily on what she calls a "compositional argument"—that is, a cultural narrative about the "bullish CEO." To put it differently, the call for turning to leaders from the business sector and the military should be understood not merely as one cultural narrative but as a cultural narrative that is part of a broader ideology of corporate culture within which a series of interlocking business and military metaphors plays a central role in setting the stage for policy.

In the case of the outside leader ideal, the educational administrator as bullish CEO merges with the description of educational values through metaphors of efficiency, choice, competition, and accountability. These metaphors rely for their intelligibility on their opposites, including ascription of the public bureaucracy and the ensconced public leader as inefficient, monolithic and imposing, monopolistic, and unaccountable. The educational leader as bullish CEO hence participates in the much broader tendency found across scholarly and public discourse to imagine the school as a business, the school workers as businesspeople, and the students as consumers of private services. Within this view of privatized schooling, the leader naturally should be from the private sector or from the military.

Within this corporatized view of educational leadership found in venture philanthropy, military leadership is celebrated for its alleged link with corporate management—a focus on discipline, order, and enforcement of mandates through a hierarchy at every level of public schooling. The "natural discipline" of the market is discursively linked to the corporeal discipline of the military. The turn to military leaders of public schools began in the late 1990s with Seattle and Washington, DC, appointing military generals as "CEOs." This has picked up speed, as seen in the expansion of programs such as "Troops to Teachers," which puts veterans in the classroom; the expansion of public schools run as military academies (Chicago leads the nation with six schools so far); increases in military recruitment in schools, accompanied by slick corporate youth advertising; and the No Child Left Behind (NCLB) law, which mandated that student personal information automatically be given to military recruiters unless parents intervened. The turn to military leaders particularly for urban poor and predominantly African American and Latino student bodies belies a profoundly racialized phenomenon within which these students are framed as suffering primarily from a lack of discipline, which the military and the corporation can supply (Saltman & Gabbard, 2003).

The discourse of discipline typified by the turn to the military and corporate leader actively denies the social conditions informing the experience of schooling. Instead of acknowledging how social inequalities influence educational access, such discourse reduces the language of educational opportunity to a narrative of individual discipline. Broken schools, absent textbooks, underpaid and overworked teachers, large class sizes, communities beset by unemployment, public disinvestment, dire poverty, skyrocketing homelessness, not to mention unequal distribution of cultural capital—in short, all of the material and symbolic social conditions inside and outside of schools that render schooling difficult to impossible—are made to seem to be irrelevant when discipline frames schooling. The celebration of the disciplinarian administrator is deployed in conjunction with multiple other disciplinarian policies, such as the implementation of school uniforms, zero tolerance policies for expelling students, vast expansion of surveillance technologies in schools, surprise searches, and police school invasions (Robbins, 2008). The turn to the authoritarian disciplinarian can be found not only in policy but across public discourse in films, television shows, news stories, and advertisements about schooling that participate in what Henry Giroux, Mike Males, Lawrence Grossberg, and others have extensively detailed as a discursive and material "war on youth" being waged in the United States. In this "war," kids are blamed for a myriad of social and economic problems, while legal and public protections for kids are scaled back (Giroux, 2004a; Grossberg, 2005; Males, 1996).

Through most of the first decade of the new millennium, an unabated barrage of representations across the mass media educated Americans in the virtues of the hard-nosed CEO, from Jack Welch and his goal of regularly firing 10% of the General Electric workforce to discipline the entire company, to the return of an omnipresent Donald Trump selling viewers the fantasy of being an apprentice bullish CEO on reality TV. In this context the billionaire CEO Eli Broad and his application of business ideals to educational leadership appeared to many people to be offering the gift of corporate and military efficiencies and discipline to the beleaguered public schools. But the context for interpretation recently has changed.

As the financial crisis of 2008 hit, it became readily apparent across the political spectrum that the neoliberal idea of markets regulating themselves without state support and intervention is no longer tenable. (In a sense it never was very credible, as the neoliberal program required state support and regulation despite the ideology [see Harvey, 2005].) As waves of financial corporations collapsed or had to be saved through massive federal intervention, the assumptions behind the market fundamentalism of the past 40 years began to be called into question. Neoliberal former head of the U.S. Federal Reserve Bank Alan Greenspan appeared before Congress and admitted that the view of the economy that informed his decision to allow greater and greater deregulation of derivative markets had been wrong. Liberal economist Joseph Stiglitz came to a similar conclusion that the financial crisis could best be understood by grasping that everything came back to deregulation and the faith in markets to regulate themselves. As Henry Giroux and Susan Searls Giroux (2008) wisely point out, a consequence of the broader pedagogical effect of neoliberalism on both education and the culture at large has been a difficulty for the public to formulate and name alternative visions to the failed neoliberal ones. This is, as they rightly suggest, a significant problem. With a legacy of schooling overtaken by anti-critical approaches such as standardized testing, scripted lessons, commercialism, pay for grades, and so on, they prohibit the kinds of questioning, critical dialogue, and tools of investigation necessary for the fostering of democratic culture that citizens must learn in order to participate in reworking civil society with others.

The Broad Foundation's neoliberal approach to educational reform must be viewed with profound skepticism for two primary reasons. First, it is modeled on the same neoliberal assumptions (privatization and market deregulation) that have been thoroughly discredited as being behind the economic crisis. In other words, Broad and the other venture philanthropists assume that education is like business and should adopt the same framing language and guiding rationales. As well, neoliberal ideology forms the foundation for expanding the market metaphor to all areas of social life, conflating public and private spheres, and eradicating a sense of the public good in favor of a society composed of nothing but private consumers.

Second, in the case of Eli Broad, at issue is not simply that he, like the other venture philanthropists, adopted the language of venture capital and sought to apply it to education. Broad's fortune and hence his ability to steer educational reform, debate, and policy through his foundation derive from the two primary industries at the center of the financial crisis and subsequent economic meltdown—namely, real estate and finance. What is more, Broad made a killing in these industries specifically by using them synergistically rather than competitively. So the Broad narrative of financial success, deregulation, and idealization of corporate culture is falling apart not only due to the collapse of the neoliberal ideology that grounds it but also due to the fact Broad's neoliberal educational reform was always premised on assumptions that contradicted the origins of Broad's own wealth—namely, speculative capital in a bubble economy and monopolistic behavior. What the financial crisis reveals about Broad is that what he has sold as a narrative of skill and hard work that every schoolchild should emulate, instead ought to be understood as the result of the clever working of an economic context that was grounded in layers of gambling—an economy that was a house of cards.

The mortgage crisis of 2008 was the result of deregulation of banking compounded by the hawking of mortgage-backed securities that when made into securities were sliced and diced to appear to be secure assets but were in fact highly risky and speculative. This in turn was compounded by the linkage to these mortgage-backed securities of loan default swaps that were effectively free insurance policies on the mortgage-backed securities, which multiplied the effect of debt creation when these bad investments failed. The amount of money in the economy multiplied radically through speculation between 2001 and 2007. At their most basic, Broad's fortune was based in speculative capital made possible by the neoliberal dictate of deregulation. The removal of public controls over private capital set the stage for the amassing of Broad's personal fortune and contributed to the broader radical upward redistribution of wealth and income throughout the past 30 years. It is precisely the ideal of deregulation that Broad extrapolates as a metaphor to apply to public education. If only the public sector can be made to look like and act like the private sector, so goes the metaphor, then the public sector can be improved. And the only way to do that is to shrink public control over public institutions and hand control over to those from the private sector. But the metaphor is misleading. There are great differences between public and private institutions, their missions, and their leadership.

Educational leaders for public schools have distinctly public obligations and responsibilities that differ from the obligations and responsibilities of private sector managers. Private sector managers are responsible foremost for maximizing profit for owners or shareholders. Their decision making, skills, training, and relations with employees, in short, all that a private sector manager does, foster the financial goal of profit. Educational leaders for public schools are responsible to the public, namely, to the community and the parents, students, and teachers who form it. The end of public school administration is not profit maximization but public service. Additionally, the private corporation has a particularly hierarchical organizational structure, with the owners and managers at the top with near-absolute authority. The public school, being publicly accountable, has a considerably more democratic organizational structure, with administrators answerable to multiple constituencies within the community.

In both a practical and political sense, as BetsAnn Smith (2008) suggests, the outside private manager will not be attracted to the kinds of programs championed by Broad because although "attracted to the idea of 'running a school,' many aspirants overlook public schooling's democratic complexities and the degree to which its leadership demands are unrelenting and unrelentingly public" (p. 51). Smith's study of the case of deregulation in Michigan highlights the differences between large districts, which have been subject to anti-democratic mayoral takeovers, and the majority of districts, which remain subject to democratic oversight. The mayorally appointed CEOs sit in closed-door meetings where they generally are told that the priorities are test scores and "restoring fiscal order" (Smith, 2008, p. 51). Such set-ups subvert the messy public struggles for educational and public priorities waged in and through public institutions. Of course, in the context of an era of high-stakes standardized testing and the standardization of curricula and other anti-critical approaches to teaching and learning, such narrow imperatives for test scores and cost-cutting promoted in the name of business efficiency become above all else instruments to ensure a profoundly anti-intellectual pedagogical approach to schooling dominated by rote learning and memorization, scripted lessons, and decontextualized facts. Not only do these approaches undermine the possibilities of public schools operating as critical intellectual public spheres, but they also have implications for the kinds of social relations, identification, and identities that they produce for the activities people do outside of schools. In other words, democratic culture depends upon the built capacities for criticism, debate, and deliberation that critical intellectual public schools can develop. The corporate approach to schooling, of which the corporate bullish CEO is a part, undermines the civic possibilities that public schooling can have for communities by imagining school governance as being imposed from above and outside rather than from within the community, while suggesting that knowledge must be imposed and enforced rather than beginning with the experience of those in the community. Some educational policy writers on the political right are quite explicit in championing the corporate-style outside leader.

In the journal *Educational Policy,* Frederick Hess and Andrew Kelly (Hess & Kelly, 2005) of the neoliberal American Enterprise Institute call for a "radical" restructuring of leader preparation that would involve thoroughly importing business management and principles into the curriculum, redefining the meaning of candidate qualifications to be understood through the outside leader and primarily the business leader, stripping control of universities in leader preparation and licensure and teacher education generally, and shifting control to foundations with venture philanthropy ideals, such as Broad, NLNS, and KIPP. Hess and Kelly see as progress, although insufficiently "radical" progress, such programs as those state-based ones in Ohio and Georgia that are modeled on corporate management academies. The Ohio Principals Leadership Academy was run by a former trainer who developed management academies for companies such as Bath and Body Works. But for these authors, the problem is that they do not recruit enough middle management directly from business.

This outside leader ideal, as it is championed by Hess and Kelly, Finn, and others of the neoliberal perspective, calls for educational leadership candidates to be educated the way that NLNS does it: Having a "proven" track record of leadership experience outside education before even beginning, candidates then will be further educated by business school and education faculty and will learn educational research and "business school literature on organizational change, management, negotiation, and conflict resolution" (Hess & Kelly, 2005, p. 170). Hess and Kelly also suggest that KIPP's corporate management training model for leadership preparation is ideal. It is housed in UC Berkeley's Haas School of Business and funded by the Fisher Foundation, which is an aggressively pro-privatization venture philanthropy foundation run by the owners of the Gap, Banana Republic, and Old Navy. Students learn from business professors while "the curriculum fuses the KIPP ethos that results matter with more conventional business practices" (p. 171). "Through the examination of case studies about successful companies, such as Southwest Airlines and FedEx, students consider what lessons the private sector may hold for K–12 management" (p. 172).

Like the corporate approach of NLNS and KIPP, Broad's Academy is based in the ideal of making "great leaders." And great leaders for Broad come largely from business or accept a business view of administration.

> Dan Katzir, the Broad Foundation's managing director and an instructor in the academy, told the fellows that Southwest Airlines and the computer giant Dell Inc. are examples of how new players entered an established market, came up with innovative strategies and achieved success. The message: Urban superintendents can, and should, do the same. (Maxwell, 2006, p. 37)

The point not to be missed here is that "great managers" for Broad follow the management style, precepts, assumptions, and language from the private sector. Part of what is at issue here is the venture philanthropy approach to educational leadership that views public schools as a private market and views private corporations as the model for public institutions. The confusion between public and private institutions and values has enormous implications for educational governance, material struggles over educational resources, and especially the conceptualization of knowledge in both public schools and educational leadership programs.

This is not merely a matter of instituting a corporate style of educational leadership. Such pedagogy also involves teaching future leaders to understand their identities in reference to the private sector rather than to the public sphere, and teaching future leaders about the alleged virtues of privatization schemes such as "choice" and charter schools (Maxwell, 2006). For example, such projects encourage social relations forged through the hierarchical organizational form of the corporation and the concentrated authority of the corporate leader rather than through the collective, dialogic wielding of power found in more democratic organizational forms.

THE BROAD PROJECTS SHARE A VIEW ABOUT KNOWLEDGE

For Broad, public schools, teacher education programs, and educational leadership programs are all described as businesses. The description hangs on a metaphor of efficient delivery of a standardized product (knowledge) all along the product supply chain: The product is alleged to be high-quality, neutral, universally valuable education. The deliverable, knowledge, is positioned like a product. In the case of K–12, knowledge, which is presumed to be universal and objective, is to be standardized, measured, and tested. Test scores in this view are the ultimate arbiter of educational quality and, like units of commodity or money, can allow for the quantification of growth and progress. For Broad, this is called "achievement." Hence, one of Broad's major initiatives is the "closing of the achievement gap" and the funding of school districts and schools that improve the test scores of non-White students. The presumption is that the unequal distribution of the product, knowledge, can be remedied through methodological interventions such as the introduction of rigid pedagogical reforms, the introduction of proper business incentives such as teacher bonus pay, or paying students for grades, as well as management reforms such as installing businesspeople to manage schools and getting unions and school boards out of the way of these business-based, "achievement-oriented" reform efforts. The moment the goal of education becomes "achievement," the crucial ongoing conversation about the purposes and values of schooling stops, as does the struggle over whose knowledge and values and ways of seeing should be taught and learned.

This perspective about knowledge as measurable, quantifiable, universally valuable, and neutral directs Broad's biggest initiatives: the leadership agenda, the "Broad Prize," and the database project. The leadership agenda imagines educational leaders as business managers who can increase test-based achievement like increasing financial revenue and who can decrease the "achievement gap" like a CEO seeking to close the earnings gap with business competitors.

As Fenwick English argues, the movement in educational leadership to standardize a knowledge base (and then enforce it through ISLLC/ELCC standards applied in NCATE/National Policy Board for Educational Administration) destroys the most valuable dimension of intellectual preparation offered by university leadership programs, effectively lowering standards in educational administration preparation by encouraging the proliferation of weak programs that offer advanced degrees. English (2006) contends that Broad typifies the "back door" to "a neoliberal global policy agenda to privatize educational preparation as advanced by right-wing, corporate-backed think tanks and foundations that proffer that free market approaches (i.e., marketization) are a better way to prepare educational leaders" (p. 461). What makes these programs weak for English is that they are based in standards that form a "knowledge base." The standards represent a mistaken view of knowledge as static rather than dynamic. Such standards are anti-democratic, work against historically marginalized groups, and secure the authority of those with the most political power. They are grounded in a "knowledge base" that functions primarily to exercise political power; are ahistorical and conceptually incoherent, representing "disembodied skills, concepts, and ideas distanced from the theories that spawned them" (English, 2006, p. 461) that artificially ground existing relations of power; and are anti-scientific and anti-intellectual, denying the necessity for research beyond what is encoded in the standards. Together, these problematic underlying assumptions set the stage for a radical venture philanthropy transformation of administrator preparation defined by market competition, with students shopping for the most convenient certification program. Meanwhile, vacuous programs lacking in intellectual rigor proliferate. As English argues, the NCATE standards make challenging the assumptions of the field irrelevant or a problem for professors of administration. These standards as currently conceived do not conceptualize the field as dynamic and contested.

The bad assumption of a standardized knowledge base results in the stunted intellectual development of the field of administrator preparation. Consequently, the university's role in intellectual or critical preparation appears tenuous, as off-campus, "onsite" preparation programs rapidly expand. The theoretical and intellectual content of administration preparation shifts largely to efficacy-oriented literature from business management, or it is evacuated altogether. As well, this plays into the longstanding confusion in the field of education over the relationship between theory and practice, as onsite learning takes precedence and an anti-critical practicalism takes over. Practice is positioned as the real stuff of administrator preparation, grounded by the ultimate goal of "changing outcomes" measured by "increasing student achievement," which means raising test scores. Of course, such a conceptualization of educational leadership through the static knowledge base conceals who makes the content of such tests and the symbolic and material interests tied to such claims to truth. The positivism of this approach to knowledge separates facts from the assumptions, values, and ideologies that inform the selection and arrangement of facts.

The Broad approach typifies a much larger movement across the field of education to tie the preparation of teachers and administrators to the test outcomes of candidates' students. In other words, the value of an education professor or person preparing teachers can be boiled down to the test scores of the student's students. The Carnegie Corporation recently has championed such thinking, and one variation of it goes by the title "value-added" education. The measure of the value of preparation programs is the "value" they have in upping scores. This way of thinking about teacher and administrator preparation exemplifies this resurgent positivism and its anti-intellectual bent. In this view, there can be no place for educational study that does not result in test score improvement two levels down. So educational theory, sociology and philosophy of education, curriculum theorizing, pedagogical theory—those approaches in education that address the underlying assumptions and ethical, historical, and political aspects of what is taught and learned—none has a place in the value-added perspective because all that matters is "delivery" of "content knowledge" through the use of the "best" "instructional methods."[4] As English rightly contends, educational leadership instruction and knowledge ought to be dynamic rather than static, and ought to link research into educational problems with research into social problems.

THE SCHOLARSHIP AGENDA

Broad created the Broad Prize for Urban Education. The foundation claims that what it has promoted as a "Nobel prize for education" is intended to support public schooling and increase confidence in public education. The media has picked up the mantra "Nobel prize for education" from Broad, and it has been repeated endlessly in the popular press. Broad divides a million dollars among five urban school districts that it has deemed as making improvements in "student performance" and "closing the racial achievement gap." One winning district gets $500,000 and four runners up get $125,000 each to be used for university scholarships for graduating seniors. Broad evaluates urban districts for the prize money by looking at state standardized tests, graduation rates, and SAT and ACT scores, among other national tests.

Broad's educational reform agenda applies the same assumptions to rewarding schools and students as it does to training principals and superintendents. While in the case of the administrator there is a "knowledge base" that can collect and apply knowledge regardless of social context, in the case of promoting particular school policy through the prize, it rewards standardized and largely decontextualized knowledge that is alleged to be of universal value. In this perspective, those students and schools that do not score highly on the standardized achievement tests can be "incentivized" through the promise of scholarship funds. One of the most obvious basic problems is the fact that the scholarship prize does not address the skyrocketing costs of higher education and that higher education could be publicly funded. The prize assumes that all students somehow will be able to afford to go to college. There are numerous other problems with this line of thinking animating the scholarship.

First, the prize assumes that genuine learning should be measured principally by standardized tests composed of knowledge formulated by specialists. Second, it assumes that the tested knowledge is of universal value and expresses no class or cultural values or perspectives and should be of universal interest. When poor and non-White students score poorly on these tests, Broad frames this as a deficit in those students. Such a deficit ought to be remedied by figuring out how to raise test scores. Broad's perspective runs contrary to more critical approaches to teaching and learning. According to these perspectives, learning ought to begin with what the learners know; those meaningful student experiences then should be problematized in relation to broader questions and problems to help students develop a greater understanding of what has produced their experiences. This means that students in a more critical approach must learn to approach knowledge not as decontextualized bytes to be unthinkingly consumed and regurgitated, but in ways that comprehend that knowledge and versions of truth are struggled over, and that different interpretations are informed by material and symbolic power struggles. In this critical perspective, learning as an act of interpretation must be understood as inevitably linked to acts of intervention in the sense that there can be no neutral interpretations and in the sense that how students come to see the world informs how they act on the world. Rather than primarily developing the tools for repeating official knowledge, from a critical perspective students must learn to analyze, in social, political, ethical, and historical ways, what they come to know from experience and texts. Crucial questions at the center of this critical approach include who is making this knowledge, why does the person claim this, how are these claims related to the position of the claimant, and what kinds of broader structural forces inform the claim to truth? Broad's rewarding of knowledge that is foremost confirmable through standardized tests denies all of these crucial questions and shuts down the critical approach to knowledge.

Nothing better illustrates the stakes in these different approaches to learning than Broad's own involvement in educational reform following Hurricane Katrina in New Orleans. When Katrina devastated the city and its schools, long-standing politically failed privatization plans were put in place (spearheaded by right-wing think tanks like the Urban Institute and Heritage), including vouchers and charter schools, the carving up of the school district, the dismantling of the teachers union, and the refusal to rebuild the public schools as part of the business-led BNOBC plan to keep poor and predominantly African American citizens from returning to their communities, homes, and schools. New Orleans was an experiment in neoliberal urban rebuilding. (I detail neoliberal educational rebuilding in New Orleans in Saltman, 2007a.) The fate of the schools was struggled over. The history of systematic disinvestment in the New Orleans schools, the history of White flight, the failure of the corporate sector to contribute adequately to the public schools—these histories were conveniently erased as the Broad Foundation and the other venture philanthropies, including Gates, Fisher, and Walton, showed up to offer their generosity. The cash on hand came with strings. Rather than supporting the rebuilding of the public system in a better form, the venture philanthropies targeted their money at the creation of charter schools, alternative administrator preparation of the sort discussed above, and the Teach for America program that expands an uncertified, undereducated, and de-unionized teacher workforce. Totaling $17.5 million, these initiatives contributed significantly to the carving out of an elite charter network in the city for more privileged residents, the solidifying of the dispossession of predominantly poor and African American former residents, and the continuing attack on the teachers union (Associated Press, 2007).

The kinds of "achievement-oriented" standardized schooling fostered by such gifts will prohibit the kinds of critical teaching and learning that would encourage students to understand how Katrina, the city, and the schools became disputed terrains of class and racial struggles. Indeed, if public schooling is to offer democratic possibilities, such critical knowledge becomes crucial in order for students to develop the skills to engage as public citizens in the formation of both community and knowledge-making about it. Eli Broad's own words help to illuminate this. Speaking of Miami-Dade, Florida, Broad said, "Miami-Dade is doing what some say is impossible—improving students' performance, regardless of their race or family income—while at the same time closing persistent achievement gaps" (Pinzur, 2006, p. 3B). Broad frames class position and cultural difference as needing to be erased or seen as impositions to students' learning the right knowledge. What this view completely misses is how school rewards the knowledge and cultural capital of students of class and cultural privilege, while disaffirming the knowledge of students of oppressed classes and cultural groups.

Third, while Broad claims that the prize increases confidence in public education (Hurst, 2003), it undermines many of the public aspects of public education. One of the ways it does so is by misrepresenting knowledge, as discussed above. However, it also "de-publicizes" public schooling by suggesting that private businesspeople should have the power to designate and influence the determination of what is valuable knowledge for students to learn. Furthermore, these private businesspeople use a series of private for-profit companies, such as MPR Associates, Inc., to manage the prize selection process and another company, Schoolworks, an educational consulting firm, to do site visits and collect information on prize candidates. Rather than the values of a community guiding reform, the values of the billionaire and the private educational consultants do. The very idea that the value and vision of public education should be steered and influenced by one who can fund the "education Nobel prize" aligns the values of learning less with enriching individual lives and collective social purpose defined by the love of learning or the social implications of it, than with learning for extrinsic rewards, possessive individualism, and even celebrity adoration. Should the point be missed, Secretary of Education Margaret Spellings announced a $125,000 Broad award in Bridgeport, Connecticut: "This is like the Oscars for public education." Of course, mass media sells products by offering celebrity identifications and educating viewers to imagine themselves in celebrity relationships. As Zygmunt Bauman (2007) discusses, the cultural pedagogies of new media, TV, and film beset us with the problem of subjectivity fetishism—a world of people subjectified as commodities who misunderstand their commoditized selves as authentic and free of the market. What public schooling as a public site can offer us in this context is one place where commercialized forms of address and modes of identification can be criticized and where non-commodified versions of selfhood and values can be taught and learned. Not only does the Broad prize contribute to an expansion into public schools of the commercialism found nearly everywhere else in society, but it also promotes the kind of learning in formal schooling that does not foster interpretation and questioning of commercial pedagogies that promote a privatized and individualized society outside of schooling. In other words, forms of schooling that make central social, cultural, political problems in the world ought to be brought into formal schooling, while the test-oriented pedagogical approaches that Broad supports do just the opposite.

Fourth, Broad's funding of scholarships for students to go to college obscures some crucial public policy issues regarding public funding for higher education, the skyrocketing costs of tuition, and the increasing corporatization of the university. Rather than advocating for a greater role of the federal government in funding universal higher education, Broad instead promotes an exclusionary and lottery-style system of funding that resembles social Darwinist reality TV programs like *Survivor*. While the aim of providing some students with access to college appears to be an admirable one, what needs to be recognized is that the Broad Foundation's actions function to sanction and legitimate a highly exclusionary system of access to higher education. As Stanley Aronowitz (2008) wisely writes, criticizing one of the "crucial precepts of progressive educational philosophy" (specifically Dewey):

> Under the sign of egalitarianism, the idea [is] that class deficits can be overcome by equalizing access to school opportunities without questioning what those opportunities have to do with genuine education. . . . The structure of schooling already embodies the class system of society, and for this reason the access debate is mired in a web of misplaced concreteness. To gain entrance into schools always entails placement into

that system. "Equality of opportunity" for class mobility is the system's tacit recognition that inequality is normative. (p. 18)

What Aronowitz means by genuine learning is what, drawing on Hannah Arendt, he calls transmitting a "love for the world" and "love for our children." He develops this to mean that radical imagination must stem from radical criticism. Instead, as Aronowitz (2008) laments, all too commonly schools teach "conformity to the social, cultural and occupational hierarchy" (p. 23) rather than the democratic values that are often the official but unfulfilled principles guiding schools. Broad's scholarship prize represents the reduction of the possibilities of schooling to work, and through universal schooling, *access to social mobility*, which, as Aronowitz points out, is not egalitarian at all.

Broad's scholarship prize promises equality through the potential of individual upward mobility through graduation. By setting such bait, Broad fails to acknowledge the structural economic limits of job markets. The existing global economy cannot accommodate good employment for a fully educated population. Consequently, the real fulfillment of educational and economic uplift can come only through collective action to change the conditions and standards of work to provide full employment at fair pay, security, and so on. Students can be educated for such collective struggle rather than merely for compliance to the current economic arrangement of "casino capitalism" (Giroux, 2011; Saltman, 2007b).

THE DATABASE PROJECT

Broad supports the School Information Partnership and the more expansive Data Partnership. These are efforts to compile, track, aggregate, and analyze student test scores, with the long-term goal of influencing school and teacher education policy based in the data. The U.S. Department of Education provided $4.7 million, and $50.9 million came from private organizations. Of this, Broad provided half. One explicit goal is to foster the aims of NCLB to provide schools and parents with test score information.

The literature on the database project suggests that data offer parents and students information for "school choice"—that is, privatization. As with the Broad prize, the foundation's justification in supporting this project is to narrow the racial "achievement gap." This is also a lucrative opportunity for information technology companies (including Data Partnership collaborators CELT Corp., which designs information technology systems for schools; the school evaluation division of Standard & Poors; and the influential Achieve Inc., a non-profit organization that was founded by corporations and governors) to promote "standards-based" education. In addition to Broad, the Gates Foundation is heavily supporting the Database Partnership.

Mass data collection of student test scores appeals to many who embrace an understanding of learning through numerically quantifiable "standards" imposed from above. Longitudinal tracking of test scores appeals to those who want to boil down successful teaching practice to "efficient delivery" of curriculum. In this perspective, instructional methodologies become the primary concern of teacher practice, and methodologies are disconnected from the matter of what is taught. The experts who know, determine what students should learn. The teacher becomes a routinized technician proficiently executing what has been determined to be the most efficient instructional methods to raise test scores. In the tradition of Taylorism's scientific management, the classroom becomes "teacher proof."

The database project aims to track and identify which teachers and teacher approaches raise standardized test scores despite racial, ethnic, class, or linguistic differences. Then, once the instructional methods that most raise test scores can be identified, the teacher education approaches that those test-improving teachers were exposed to can be replicated. The database promises to highlight which schools' methods are resulting in raised test scores by minorities and hence purports to provide information that will enable administrators to work to "close the achievement gap." Another promise is that the schools that score the highest on tests will be attractive "choices" for parents. Hence the database project appears to work in conjunction with the way that NCLB set the stage for transforming public education into a national market by requiring local schools to allow enrollments by anyone who chooses to go to the schools.

What is wrong with the database project is that it reduces the value of schooling to standardized test scores while effacing the ways that standardized tests correlate most closely with family income and cultural capital. The emphasis on instructional methodologies, paired with the delivery of standardized units of curriculum, rewards and promotes approaches to teaching that thoroughly ignore the social contexts within which students learn, as well as the identities of the students. As a consequence, such approaches encourage teaching to be viewed not as an intellectual practice or as critical practice, but rather as a technical skill. The overemphasis on testing as the definition of student achievement has practical and social costs. It compromises pedagogical approaches oriented toward creative problem solving while rendering pedagogical content estranged. Critical educators emphasize that learning ideally ought to begin with meaningful knowledge that students have experienced and that can be problematized in relation to broader social, political, and cultural contexts and forces to help students both comprehend how their experiences, under-standings, and assumptions are produced and also theorize how to confront those forces that produce their experiences. The standards-based approach undermines critical confrontation with both student experience and the social forces and actors that tell students what is valuable to know.

When it comes to policy, the database project lends itself to a positivist separation of fact from the values and assumptions that organize facts.

> Participating states will each receive a customized analysis of data needs and how to close any gaps from the CELT Corp. Over time, the partnership could help states build the architecture for a more robust data system, including detailed implementa-tion plans, joint requests for proposals, procurement, and contractor oversight and management. CELT also plans to identify and share best practices across participating states. (Olson, 2004, p. 16)

The point not to be missed here is that policy will be "data driven." In reality, data cannot "drive" policy. The very expression conceals the motives and poli-tics undergirding human beings' decisions about curriculum, pedagogy, teacher education, and administration. Implementing in low-scoring schools practices used in high-scoring schools not only will result in misapplications of pedagogi-cal approaches, but naturalizes the unthinking consumption of information as the essence of achievement, while imagining teachers as little more than fleshy delivery machines. What does not get interrogated in all this, is the process whereby some people with particular values, perspectives, and ideological con-victions determine what is important for students to know. Belied is the ques-tion of who has the power to distribute and universalize this knowledge, whose material and symbolic interests it represents, who profits from it financially, and what is lost in terms of schooling as dialogic and intellectually dynamic. The database project promises inclusion and access. Yet, it is highly exclusionary by universalizing approaches to learning that refuse to engage with the different contexts that students bring to the learning situation. Context-based pedagogi-cal approaches enable students who traditionally are excluded from the curricu-lum and who come from historically oppressed groups to problematize claims to truth in relation to their experiences. As in colonialist education policies, the learner must assimilate or perish (see, for example, the works of Donaldo Macedo and John Willinsky).

There is a grand irony in the Data Partnership. Its website was developed by the National Center for Educational Accountability and Standard & Poor's school evaluation services division. Standard & Poor's, along with the other credit rating agencies, came under intense criticism in 2007 and 2008 as the collateralized debt obligation (CDO) markets that S&P had rated highly, collapsed. These CDOs are understood largely as triggering the broad-based global financial meltdown following their implication in the radical expansion of a speculative economic bubble (Tomlinson & Evans, 2007). As well, S&P continued to rate the government of Iceland highly right up to its financial collapse in 2008. The point not to be missed here is that the database project in education is driven by a number of neoliberal assumptions that ought to be seen as thoroughly discredited. The unquestionable efficiency of business, the model of the numerically quantifiable progress derived in part from industry and the financial sector, the rating of students and teachers through quasi-credit ratings—all of these are called into question not by the financial crisis but by the failure of the neoliberal dictates that tell people to think of all social goods through the logic of economics. Rather than using dubious credit rating tactics to measure schoolchildren, teachers, and knowledge as if they were investments and commodities, human measures of the value of teaching, learning, and knowledge must be expanded. Perhaps as well, to turn it around, financial investments can be rated through their social values and social costs on a human index.

CONCLUSION

Venture philanthropy initiatives, including those of the Broad Foundation, need to be recognized for their hostility to public and critical forms of schooling as well as their alignment with the broader movement to privatize and dismantle public schooling. It is incumbent upon educators to challenge the promotion of retrograde positivism, the use of private money to steer public educational reform debates, and the corporate hijacking of public institutions, especially at a moment when the central tenets of neoliberal ideology are revealed to be utterly untenable. The wealth of the venture philanthropies is made possible only by public subsidy in the form of tax incentives through which the public pays to have public control over public services given over to elite private interests. Private foundation wealth, including that of the Broad, Gates, and Walton foundations, ideally ought to be nationalized and channeled into public institutions with strong public governance, oversight, and control. Public schools are crucial for making publicly minded citizens capable of interpreting and acting on matters of public importance. Consequently, the preparation of teachers and administrators cannot be turned over to elite private interests promoting corporate ideologies, but must become increasingly determined in public domains and institutions. The struggle for critical and public democratic forms of administrator preparation must be waged not only discursively but also through accreditation bodies, state boards of education, and state legislatures, as well as in university education program development.

NOTES

1. *Neoliberalism* involves redistributing public goods to private control while espousing market triumphalism. As David Harvey explains, it is a project of class warfare.

2. Notable early exceptions to this include Frederick Hess's edited collection *With the Best of Intentions* (1995) from a neoliberal perspective, the liberal work of Janelle Scott (e.g., 2009), and the work of Rick Cohen of the Center for Responsive Philanthropy. Mike and Susan Klonsky's book *Small Schools* (2008) and Philip Kovacs's scholarship on Gates stand out as some of the rare critical work on venture philanthropy. See, for example, Kovacs and Christie (2008).

3. For some of the literature criticizing neoliberal education, see Giroux (2004b), Apple (2001), and Saltman (2000, 2007a).

4. Attempts at longitudinal tracking of administrator "performance" and teacher "performance," and then isolating individual behaviors or methodological approaches, have been funded by the Carnegie Corporation and the U.S. Department of Education under the Bush administration without success. Meanwhile, the Broad and Gates foundations are continuing to fund these kinds of positivist projects that share the same assumptions.

REFERENCES

Apple, M. (2001). *Educating the right way: Markets, standards, God, and inequality.* New York: Routledge.

Aronowitz, S. (2008). *Against schooling for an education that matters.* Boulder, CO: Paradigm.

Associated Press (AP). (2007, December 14). Louisiana: Grants for schools. *New York Times*, p. 33.

Bauman, Z. (2007). *Consuming life.* New York: Polity Press.

English, F. W. (2006, August). The unintended consequences of a standardized knowledge base in advancing educational leadership preparation. *Educational Administration Quarterly, 42*(3), 461.

Giroux, H. A. (2004a). *Abandoned generation: Democracy beyond the culture of fear.* New York: Palgrave Macmillan.

Giroux , H. A. (2004b). *The terror of neoliberalism.* Boulder, CO: Paradigm Publishers.

Giroux, H. A. (2011). American Democracy beyond casino capitalism and the torture state. Available at http://www.truth-out.org/american-democracy-beyond-casino-capitalism-and-torture-state/1305143581

Giroux, H. A., & Giroux, S. S. (2008). Beyond bailouts: On the politics of education after neoliberalism. *Truthout.org*. Available at http://www.truthout.org/123108A

Grossberg, L. (2005). *Caught in the crossfire*. Boulder, CO: Paradigm.

Harvey, D. (2005). *A brief history of neoliberalism*. Oxford: Oxford University Press.

Hess, F. (Ed.). (1995). *With the best of intentions: How philanthropy is reshaping K–12 education*. Cambridge, MA: Harvard Education Press.

Hess, F., & Kelly, A. (2005, January & March). An innovative look, a recalcitrant reality: The politics of principal preparation reform. *Educational Policy, 19*(1), 158–172.

Hurst, M. (2003, October 1). California district awarded urban education prize. *Education Week*.

Klonsky, M., & Klonsky, S. (2008). *Small schools*. New York: Routledge.

Kovacs, P., & Christie, H. K. (2008, December). The Gates Foundation and the future of U.S. public education: A call for scholars to counter misinformation campaigns. *The Journal for Critical Education Policy Studies, 6*(2).

Males, M. (1996). *Scapegoat generation: America's war on adolescents*. Monroe, ME: Common Courage Press.

Maxwell, L. A. (2006, June 21). Challenging the status quo. *Education Week, 25*(41), 36–40.

Olson, L. (2004, July 14). State chiefs, businesses forge $45 million data venture. *Education Week, 23*(42), 16.

Pinzur, M. (2006, April 6). Dade selected as one of 5 most-improved urban school districts. *The Miami Herald*.

Robbins, C. G. (2008). *Expelling hope: The assault on youth and the militarization of schooling*. Albany: State University of New York Press.

Saltman, K. J. (2007a). *Capitalizing on disaster: Taking and breaking public schools*. Boulder, CO: Paradigm.

Saltman, K. J. (2007b). Gambling with the future of public education: Risk, discipline, and the moralizing of educational politics in corporate media. *Policy Futures in Education, 5*(1).

Saltman, K. J. (2000). *Collateral damage: Corporatizing public schools—a threat to democracy*. Lanham, MD: Rowman & Littlefield.

Saltman, K. J., & Gabbard, D. (2003). *Education as enforcement: The militarization and corporatization of schools*. New York: Routledge.

Scott, J. (2009). The politics of venture philanthropy in charter school policy and advocacy. *Educational Policy, 23*(1), 106–136.

Smith, B. A. (2008). Deregulation and the new leader agenda: Outcomes and lessons from Michigan. *Educational Administration Quarterly, 44*(1), 51.

Tomlinson, R., & Evans, D. (2007, March 31). CDO boom masks subprime losses, abetted by S&P, Moody's, Fitch. Available at http://www.bloomberg.com/apps/news?pid=newsarchive&sid=ajs7BqG4_X8I

Willinsky, J. (1998). *Learning to divide the world: Education at empire's end*. Minneapolis: University of Minnesota Press.

CHAPTER 4

Test Today, Privatize Tomorrow
Using Accountability to "Reform" Public Schools to Death

Alfie Kohn

The mantle of school reform has been appropriated by those who oppose the whole idea of public schooling. Their aim is to paint themselves as bold challengers to the current system and to claim that defenders of public education lack the vision or courage to endorse meaningful change. This rhetorical assault seemed to come out of nowhere, as though a memo had been circulated one day among those on the right: "Attention. Effective immediately, all of our efforts to privatize the schools will be known as 'reform,' and any opposition to those efforts will be known as 'anti-reform.' That is all."

Silver-lining hunters may note that this strategy pays a backhanded compliment to the very idea of change. It implicitly acknowledges the inadequacy of conservatism, at least in the original sense of that word. These days everyone insists there's a problem with the way things are. (On one level, this posture is familiar: Polemicists across the political spectrum frequently try to describe whatever position they're about to criticize as "fashionable." The implication is that only the bravest soul—that is, the writer—dares to support an unfashionable view.) But the word *reform* is particularly slippery and tendentious. The *Associated Press Guide to Newswriting* urges journalists to exercise caution about using it, pointing out that "one group's reform can be another group's calamity" (cited in Freeman, 2004, p. L3). At the same time, conservative politicians are being exhorted (for example, by a like-minded *New York Times* columnist) to embrace the word. "For my money," David Brooks (2004) wrote earlier this year, "the best organizing principle for Republicans centers on the word 'reform'"—which can give the impression that they want to "promote change, while Democrats remain the churlish defenders of the status quo" (p. 15).

Of course, this begs the question of what kind of change actually is being promoted, but begging the question is really the whole point, isn't it? The "reform" of environmental laws often has meant diluting them or simply washing them away. And just ask someone who depends on public assistance what "welfare reform" really implies. The privatizers and deregulators have gone after healthcare, prisons, banks, airlines, and electric utilities. Now they're setting their sights on Social Security. I recently was reading about the added misery experienced by desperately poor families in various parts of the world as a result of the privatization of local water supplies. The clarity of language be damned: They come to bury a given institution rather than to improve it, but they describe their mission as "reform." As Lily Tomlin once remarked, "No matter how cynical you become, it's never enough to keep up."[1]

THE NATURE OF "SCHOOL REFORM"

But back to education. People with an animus against public schooling typically set the stage for their demolition plans by proclaiming that there isn't much there worth saving. Meanwhile, those who object are portrayed as apologists for every policy in every school. It's a very clever gambit, you have to admit. Either you're in favor of privatization or else you are inexplicably satisfied with mediocrity.

Let's state what should be obvious, then. First, a defense of public education is wholly consistent with a desire for excellence. Second, by most conventional criteria, public schools have done surprisingly well in managing with limited resources to educate an increasingly diverse student population (see Berliner & Biddle, 1995; Rothstein, 1998; the collected works of Gerald Bracey [e.g., 2003, 2004]). Third, notwithstanding that assessment, there's plenty of room for dissatisfaction with the current state of our schools. An awful lot is wrong with them: the way conformity is valued over curiosity and enforced with rewards and punishments, the way children are compelled to compete against one another, the way curriculum so often privileges skills over meaning, the way students are prevented from designing their own learning, the way instruction and assessment are increasingly standardized, the way different avenues of study are rarely integrated, the way educators are systematically deskilled . . . and I'm just getting warmed up.

Notice, however, that these criticisms are quite different from—in fact, often the exact opposite of—the particulars cited by most proponents of vouchers and similar "reforms." To that extent, even if privatization worked exactly the way it was supposed to, we shouldn't expect any of the defects I've just listed to be corrected. If anything, the micro-level impact (on teaching and learning) of such a macro-level shift is likely to exacerbate such problems. Making schools resemble businesses often results in a kind of pedagogy that's not merely conservative but reactionary, turning back the clock on the few changes that have managed to infiltrate and improve classrooms. Consider the stultifyingly scripted lessons and dictatorial discipline that pervade for-profit charter schools. Or have a look at some research from England showing that "when schools have to compete for students, they tend to adopt 'safe,' conventional and teacher-centered methods, to stay close to the prescribed curriculum, and to tailor teaching closely to test-taking" (Delhi, 1998).[2] (One more example of the destructive effects of competition.)

This is a point worth emphasizing to the handful of progressive-minded individuals who have made common cause with those on the right by attacking public education. John Taylor Gatto is an example here. In a *Harper's* essay entitled "Against School" (Gatto, 2003), he asserts that the goal of "mandatory public education in this country" is "a population deliberately dumbed down," with children turned "into servants."

In support of this sweeping charge, Gatto names some important men who managed to become well educated without setting foot in a classroom. (However, he fails to name any defenders of public education who have ever claimed that it's impossible for people to learn outside of school or to prosper without a degree.) He also cites a few "school as factory" comments from long-dead policymakers, and observes that many of our educational practices originated in Prussia. Here he's right. Our school system is indeed rooted in efforts to control. But the same indictment could be leveled, with equal justification, at other institutions. The history of newspapers, for example, and the intent of many powerful people associated with them, has much to do with manufacturing consent, marginalizing dissent, and distracting readers. But is that an argument for no newspapers or better newspapers?

Ideally, public schools can enrich lives, nourish curiosity, and introduce students to new ways of formulating questions and finding answers. Their existence also has the power to strengthen a democratic society, in part by extending those benefits to vast numbers of people who didn't fare nearly as well before the great experiment of free public education began.

Granted, "ideally" is a hell of a qualifier. But an attack on schooling as we know it generally is grounded in politics rather than pedagogy, and is advanced most energetically by those who despise not just public schools but all public institutions. The marketplace, which likely would inherit the task of educating our children if Gatto got his way, is (to put it gently) unlikely to honor the ideals that inform his critique. Some folks will benefit from that kind of "reform," but they certainly won't be kids.[3]

People who want to strike a blow for individual liberty understandably lash out against the government—and these days they don't want for examples of undue interference from Washington and state capitals. But in education, as in other arenas of contemporary American life, there is an equal or greater danger from concentrating power in *private* hands, which is to say in enterprises that aren't accountable to anyone (except their own shareholders) or for anything (except making a profit).

Worst of all is a situation where public entities remake themselves in the image of private entities, where politicians pass laws to codify corporate ideology and impose it on our schools (see Kohn, 2002; Kohn & Shannon, 2002). Perhaps the two most destructive forces in education these days are the tendency to view children as "investments" (whose ultimate beneficiary is business) and a market-driven credentialism in which discrete individuals struggle for competitive distinctions. To attack the institution of public education is like hollering at the shadows on the wall. The source of the problem is behind you, and it grows larger as you train your rage on the flickering images in front.

"FREEDOM" FROM PUBLIC EDUCATION

I try to imagine myself as a privatizer. How would I proceed? If my objective were to dismantle public schools, I would begin by trying to discredit them. I probably would refer to them as "government" schools, hoping to tap into a vein of libertarian resentment. I would never miss an opportunity to sneer at researchers and teacher educators as out-of-touch "educationists." Recognizing that it's politically unwise to attack teachers, I would do so obliquely, bashing the unions to which most of them belong. Most important, if I had the power, I would ratchet up the number and difficulty of standardized tests that students had to take, so that I then could point to the predictably pitiful results. I then would defy my opponents to defend the schools that had produced students who did so poorly.

How closely does my thought experiment match reality? One way to ascertain the actual motivation behind the widespread use of testing is to watch what happens in the real world when a lot of students manage to do well on a given test. Are schools credited and teachers congratulated? Hardly. The response, from New Jersey to New Mexico, is instead to make the test harder, with the result that many more students subsequently fail.

> **Addendum 2009**: "Math scores are up on Long Island and statewide—enough so that state educational leaders could soon start raising the bar," Meryl Tisch of Manhattan, the new Chancellor of the state's Board of Regents, said. "What today's scores tell me is not that we should be celebrating but that New York State needs to raise its standards." (*Newsday*, June 1, 2009)

Consider this item from the *Boston Globe:*

> As the first senior class required to pass the MCAS exam prepares for graduation, state education officials are considering raising the passing grade for the exam. State Education Commissioner David Driscoll and Board of Education chairman James Peyser said the passing grade needs to be raised to keep the test challenging, given that a high proportion of students are passing it on the first try. . . . Peyser said as students continue to meet the standard, the state is challenged to make the exam meaningful. (Redd, 2003, p. B2)

You have to admire the sheer Orwellian chutzpah represented by that last word. By definition, a test is "meaningful" only if large numbers of students (and, by implication, schools) fare poorly on it. What at first seems purely perverse—a mindless acceptance of the premise that harder is always better—reveals itself instead as a strategic move in the service of a very specific objective. Peyser, you see, served for 8 years as executive director of the conservative Pioneer Institute, a Boston-based think tank devoted to "the application of free market principles to state and local policy" (in the words of its website, http://www.pioneerinstitute.org/). The man charged with overseeing public education in Massachusetts is critical of the very idea of public education. And how does he choose to pursue his privatizing agenda? By raising the bar until alarming failure[4] is ensured.

Of course, tougher standards are usually justified in the name of excellence—or, even more audaciously (given the demographics of most of the victims), equity. One doesn't expect to hear people like Peyser casually concede that the real point of this whole standards-and-testing business is to make the schools look bad, the better to justify a free-market alternative. Now and then, however, a revealing comment does slip out. For example, when the *School Choice Advocate*, the newsletter of the Milton and Rose Friedman Foundation, approvingly described Colorado's policy of publishing schools' test scores, a senior education advisor to Republican Governor Bill Owens remarked that the motive behind reporting these results was to "greatly enhance and build pressure for school choice" ("In the Spotlight: Colorado," 2001, p. 7).

An op-ed published in the *Wall Street Journal* by William Bennett and Chester Finn underscored the integral relationship between the push for high-stakes testing (which they call "standards") and the effort to undermine public schooling (which they call "freedom"). The latter bit of spin is interesting in its own right: Vouchers, having been rejected decisively by voters on several occasions, were promptly reintroduced as "school choice" to make them sound more palatable.[5] But apparently an even more blatant appeal to emotionally charged values is now called for. In any case, the article notes (correctly, I fear) that "our two political parties . . . can find common ground on testing and accountability," but then goes on to announce that "what Republicans have going for them in education is freedom." They understand this value "because of their business ties"; unlike Democrats, they are "not afraid of freedom."

Even in an era distinguished by unpleasantly adversarial discourse, Bennett and Finn redefine its lower depths with the charge that freedom is a "domain that few Democrats dare to visit." (Their evidence for this charge is that most Democrats exclude private schools from choice plans.) But this nasty little essay, headlined "No Standards Without Freedom," serves primarily to remind us that the most vocal proponents of accountability—defined, as it usually is these days, in terms of top-down standards and coercive pressure to raise scores on an endless series of standardized tests—have absolutely no interest in improving the schools that struggle to fulfill these requirements. Public education, in their view, is not something to be made better; it is something from which we need to be freed.

MANY CHILDREN LEFT BEHIND

None of this is exactly new. "Standards" have been used to promote "freedom" for some time. But if that picture slowly has been coming into focus as education policies are enacted at the state level, it now attains digital clarity as a result of federal involvement—in particular, the law that some have rechristened No Child Left Untested (or No Corporation Left Behind, or No Child's Behind Left). Even those observers who missed, or dismissed, the causal relationship until now, are coming to realize that you don't have to be a conspiracy nut to understand the real purpose of this new law. Indeed, you have to be vision-impaired *not* to see it.

Jamie McKenzie, a former superintendent, put it this way on his website, NoChildLeft.com: "Misrepresented as a reform effort, NCLB is actually a cynical effort to shift public school funding to a host of private schools, religious schools and free-market diploma mills or corporate experiments in education." The same point has been made by Jerry Bracey, Stan Karp, and a number of others. Lately, even some prominent politicians are catching on. Senator James Jeffords, who chaired the Senate committee that oversees education from 1997 to 2001, has described the law as a back-door maneuver "that will let the private sector take over public education, something the Republicans have wanted for years."[6] Former senator Carol Moseley Braun recently made the same point.

Addendum 2008: We now have corroboration that these fears were entirely justified. Susan Neuman, an assistant secretary of education during the rollout of NCLB, admitted that others in Bush's Department of Education "saw NCLB as a Trojan horse for the choice agenda—a way to expose the failure of public education and 'blow it up a bit.'" (Wallis, 2008)

So what is it about NCLB in particular that has led a growing number of people to view it as a stalking horse for privatization? While any test can be, and many tests have been, rigged to create the impression of public school failure, nothing has ever come close to NCLB in this regard. Put aside for a moment the rather important point that higher scores on standardized tests do not necessarily reflect meaningful improvement in teaching or learning—and may even indicate the opposite (see, e.g., Kohn, 2000). Let's assume for the sake of the argument that better performance on these tests *was* a good sign. This law's criteria for being judged successful—how fast the scores must rise, and how high, and for how many subgroups of students—are nothing short of ludicrous. NCLB requires every single student to score at or above the proficient level by 2014, something that has never been done before and that few unmedicated observers believe is possible (see, e.g., Linn, 2003).

As Monty Neill (2003) of FairTest explained, even the criteria for making "adequate yearly progress" toward that goal are such that "virtually no schools serving large numbers of low-income children will clear these arbitrary hurdles." Consequently, he adds, "many successful schools will be declared 'failing' and may be forced to drop practices that work well. Already, highly regarded schools have been put on the 'failing' list." Schools that do manage to jump through these hoops, which include a 95% participation rate in the testing, then must contend with comparable hurdles involving the qualifications of their teachers.

The party line, of course, is that all these requirements are meant to make public schools improve, and that forcing every state to test every student every year (from 3rd through 8th grades and then again in high school) is intended to identify troubled schools in order to "determine who needs extra help," as President Bush put it (quoted in Robelen, 2004). To anyone who makes this claim with a straight face, we might respond by asking three questions.

1. *How many schools will NCLB-required testing reveal to be troubled that were not previously identified as such?* I have challenged defenders of the law to name a single school anywhere in the country whose inadequacy was a secret until yet another wave of standardized test results was released. So far I have had no takers.

2. *Of the many schools and districts that are obviously struggling, how many have received the resources they need, at least without a court order?* If conservatives are sincere in saying they want more testing in order to determine where help is needed, what has their track record been in providing that help? The answer is painfully obvious, of course: Many of the same people who justify more standardized tests for information-gathering purposes also have claimed that more money doesn't produce improvement. The Bush administration's proposed budgets have fallen far short of what states would need just to implement NCLB itself, and those who point this out are dismissed as malcontents. (Thus Bennett and Finn: "Democrats are now saying that Republicans are not spending enough. But that is what they always say—enough is never sufficient for them when it comes to education spending.")

3. *What have the results been of high-stakes testing to this point?* To the best of my knowledge, no positive effects have ever been demonstrated, unless you count higher scores on these same tests. More low-income and minority students are dropping out, more teachers (often the best ones) are leaving the profession, and more mind-numbing test preparation is displacing genuine instruction. Why should anyone believe that annual do-or-die testing mandated by the federal government will lead to anything different? Moreover, the engine of this legislation is punishment. NCLB is designed to humiliate and hurt the schools that, according to its own warped standards, most need help. Families at those schools are given a green light to abandon them— and, specifically, to transfer to other schools that don't want them and probably can't handle them. This, it quickly becomes clear, is an excellent way to sandbag the "successful" schools, too.

So who will be left undisturbed and sitting pretty? Private schools and companies hoping to take over public schools. In the meantime, various corporations already are benefiting. The day after Bennett and Finn's rousing defense of freedom appeared on its op-ed page, the *Wall Street Journal* published a news story that began as follows: "Teachers, parents, and principals may have their doubts about No Child Left Behind. But business loves it." Apart from the obvious bonanza for the giant companies that design and score standardized tests, "hundreds of 'supplemental service providers' have already lined up to offer tutoring, including Sylvan, Kaplan Inc. and Princeton Review Inc. . . . Kaplan says revenue for its elementary- and secondary-school division has doubled since No Child Left Behind passed" (Kronholz, 2003, p. B1).

THE ACCOUNTABILITY–PRIVATIZATION CONNECTION

Ultimately, any attempt to demonstrate the commitment to privatization lurking behind NCLB doesn't require judgments about the probability that its requirements can be fulfilled, or speculation about the significance of which companies find it profitable. That commitment is a matter of public record. As originally proposed by the Bush administration, the legislation would have used federal funds to provide private school vouchers to students in Title I schools with lagging test results. This provision was dropped only when it threatened to torpedo the whole bill; instead, the stick used to beat schools into raising their scores was limited to the threat that students could transfer to other public schools.

Subsequently, Bush's Department of Education (DOE) took other steps to pursue its agenda, such as allocating money hand over fist to private groups that shared its agenda. People for the American Way reported that the administration funneled more than $75 million in taxpayer funds to pro-voucher groups and miscellaneous for-profit entities. Among them was William Bennett's latest gamble, known as K12—a company specializing in online education for home schoolers. (Finn sits on the board of directors.) "Standards" plus "freedom" eventually may add up to considerable revenue, then. In the meantime, the DOE is happy to ease the transition: A school choice pilot program in Arkansas received $11.5 million to buy a curriculum from Bennett's outfit, and a virtual charter school in Pennsylvania affiliated with K12 got $2.5 million.[7]

At the center of the conservative network receiving public funds to pursue what is arguably an antipublic agenda, is the Education Leaders Council (ELC), which was created in 1995 as a more conservative alternative to the Council of Chief State School Officers (which itself is not all that progressive). One of its founders was Eugene W. Hickok, formerly Pennsylvania's secretary of education and then the second-ranking official in the U.S. Department of Education. Hickok brushed off the charge that the DOE is promoting and funding privatization. If there's any favoritism reflected in these grants, he said, it's only in that "we support those organizations that support No Child Left Behind" (Dobbs, 2004).

But that's exactly the point. A hefty proportion of those who support vouchers also support NCLB, in large part because the latter is a means to the former. Take Lisa Graham Keegan, who was Arizona's school superintendent and then ELC's executive director. She was a bit more forthcoming about the grants than Hickok, telling a reporter that it was only natural for the Bush administration to want to correct a "liberal bias" in American education by giving grants to groups that shared its philosophy. "It is necessary to be ideological in education these days if you want to promote academic standards, school choice, and new routes to certifying teachers" (Dobbs, 2004). Notice again the juxtaposition of "standards" and "choice," this time joined by another element of the conservatives' agenda: an initiative, undertaken jointly by the ELC and a group set up by Finn's Thomas B. Fordham Foundation—and, again, publicly funded thanks to the DOE—to create a new quasi-private route to teacher credentialing.

For that matter, take former Secretary of Education Rod Paige, who appeared at an ELC conference to assure its members that they were "doing God's work" (Sack, 2001), and has been quoted as saying that "the worst thing that can happen to urban and minority kids is that they are not tested" (Johnston, 2001). Indeed, Paige spent his years as superintendent in Houston doing anything and everything to raise test scores (or, rather, as it turns out, to give the appearance of raising test scores). At the same time, his "tenure as superintendent was marked by efforts to privatize or contract out not only custodial, payroll, and food services, but also educational services like 'alternative schools' for students with 'discipline problems'" (Karp, 2001, p. 4).

Paige made his way around the perimeter of the U.S. Capitol to speak at the conservative Heritage Foundation, whose headquarters stand about a dozen blocks from the Department of Education. His purpose was twofold: to laud NCLB for injecting "competition into the public school system" and to point out that vouchers—which he called "opportunity scholarships"—are the next logical step in offering "educational emancipation" from "the chains of bureaucracy."

The arguments and rhetoric his speechwriters employed on that occasion are instructive. For example, he explained that the way we improve education is "one child at a time"—a phrase both more substantive and more dangerous than it may seem at first hearing. And he demanded to know how anyone could oppose vouchers in light of the fact that the GI Bill was "the greatest voucher program in history." Paige was particularly enthusiastic about the legislation that earmarks $14 million in public funds—federal funds, for the first time—for religious and private schools in Washington, DC, which he hoped would turn out to be "a model program for the nation." (However, "this isn't a covert plan to finance private, especially Catholic, schools," he assured his audience. The proof? "Many of the students in Catholic schools are not Catholic.")

Paige couldn't restrain himself from gloating over how the passage of this law represented a triumph over "special interests"—that is, those who just "ask for more money" and want "to keep children in schools in need of improvement." These critics are "the real enemies of public schools." In fact, they put him in mind of France's determined opposition to the Bush administration's efforts to secure UN approval for an invasion of Iraq.[8] (At another gathering, a few weeks later, he compared opponents of the law to terrorists.[9])

Notice that Paige chose to deliver these remarks at the Heritage Foundation, which publishes "No Excuses" apologias for high-stakes testing while simultaneously pushing vouchers and "a competitive market" for education. (Among its other reports: "Why More Money Will Not Solve America's Education Crisis.") Nina Shokraii Rees, a key education analyst at Heritage who helped draft the blueprint for NCLB and pressed for it to include annual high-stakes testing, was then working for Paige, implementing the plans that she and her group helped to formulate. So it goes for the Hoover Institution in California, the Manhattan Institute in New York, the Center for Education Reform in Washington, and other right-wing think tanks. All of them demand higher standards and more testing, and all of them look for ways to turn education over to the marketplace where it will be beyond the reach of democratic control. Over and over again, accountability and privatization appear as conjoined twins.

To point out this correlation is not to deny that there are exceptions to it. To be sure, some proponents of public schooling have, with varying degrees of enthusiasm, hitched a ride on the Accountability Express. In fact, I've even heard one or two people argue that testing requirements in general—and NCLB in particular—represent our last chance to *save* public education, to redeem schools in the public's mind by insisting that they be held to high standards.

But the idea that we should scramble to feed the accountability beast is based on the rather desperate hope that we can satisfy its appetite by providing sufficient evidence of excellence. This is a fool's errand. It overlooks the fact that the whole movement is rooted in a top-down, ideologically driven contempt for public institutions, not in a grassroots loss of faith in neighborhood schools. The demand for accountability didn't start in living rooms; it started in places like the Heritage Foundation. After a time, it's true, even parents who think their own children's school is just fine may swallow the generalizations they've been fed about the inadequacy of public education in general. But do we really think that the people who have cultivated this distrust, who holler about the need for more testing, who brush off structural barriers like poverty and racism as mere "excuses" for failure, will be satisfied once we agree to let them turn our schools into test prep factories?

COLLATERAL DAMAGE

In any event, if we did so we'd be destroying the village in order to save it. No, scratch the conditional tense there: The devastation is already underway. Every few days there is fresh evidence of how teaching is being narrowed and dumbed down, standardized and scripted—with poor and minority students getting the worst of the deal as usual. I have an overstuffed file of evidence detailing what we're sacrificing on the altar of accountability, from developmentally appropriate education for little children to rich, project-based learning for older ones, from music to field trips to class discussions (see Jones, Jones, & Hargrove, 2003; www.susanohanian.org).

Lately, it has become clear that piling NCLB on top of the state testing that already was assuming nightmarish proportions is producing still other sorts of collateral damage. For example, there is now increasing pressure to:

1. Segregate schools by ethnicity. A California study confirms what other scholars have predicted: NCLB contains a "diversity penalty" such that the more subgroups of students that attend a given school, the lower the chance that it will be able to satisfy all the federally imposed requirements for adequate progress (see Novak & Fuller, 2003).
2. Segregate classes by ability. While there are no hard data yet, it appears that schools may be doing more grouping and tracking in order to maximize test prep efficiency.[10] All children lose out from less heterogeneity, but none more than those at the bottom—yet another example of how vulnerable students suffer the most from the shrill demands for accountability.
3. Segregate classes by age. Multiage education reportedly is becoming less common now—not because its benefits haven't been supported by research and experience (they have), but because of "grade-by-grade academic standards and the consequences tied to not meeting those targets as measured by state tests" (Jacobson, 2003).

4. Criminalize misbehavior. "In cities and suburbs around the country, schools are increasingly sending students into the juvenile justice systems for the sort of adolescent misbehavior that used to be handled by school administrators" (Rimer, 2004, p. 1). There are many explanations for this deeply disturbing trend, including the loss of school-based mental health services due to budget cuts. But Augustina Reyes of the University of Houston observes, "If teachers are told, 'Your scores go down, you lose your job,' all of a sudden your values shift very quickly. Teachers think, 'With bad kids in my class, I'll have lower achievement on my tests, so I'll use discretion and remove that kid.'"[11] Moreover, attempts to deal with the kinds of problems for which children are now being hauled off by the police—programs to promote conflict resolution and to address bullying and other sorts of violence—are being eliminated because educators and students are themselves being bullied into focusing on test scores to the exclusion of everything else.[12]

5. Retain students in grade. The same get-tough sensibility that has loosed an avalanche of testing has led to a self-congratulatory war on "social promotion" that consists of forcing students to repeat a grade. The preponderance of evidence indicates that this is just about the worst course of action to take with struggling children in terms of both its academic and social-psychological effects. And the evidence *uniformly* demonstrates that retention increases the chance that a student will leave school; in fact, it's an even stronger predictor of dropping out than is socioeconomic status (see, e.g., Heubert [2003]).

If flunking kids is a terrible idea, flunking them solely on the basis of their standardized test scores is even worse. But that's precisely what Chicago, Baltimore, and the state of Florida are doing, harming tens of thousands of elementary schoolchildren in each case. And even that isn't the whole story. Some students are being forced to repeat a grade not because this is believed (however inaccurately) to be in their best interest, but because pressure for schools to show improved test results induces administrators to hold back potentially low-scoring children the year before a key exam is administered. That way, students in, say, 10th grade will be a year older, with another year of test prep under their belts, before they sit down to start bubbling in ovals.

Across the United States, according to calculations by Walt Haney and his colleagues at Boston College (2004), there were 13% more students in 9th grade in 2000 than there were in 8th grade in 1999. Retention rates are particularly high in states like Texas and North Carolina, which helps to explain their apparently impressive NAEP scores.[13] The impact on the students involved, most of whom end up dropping out, is incalculable, but it makes schools and states look good in an age where accountability trumps all other considerations. Moreover, Haney predicts, "Senseless provisions of NCLB likely will lead to a further increase of 5 percent or more in grade nine retention. And of those who are flunked," he adds, "70 to 75 percent will not persist to high school graduation."[14]

CONCLUSION: THE DANGERS OF COMPLYING WITH NCLB

Take a step back and consider these examples of what I'm calling collateral damage from high-stakes testing: a more traditional, back-to-basics curriculum; more homogeneity; a retreat from innovations like multiage classrooms; more tracking and retention; and harsher discipline. What's striking about these ostensibly accidental by-products of policies designed to ensure accountability, is that they, themselves, are on the wish list of many of the same people who push for more testing—and, often, for vouchers.

In fact, we can add one more gift to the right: By virtue of its definition of a qualified teacher, NCLB helps to cement the idea that education consists of pouring knowledge into empty receptacles. We don't need people who know how to help students become proficient learners (a skill that they might be helped to acquire in a school of education); we just need people who know a lot of stuff (a distinction that might be certified simply by a quasi-private entity—using, naturally, a standardized test). Or, as Bennett and Finn explain things to the readers of the *Wall Street Journal*, "A principal choosing teachers will make better informed decisions if she has access to comparable information about how much history or math or science each candidate knows." This nicely rounds out the "reform" agenda, by locking into place a model that not only deprofessionalizes teachers but confuses teaching with the transmission of facts.

The upshot of all this is that the right has constructed a single puzzle of interlocking parts. It is hoping that some people outside its circle will be persuaded to endorse some of those parts (specific, uniform curriculum standards, for example, or annual testing) without understanding how they are integrally connected to the others (for example, the incremental dissolution of public schooling and the diminution of the very idea that education is a public good).

It is succeeding largely because decent educators are playing into its hands. That's why we must quit confining our complaints about NCLB to peripheral problems of implementation or funding. Too many people give the impression that there would be nothing to object to if only their own school had been certified as making adequate progress, or if only Washington were more generous in paying for this assault on local autonomy. We have got to stop prefacing our objections by saying that, while the execution of this legislation is faulty, we agree with its laudable objectives. No. What we agree with is some of the rhetoric used to *sell* it, invocations of ideals like excellence and fairness. NCLB is not a step in the right direction. It is a deeply damaging, mostly ill-intentioned law, and no one genuinely committed to improving public schools (or to advancing the interests of those who have suffered from decades of neglect and oppression) would want to have anything to do with it.

Ultimately, we must decide whether we will obediently play our assigned role in helping to punish children and teachers. Every inservice session, every article, every memo from the central office that offers what amounts to an instruction manual for capitulation slides us further in the wrong direction until finally we become a nation at risk of abandoning public education altogether. Rather than scrambling to comply with its provisions, our obligation is to figure out how best to resist.

NOTES

The beginning of this chapter was adapted from the introduction to Kohn's book, *What Does It Mean to Be Well Educated? And More Essays on Standards, Grading, and Other Follies*, published by Beacon Press in 2004.

1. To be precise, those who decry these semantic misrepresentations should be described as "skeptical" or "critical." It's those responsible for them who more accurately are described as cynical. (And while we're being precise, the line I've quoted, like much of Tomlin's material, actually was written by Jane Wagner.)

2. The author cites three studies from the UK in support of this conclusion.

3. After I made some of these points in a letter to the editor that appeared in *Harper's*, Gatto wrote to tell me I had missed the point of his essay because he actually doesn't support "the elimination of public education." However, he does "hope to undermine centralized institutional schooling which uses the police power of the state to impose habits, attitudes, etc." I can only assume that he is using the word *public* in a way I don't understand. In any case, his furious attack on "mandatory" education—on universal schooling that is supported by the public treasury and administered by elected authorities—is one that has been warmly received by those on the right. Indeed, Gatto was one of the first endorsers of the Alliance for the Separation of School and State, which repudiates the idea of a "common school" and calls for "the end of federal, state, and local involvement with schooling." (A conference sponsored by the Alliance "featured a wide variety of conservative speakers, including John Taylor Gatto," according to a newsletter of Phyllis Schlafly's Eagle Forum.)

Elsewhere, Gatto has written that he is "deeply depressed by Jonathan Kozol's contention that money would improve the schools of the poor. It would not."

4. Alarming failure, not universal failure. As education policymakers across the country have learned, there are political costs to having too many students flunk the tests, particularly if an unseemly number of them are White and relatively affluent. At that point, politically potent parents—and, eventually, even education reporters—may begin to ask inconvenient questions about the test itself. Fortunately, by tinkering with the construction of items on the exam and adjusting the cut score, it is possible to ensure virtually any outcome long before the tests are scored or even administered. For the officials in charge, the enterprise of standardized testing is reminiscent of shooting an arrow into a wall and then drawing the target around it.

5. For an account of the carefully coordinated decision to stop using the V word, see Bowman (2001).

6. The McKenzie quotation is from "The NCLB Wrecking Ball," an essay first posted on www.nochildleft.com in November 2003. The Jeffords quotation is from Johnson (2003).

7. The report by People for the American Way is entitled "Funding a Movement."

8. Paige's January 28, 2004 speech, "A Time for Choice," is available at www.ed.gov/news/speeches/2004/01/01282004.html

9. Here Paige was referring to the National Education Association, which he likened to "a terrorist organization" because it opposes some provisions of NCLB. He apologized, under pressure, for a poor choice of words but then immediately resumed his virulent criticisms of the union. See Pear (2004).

10. "The federal No Child Left Behind Act demands that schools show proficient test scores for every student. One approach to achieve that, some argue, is to tailor instruction in groups of similarly skilled students." See Pappano, 2003.

11. That explanation also makes sense to Mark Soler of the Youth Law Center, a public interest group that protects at-risk children: "Now zero tolerance is fed less by fear of crime and more by high-stakes testing. Principals want to get rid of kids they perceive as trouble." Both Reyes and Soler are quoted in Fuentes, 2003.

12. Scott Poland, a school psychologist and expert in crisis intervention, writes: "School principals have told me that they would like to devote curriculum time to topics such as managing anger, violence prevention and learning to get along with others regardless of race and ethnicity, but . . . [they are] under tremendous pressure to raise academic scores on the state accountability test" (see "The Non-Hardware Side of School Safety," 2000). Poland made the same point while testifying at a congressional hearing on school violence in March 1999—a month before the shootings at Columbine.

13. That's triple the rate for the disparity between 9th and 8th grades during the 1970s. See Haney et al., 2004.

14. Walt Haney, personal communication, January 15, 2004. Haney's study also found that there was a substantial drop in high school graduation rates, beginning, as a reporter noticed, "just as President Bill Clinton and Congress ushered in the school accountability

measures [that were later] strengthened in the No Child Left Behind Act." Haney is quoted in that same article (see Schemo, 2004) as saying, "The benign explanation is that this whole standards and reform movement was implemented in an ill-conceived manner" (p. 23). This, of course, invites us to consider explanations that are less benign.

REFERENCES

Berliner, D. C., & Biddle, B. J. (1995). *The manufactured crisis: Myths, fraud, and the attack on America's public schools*. Reading, MA: Addison-Wesley.

Bowman, D. H. (2001, January 31). Republicans prefer to back vouchers by any other name. *Education Week*.

Brooks, D. (2004, January 3). Running on reform. *New York Times*, p. 15.

Delhi, K. (1998). Shopping for schools. *Orbit*, 25(1), 32.

Dobbs, M. (2004, January 2). Critics say education dept. is favoring political right. *Washington Post*, p. A-19.

Freeman, J. (2004, January 11). Reform school. *Boston Globe*, p. L3.

Fuentes, A. (2003, December 15). Discipline and punish. *The Nation*, pp. 17–20.

Gatto, J. T. (2003, September). Against school. *Harper's*, pp. 33–38.

Haney, W., et al. (2004, January). *The education pipeline in the United States, 1970–2000*. Boston: National Board on Educational Testing and Public Policy. Available at www.bc.edu/research/nbetpp/statements/nbr3.pdf

Heubert, J. P. (2003, December/January). First, do no harm. *Educational Leadership*, p. 27.

In the spotlight: Colorado. (2001, December). *School Choice Advocate*, p. 7. Available at www.friedmanfoundation.org/downloadFile.do?id=222

Jacobson, L. (2003, September 10). Once-popular "multiage grouping" loses steam. *Education Week*, pp. 1, 15.

Johnson, S. W. (2003, February 5). Mathis rips feds over school act. *Rutland* [Vermont] *Herald*.

Johnston, R. C. (2001, February 7). Urban leaders see Paige as "our own." *Education Week*.

Jones, M. G., Jones, B. D., & Hargrove, T. (2003). *The unintended consequences of high-stakes testing*. Lanham, MD: Rowman & Littlefield.

Karp, S. (2001, Spring). Paige leads dubious cast of education advisors. *Rethinking Schools*, p. 4.

Kohn, A. (2000). *The case against standardized testing: Raising the scores, ruining the schools*. Portsmouth, NH: Heinemann.

Kohn, A. (2002, October). The 500-pound gorilla. *Phi Delta Kappan*, 113–119.

Kohn, A., & Shannon, P. (2002). *Education, Inc.: Turning learning into a business* (Rev. ed.). Portsmouth, NH: Heinemann.

Kronholz, J. (2003, December 24). Education companies see dollars in Bush school-boost law. *Wall Street Journal*, p. B1.

Linn, R. L. (2003). *Accountability: Responsibility and reasonable expectations* [Presidential address to the American Educational Research Association]. Available at www.aera. net/uploadedFiles/Journals_and_Publications/Journals/Educational_Researcher/320 7/3207_03PresAddress.pdf

Neill, M. (2003, November). Leaving children behind. *Phi Delta Kappan,* 225–226.

The non-hardware side of school safety. (2000, March). NASP [National Association of School Psychologists]. *Communique, 28*(6).

Novak, J. R., & Fuller, B. (2003, December). *Penalizing diverse schools* [University of California at Berkeley and Stanford University, Policy Analysis for California Education]. Available at http://gse.berkeley.edu/research/pace/reports/PB.03-4.pdf

Pear, R. (2004, February 24). Education chief calls union "terrorist," then recants. *New York Times,* p. A20.

Pappano, L. (2003, December 14). Grouping students undergoes revival. *Boston Globe.*

Redd, C. K. (2003, April 30). Raising of MCAS bar is weighed. *Boston Globe,* p. B2.

Rimer, S. (2004, January 4). Unruly students facing arrest, not detention. *New York Times,* p. 1.

Robelen, E. W. (2004, January 14). Bush marks school law's 2nd anniversary. *Education Week,* p. 20.

Rothstein, R. (1998). *The way we were?: The myths and realities of America's student achievement.* New York: Century Foundation Press.

Sack, J. L. (2001, October 10). ELC receives grant to craft tests to evaluate teachers. *Education Week.*

Schemo, D. J. (2004, January 18). As testing rises, 9th grade becomes pivotal. *New York Times,* p. 23.

Wallis, C. (2008, June 8). No Child Left Behind: Doomed to fail? *Time.*

CHAPTER 5

The Neoliberal Agenda and the Response of Teachers Unions

Jack Gerson

The neoliberal agenda of the past 30 years has included the dismantling of the Keynesian welfare state; the disenfranchisement of the public—notably working and poor people—from economic entitlements, civil rights, and basic civil liberties; and a sustained campaign to weaken labor unions. This chapter argues that:

1. The core of these neoliberal policies remains in place today, notwithstanding the view of some that the coordinated deficit spending of 2008–2010 represented a shift from "free market" to "Keynesianism";
2. The neoliberal policies have not meant a diminished role for the state but, rather, a growth of the repressive/regulatory state apparatus to ensure conditions of profitability;
3. This is a bipartisan agenda, supported by congressional Democrats and Republicans;
4. Labor unions' strategy of reliance on the Democratic Party has failed in the context of the bipartisan support for the neoliberal agenda;
5. The assault on public education, teachers, and teachers unions exemplifies the neoliberal agenda in practice;
6. National Education Association (NEA) and American Federation of Teachers (AFT) leaderships have moved from resistance to compromise to collaboration with the educational reform agenda;
7. New resistance based on new strategies can succeed and new strategies are beginning to emerge.

A NEOLIBERAL AGENDA

Harvey (2005) defines *neoliberalism* as the theory that "human well-being can best be advanced by liberating individual skills and entrepreneurial freedoms and skills within an institutional framework characterized by strong private property rights, free markets, and free trade" (p. 2). And indeed, prior to the financial panic of Fall 2008, it appeared to many that unregulated capitalism had triumphed on an intellectual and ideological level.

> The free market stopped being one way of arranging the world, subject to argument and comparisons with other systems: it became an item of faith, a near-mystical belief. In that belief system, the finance industry made up the class of priests and magicians and began to be treated as such. (Lanchester, 2010, p. 21)

Unproven and indecipherable quantitative models ruled the world's financial markets. The "bottom line" was applied to areas from which it ought to be permanently quarantined: pensions, public health and healthcare, and public education. Instead of guaranteeing certain basics as the inalienable rights of all its citizens—first among these being food, shelter, medical care, and quality education—our society put profit (masquerading as "individual initiative") first, and basic needs last if at all. Dog eat dog.

Two years ago, the financial markets nearly brought down the world economy. Today, that economy is in the throes of the Great Recession, while the financial wizards have fallen into disgrace. Yet the laissez-faire mumbo jumbo continues to assert its destructiveness. For example, the idea of a national health service continues to be vilified as "government interfering with our freedom to choose." Another example: Just months before BP's catastrophic Gulf of Mexico oil spill, the Obama administration announced plans to allow drilling in more offshore waters. In public education, under the banner of "narrowing the achievement gap" and encouraging "individuals' right to choose," corporate billionaires posing as "educational reformers" continue to advance their program of punitive high-stakes testing (using student test scores as the basis for evaluating, paying, and retaining or firing teachers, as well as for closing or sanctioning schools); union-curbing; cuts to vital programs; and privatization (contracting out, proliferation of charter schools). Their influence is, if anything, stronger under Barack Obama and his secretary of education, Arne Duncan, than it was under George W. Bush and Margaret Spellings.

The neoliberal economic and social policies in place for the past 30-odd years remain largely intact. Free market rhetoric was replaced partially and briefly by Keynesian rhetoric ("deficit spending to increase effective demand"), but not by the Keynesian welfare state. In the 1930s, a large part of government deficit spending was channeled into massive public works programs and combined with measures to reign in and regulate the big banks (the Glass-Steagall Act, which established the Federal Deposit Insurance Corporation and separated commercial banks from stock brokerages; the Emergency Banking Act, which enabled the closing of insolvent banks; the Home Owners' Loan Corporation, the New Deal Agency established to refinance home mortgages and prevent foreclosures, etc.). In contrast, the Bush/Paulson/Bernanke/Obama/ Geithner deficit-spending program has focused on subsidizing the big Wall Street banks by giving them trillions of dollars in outright handouts, near-zero interest loans, and loan guarantees. Meanwhile, programs that provide essential services have been cut at the federal, state, and municipal levels. In effect, the government is operating a giant pump that sucks money away from essential public programs and from the public treasury, and delivers that money to the big financial institutions and to the war machine. This is a gross transfer of wealth from workers and the poor to the big banks and big corporations of the military-industrial complex. The poor subsidize the rich.

Worse may be in store. The bipartisan "deficit hawks" argue that rapid expansion of government debt can trigger runaway inflation, and this can be combated—no, not by ending the subsidization of big finance, not by pulling out of Iraq and Afghanistan and ending the subsidization of the war machine, but—only by cutting back still more on public programs and the social wage. Plans are in the works to make deep cuts to Social Security, Medicare, and state workers' pension plans.

Harvey (2005) explains:

> As the state withdraws from welfare provision and diminishes its role in areas such as health care, public education, and social services, which were once so fundamental to embedded liberalism, it leaves larger and larger segments of the population exposed to impoverishment. The social safety net is reduced to a bare minimum in favor of a system that emphasizes personal responsibility. Personal failure is generally attributed to personal failings, and the victim is all too often blamed. (p. 76)

In other words, this is class war.

According to the prevailing wisdom, the 30-year period beginning with (then-chairman of the Federal Reserve Bank) Paul Volcker's anti-inflationary policies (1979) and ending with the collapse of Bear Stearns and Lehman Brothers (2008) was a period of intense deregulation. However, throughout this period the size of the state sector and its regulatory role grew substantially. In particular, there was disproportionate, even qualitative, growth in the state's repressive apparatus: prisons, prison guards, cops, military, border patrol, and ICE. There was a corresponding growth in *regulations*—especially those aimed at restricting civil liberties (e.g., the Homeland Security Act) and those aimed punitively at students, teachers, and schools (e.g., No Child Left Behind, Race to the Top). There was indeed deregulation—mainly, elimination of regulations that got in the way of corporations, including those that restricted dangerous and predatory practices that had accelerated economic collapse in the 1930s. Thus, Congress repealed the Glass-Steagall legislation, which had kept banks and brokerages separate since the 1930s. In education, charter schools were exempted from state education code regulations that protect students, teachers, and popular oversight.

No Child Left Behind and Race to the Top illustrate the state's expanded regulatory role in carrying out the neoliberal agenda. NCLB incorporated punitive measures against students, teachers, and schools for "poor performance" on high-stakes standardized tests, up to and including an option to replace "failed schools" with charter schools. Race to the Top, the Obama/Duncan creation, makes funding contingent on states agreeing to allow more charter schools and to make teacher evaluations, pay, and continued employment dependent on student test scores.

So this has been not simply a question of deregulation and a shrinking of the state's role. Rather, the state has stepped forward to enforce profitability and privatization via *deregulation of things* (banks, corporations, charter schools) and the *elimination of regulations that protect people and basic rights* (labor, students, teachers, protestors, immigrants, etc.), while simultaneously *increasing punitive and disciplinary regulation of people* (Homeland Security, NCLB).

Robertson (2008) puts it this way:

> Neoliberalism demands that freedom of the market, the right to free trade, the right to choose, and protection of private property be assured by the state. (p. 13)

Hudson (2007) observes:

> The slogan of free markets is merely a euphemism for centralizing planning power in the hands of financial and other vested interests that are seeking to break free of oversight, regulation and taxation by elected officials. . . . Thanks largely to the privatization of election financing and its rising media advertising costs in today's political campaigns, the vested property and financial interests have succeeded in un-taxing and deregulating themselves. (p. 2)

A BIPARTISAN AGENDA

During the heyday of the Keynesian welfare state (the postwar boom), the corporations and the state were able to grant expanded public services and a moderate increase in real wages in exchange for labor peace. The labor leadership for the most part enforced that peace. Consequently, labor's strategy of appealing to Democrats *seemed* viable (although failure to organize the unorganized already spelled a decline in private sector union membership).

The end of the postwar boom brought an end to the era of labor peace, as Ronald Reagan drove home when he broke the PATCO union's air controller strike in 1981 by firing the strikers. At the same time, big business launched a systematic campaign to change state policy in their favor, as Jacob Hacker and Paul Pierson (2010) document in their recent book. From Bob Herbert's book review:

> The authors argue persuasively that the economic struggles of the middle and working classes in the U.S. since the late-1970s were not primarily the result of globalization and technological changes but rather a long series of policy changes in government that overwhelmingly favored the very rich. . . . Those changes were the result of increasingly sophisticated, well-financed and well-organized efforts by the corporate and financial sectors to tilt government policies in their favor, and thus in favor of the very wealthy. . . . Big business mobilized on an enormous scale to become much more active in Washington, cultivating politicians in both parties and fighting fiercely to achieve shared political goals. This occurred at the same time that organized labor, the most effective fighting force on behalf of the middle class and other working Americans, was caught in a devastating spiral of decline. (Herbert, 2010, p. A31)

Indeed, from its inception, the neoliberal agenda has been a bipartisan agenda. Paul Volcker, the Federal Reserve chairman whose anti-inflationary policies (the "Volcker Shock") in 1979–1982 are widely credited with ending the stagflation of the 1970s, was appointed to head the Fed in 1978 by Democrat Jimmy Carter and was reappointed in 1982 by Republican Ronald Reagan. The bipartisan bleeding of the public treasury to recapitalize the banks and fuel the war machine has meant reduced federal aid to states and municipalities, which in turn impose harsh cutbacks on jobs and programs that working and poor people depend upon for their survival. Nobel laureate Joseph Stiglitz and Harvard professor Linda Bilmes estimate that the cost of the Iraq and Afghan wars will total $3 trillion (Stiglitz & Bilmes, 2008). The Federal Reserve Bank has shoveled an even larger sum to the banks over the past 2 years. (As a point of reference, $1 trillion would pay the salaries of 1 million teachers for 15 years.)

Labor unions continue to contribute millions of dollars to Democratic Party politicians—but these politicians support the prioritization of banks and the war machine over education and other essential programs, and have done so for years. So in funding the Democrats, labor funds the strengthening of the repressive state apparatus and the punitive regulatory apparatus, while doing little or nothing to stop the shredding of the social safety net.

This is clearly the case in public education. NEA and AFT have played critical roles in Democratic Party election campaigns for decades, providing phone banking, precinct walking, and hard cash. In return, the Democrats overwhelmingly supported and stood behind the No Child Left Behind legislation. (Although NCLB was drafted by G.W. Bush appointees, it was promoted and co-sponsored in Congress by very liberal Democrats Senator Ted Kennedy and Representative George Miller. It received overwhelming bipartisan support.) The Obama/Duncan Race to the Top and Blueprint for Reform likewise are supported by both Democrats and Republicans. Virtually identical educational policies have been and are being carried out at state and local levels by Republicans (e.g., ex-Los Angeles Mayor Riordan, New York Mayor Bloomberg) and Democrats (e.g., Chicago Mayor Daley, Michigan Governor Grantholm). Eli Broad, the Los Angeles billionaire who acts as point person for the corporate education "deform" agenda, is a power in California Democratic Party politics. Thus labor's main—virtually only—strategy, that of funding, promoting, and relying on elected Democratic Party politicians, has hit the wall. Continuing with that strategy cannot lead to success. Another strategy is needed. We will return to this after we examine the crisis in public education in more detail.

CRISES IN PUBLIC EDUCATION— REAL AND MANUFACTURED

In education, the neoliberal campaign initially based itself on two claims:

- That public education as a whole was declining rapidly, putting the "nation at risk" of falling behind other industrial nations economically and technologically.
- That this decline was caused by bad teaching and lack of uniformity, and could be fixed by introducing standards, mandatory statewide tests aligned with those standards, and punishment or rewards for schools and teachers based on students' test scores (test-based accountability).

Later, a third claim was added, building on the second:

- That the "achievement gap" between low-achieving schools and high-achieving schools is caused by bad teaching and lack of uniformity, and could be eliminated by standards, test-based accountability, application of corporate management methods to school districts and schools, and promotion of "choice" (especially, more charter schools).

Let's address these.

First, on the "nation at risk": U.S. students appear to have mediocre scores when compared with students from other industrial nations—until the data are broken down by poverty level and by race. Such a stratified comparison is important, because the United States has the highest rate of poverty among industrial nations (Berliner, 2006) and has fewer public programs to support the poor than many other industrial countries (e.g., the United States alone fails to provide nationalized healthcare). When data are stratified by income level, the average score for schools with more than half their students above the poverty level is above the U.S. average score and far above the international average score. When data are broken down by race and then compared with the average scores, U.S. White students repeatedly score in the top five internationally for the 25 to 30 industrial countries studied, while Black and Latino students repeatedly score in the bottom five. These results have been shown for multiple studies of math, reading, and science scores (Berliner, 2006; Bracey, 2004). To underscore this: Public schools in middle- and upper income areas do well in comparison to the corresponding schools in other industrial countries. Schools in low-income areas do poorly.

On the second and third points, which blame low achievement and the "achievement gap" on bad teaching, lack of standards, lack of test-based accountability, and lack of "choice": All of these avoid identifying and doing something about the main problem, which is poverty. Dating as far back as the 1966 Coleman Report, researchers have found that "non-school" factors (overwhelmingly poverty-related) are at least twice as responsible for low student achievement as "in-school" factors. The evidence is overwhelming:

> Decades of social science research have demonstrated that differences in the quality of schools can explain about one-third of the variation in student achievement. But the other two-thirds is attributable to non-school factors . . . making teacher quality the focus distracts us from the biggest threat to student achievement in the current age:

our unprecedented economic catastrophe and its effect on parents and their children's ability to gain from higher-quality schools. (Rothstein, 2010, pp. 1–2)

Teachers see the effects of poverty on learning every day. Thus, a staggering percentage of students in schools like East Oakland's Castlemont High School (where I teach) live in group homes (some are homeless), come to school not having eaten since yesterday's school lunch, have been in lockup or are on probation, have chronic health conditions affecting their ability to concentrate and learn but that go untreated (hearing loss, vision problems, asthma, etc.), lack good role models, are subject to negative peer pressure, and/or have no family support system.

Rothstein actually *underestimates* the poverty effect, because many "in-school" factors are also poverty-related. These include large class size, under-resourced and understaffed schools, lack of administrative support, disruptive students, scripted curricula, focus on test prep and "teaching to the test" to raise test scores, and little time for planning and collaboration. In short, poverty-related effects far outweigh effects of teacher quality. Certainly, it is important to try to improve classroom instruction. But no campaign to "close the achievement gap" can succeed if it does not make its main priority to close the poverty gap by providing jobs, restoring and expanding essential public programs, and raising income levels for low-income families.

Furthermore, the reforms proposed for the in-school factors generally don't work and, in fact, have been making things worse.

Let's run through them.

Standards and Test-Based Accountability

The prevalence of test-based accountability has made raising student test scores on statewide tests the main educational goal in low-achieving schools. Teachers are told to emphasize "test-taking skills and strategies" and to spend several weeks before each exam date reviewing released questions from previous years' testing. Many low-performing schools have dropped electives and replaced them with scripted test preparation classes and scripted remedial math and reading classes, usually using workbooks and/or software from the district's favored test prep vendor. Students are encouraged to focus on "getting the right answer" as the goal, rather than encouraging curiosity, inquiry, critical thinking, conceptualization, and the problem-solving process. The effect is to sort schools by poverty level; at low-income schools, students are taught to give the right answer or get shoved out—to the military, to the street, or to prison.

Pay-for-Performance ("Merit Pay")

A recent large-scale study of performance-based pay for public school teachers, conducted by the National Center on Performance Initiatives at Vanderbilt University, found what others had found before: "Merit pay" doesn't work (Springer et al., 2010). A recent *Education Week* review of private sector experience with pay-for-performance concludes that it "nourishes short-term performance, annihilates long-term planning, builds fear, demolishes teamwork, nourishes rivalry and politics" (Gabor, 2010, p. 28).

Charter Schools

Charter schools receive public money but unlike public schools they do not have to accept all students; they are not subject to the same regulatory oversight as public schools; their boards are not elected but self-appointed; and they are overwhelmingly non-union. They are freed from "bureaucratic" regulations, including—in many states—exemption from regulations that protect the learning and teaching conditions and the well-being of students and teachers. Thus, charter schools contribute to the disenfranchisement of the public from control over public education; the deregulation of protective education codes for public education; the weakening of teachers unions; and the privatization of education overall.

Charter schools are in aggregate, if anything, outperformed by public schools, a result that has been observed in several studies, most recently in a Walton-funded multistate study by Stanford University researchers (Center for Research on Education Outcomes, 2009). To quote educational researcher Gerald Bracey (2004):

> A few charters might be laboratories of innovation, but mostly charter schools look like the schools they were supposed to replace. They don't outperform public schools and, in fact, often score lower on tests than demographically similar public schools. People were outraged by the supposedly poor performance of public schools. They should be equally outraged at the even lower achievement of charters. (p. 99)

Firing Bad Teachers

Stanford University economist Eric Hanushek (2009) asserts that "allowing ineffective teachers to remain in the classroom is dragging down the nation," and that the problem can be fixed by firing the "bottom end of the teaching force"—the 5% to 10% of teachers whose students have the lowest test scores. Hanushek makes these statements in print and as a talking head in the movie *Waiting for Superman*. However:

- Even Hanushek estimates that teacher quality explains at most 10% of student test score gains. The poverty effect is more than five times as great. Because of the poverty effect, test scores are not explained mainly by teacher quality. "Variations in teaching performance flow largely from variables that have little to do with qualities of teachers themselves. Thus, improving the quality of the nation's teachers won't come simply from trimming away the weakest performers. Nor will we attract capable teachers to failing schools simply by offering them monetary incentives" (Futernik, 2010, p. 63). So even if we accepted that student test score gains are a valid measure of student achievement, we would have to ask the same question we have asked previously: Why so little attention to poverty?
- What could help improve teacher quality?
  Reducing mis-assignment of teachers to the wrong subjects. For example, teachers without a math teaching credential or a math major teach 40% of math classes in high-poverty high schools (Futernik, 2010).
  Providing far more support to new teachers and to struggling teachers. For example, team teaching in which a capable veteran teacher is paired with a beginning teacher for a full school year can help the new teacher break into the job over time while both teachers benefit from daily feedback and collaboration.
  Increasing teacher collaboration and teacher preparation time.
  Smaller class size, particularly important in high-poverty schools (Biddle & Berliner, 2002, p. 17).
  Retaining good teachers. Most veteran teachers estimate that it takes about 5 years to become first-rate teachers. But nearly half of all teachers leave the field in their first 5 years—and the figure is considerably higher in high-poverty schools. Rather than paying teachers adequately and providing more support and resources, urban school districts are opting for the corporate reform alternative: Teach for America and New Teacher Project recruits, who come in with no experience and overwhelmingly leave in 2 or 3 years.

The campaign to fire "low-performing" teachers doesn't fix the problem. It makes the problem worse, by chasing away potentially good career teachers rather than providing them with the support and resources they need to develop and succeed. It creates a hole that at best can be filled by Teach for America and New Teacher Project interns. The consequences are the worst in high-poverty schools and communities, where the teacher turnover, and therefore the instability, is greatest. (Of course, there are a small number of ineffectual teachers who are unable or unwilling to change. They need to be identified and removed. The current campaign, though, literally throws out the baby with the bathwater, and in the process guts the protection from arbitrary harassment and dismissal that was so prevalent before the rise of teachers unions in the 1960s.)

Closing Low-Performing Schools

Much of what was said about firing low-performing teachers applies to closing low-performing schools. Fix the main problems by focusing on increasing jobs and incomes in high-poverty communities, by providing wraparound services, by providing more resources and smaller class sizes, and by creating an environment where teachers won't leave within 2 or 3 years. And as with firing teachers, closing schools increases instability and therefore accelerates the downward spiral in already unstable high-poverty communities.

In short, the neoliberal reforms do not make education in low-achieving schools better. They make things worse. Moreover, they take the place of the kind of sweeping programs that could make a real positive difference.

Two things could be done to really improve education in low-achieving schools:

1. Reduce social inequality and thereby reduce poverty.
2. Transform the goals of education from teaching obedience and memorization of arbitrary facts and rules to encouraging inquiry and understanding.

But just stating these goals is enough to understand why they are not being implemented. The corporate campaign is part of the overall neoliberal campaign, whose goals include systematically increasing the share accruing to corporations and the very wealthy at the expense of working and poor people, and increasing corporate control over society.

If the corporate-financed war against public schools continues to succeed in closing down inner-city public schools in favor of charter schools, where will the majority of young people in low-income areas be able to get an education? Since public schools are one of the few remaining permanent institutions in many inner-city neighborhoods, what will stop the cycle of instability that so often occurs when a neighborhood school is shut down?

If the corporate-financed, teacher-bashing campaign succeeds in running teachers out of teaching, where will a cadre of experienced teachers come from to take their place?

How did we get to this sorry state? How have teachers unions responded to the war on public education? What can be done to turn the situation around?

THE CORPORATE WAR AGAINST PUBLIC EDUCATION

For most Americans, exposure to the campaign against public education—what Berliner and Biddle (1995) call "the Manufactured Crisis"—came after Ronald Reagan was elected president in 1980.

> As far as the public was concerned, the Manufactured Crisis began on April 26, 1983— the date when, amidst much fanfare, the Reagan White House released its critical report on the status of American schools, *A Nation at Risk*. In many ways, this report was "the mother of all critiques" of American education. (Berliner & Biddle, 1995, p. 139)

A Nation at Risk informed the public that public education was declining rapidly, threatening American leadership in industry, science, and technology. The report blamed teachers and inadequate teaching programs. It was followed immediately by a massively financed publicity campaign, including corporate-sponsored reports and heavy media promotion (Emery & Ohanian, 2004).

In this period, the corporate program for educational reform emerged in many of the essentials that by now have become so familiar. Emery and Ohanian (2004) document how the Business Roundtable (BRT) orchestrated a heavily funded national lobbying campaign to change education policy at the state and national levels, starting with an "education summit" of 218 CEOs in January 1989.

By 1994, 19 states had adopted the BRT's call for state standards, statewide standardized tests, and punitive sanctions or rewards for schools based on student scores on the state tests. In 2001 Congress passed the No Child Left Behind legislation, much of it adapted from the BRT's 1995 "Nine Essential Components of a Successful Education System" (Emery & Ohanian, 2004).

NO CHILD LEFT BEHIND

The No Child Left Behind legislation made federal funding for public education contingent on states holding teachers and schools accountable for "achievement" as measured by student performance on standardized math and reading tests, with punitive measures for schools that don't measure up. These schools, invariably already cash and resource starved, must use some of their federal Title I funding to pay for private after-school tutoring. Schools that fail to measure up for 5 years can be closed down, put under direct state control, converted to traditional private schools, or—as is happening ever more frequently—converted to privately run, lightly regulated and generally non-union charter schools.

NCLB institutionalized high-stakes testing and pushed it to extremes. It mandated that failing schools be subjected to punitive sanctions, with the bar raised year-by-year, finally reaching the ludicrous requirement that by 2014 any school with even one student scoring below grade level in math or reading will be considered a failing school and subject to punitive sanctions. It qualitatively increased the pressure for schools in low-income areas to focus narrowly on improving test scores, with all of the negative consequences reviewed in a previous section. Its provisions that encourage replacing "failed" public schools with charter schools and hiring third-party "tutors" (in reality, usually test preparation mills) wrote socialization, routinization, and privatization of public education into federal law.

THE VENTURE PHILANTHROPIES: BROAD, GATES, WALTON, AND OTHERS

Shortly before the adoption of NCLB, a new wave of educational reformers appeared on the scene, "self-made" billionaires who established massively endowed "venture philanthropies." The most prominent of these are the Eli and Edythe Broad Foundation, the Bill and Melinda Gates Foundation, and the Walton (Walmart) Foundation.

The new venture philanthropists vigorously promoted the need for standards and high-stakes testing with punitive test-based accountability. What set them apart from earlier corporate educational reformers were:

- The ability and willingness to "invest" much more money—for example, between 2000 and 2008 Gates pumped $2 billion into creating 2,600 small schools in 45 states before abruptly abandoning the initiative (Ravitch, 2010).
- Massive funding of charter schools. Walton alone gave $82 million to charter schools in 2007 (Ravitch, 2010).
- The introduction of corporate practices, including competition between schools and between school districts and downsizing central services in favor of outsourcing to private contractors. Broad pushed this

model vigorously. Note that despite the emphasis on "competition" and "deregulation," Broad and others demanded increased state intervention to establish and enforce test-based accountability.

- Targeted investments with strict accountability. The venture philanthropists insisted on evidence of rising test scores to prove that they were getting an adequate return on their investments.

As Ravitch (2010) explains:

> Over time they converged in support of reform strategies that mirrored their own experience in acquiring huge fortunes, such as competition, choice, deregulation, incentives, and other market-based approaches. . . . Not many school districts could resist their offers . . . the offer of a multimillion-dollar grant by a foundation is enough to cause most superintendents to drop everything and reorder their priorities. (p. 200)

Despite their fetish with "evidence" and "data," the venture philanthropists ignore statistical studies that have found:

- Charter schools are in aggregate, if anything, outperformed by public schools.
- Pay-for-performance ("merit pay") does not work.
- Poverty and other "out-of-school" factors are the biggest impediment to the academic achievement of low-income students.

When the venture philanthropists insist that instruction must be "evidence-based" and "data-driven," they don't mean that schools and teachers should be guided by statistical studies. When they say "data-driven," they mean breaking down jobs into tasks, breaking tasks into components, and then measuring and quantifying each component to develop target work norms. The norms are used to establish new conditions of work and workplace discipline. These are used to impose scripted learning, narrow "teach-to-the-test" curricula, canned software, and cyber schools.

OAKLAND: A CASE STUDY

What does the "business model for education" mean in practice? Consider the case of Oakland, California.

The Oakland Unified School District (OUSD) was put into receivership by the state of California on January 1, 2003, allegedly because of a $37 million deficit. The school board was stripped of all decision-making power, which was bestowed on a state-appointed administrator, Randolph Ward, then an intern in Broad's Urban Superintendents Academy. Ward brought in Broad residents to run human resources, labor relations, finance, and the small school incubator. The Broad Foundation was effectively in charge of OUSD.

Ward immediately cut the pay of all school workers by 4%. He laid off school custodians, security guards, clerks, and food service workers, and outsourced services to private consultants. He closed the libraries in nearly all middle schools and in several high schools, "reconstituted" or shut down nearly half of all public schools, and cut electives. He drove out veteran teachers, replacing them with Teach for America and New Teacher Project interns. Consequently, OUSD now has one of the highest teacher turnover rates in the country. Teacher salaries currently fall more than 20% below the averages for California public school teachers.

By 2009, when the state returned governance to the school board, enrollment had declined to 38,000 (from 55,000 in 2002), while charter school enrollment quadrupled. Oakland now has by far the highest percentage of students in charter schools of all urban school districts in California. The cuts and downsizing notwithstanding, the district's debt tripled under the state takeover. Where did the money go? It was taken away from classroom instruction and given to contractors, consultants, and excess administrators. Oakland spends double the California school district average on contracts. A state audit found that Oakland had 78 excess administrators in 2006-07, in violation of state education code. Almost unbelievably, the state is fining the district $1.1 million for this—remember, the state was running the district!

Oakland has been a laboratory for the neoliberal education program. But it is not unique. The same program is being carried out by Broad allies and trainees in New York, Chicago, Detroit, St. Louis, Seattle, Pittsburgh, Dallas, and New Orleans, to name a few.

OBAMA, DUNCAN, AND RACE TO THE TOP

Barack Obama and his education secretary, Arne Duncan, are advocates of the corporate education agenda. In 2007 and again in 2008, Obama told NEA's annual national conventions that he was for national standards, pay-for-performance, firing "bad teachers," and increasing the number of charter schools. Duncan, a long-time Broad ally, executed the "business model" in his years as CEO of Chicago Public Schools. He closed down schools in low-income areas, increased the number of charter schools, pushed pay-for-performance, brought in hordes of consultants and contractors, harassed and fired veteran teachers, and pushed high-stakes testing, test prep, and scripted "teach-to-the-test."

Duncan is very big on competition: competition between states, between school districts, between teachers, between students. Race to the Top (RTTT) in some ways goes beyond NCLB. It establishes a competition between states for a relatively small amount of money ($5 billion in total) that is coveted in today's environment of cuts to state education funding. It requires that states applying for RTTT funding each submit detailed plans for basing teacher pay and teacher evaluations on student test scores (i.e., making teachers compete against one another). It lifts limits on the total number of charter schools permitted in the state (inducing competition between schools).

The Duncan/Obama *Blueprint for Reform* goes still further, as educator and writer Stephen Krashen (2010) explained:

> According to the *Blueprint for Reform*, released by the US Department of Education, the new standards will be enforced with new tests, which will include "interim" tests in addition to those given at the end of year. No Child Left Behind only required reading and math tests. The *Blueprint* recommends testing in other subjects as well. The *Blueprint* also insists we measure growth, which could mean testing in the fall and in the spring, doubling the number of tests.
>
> This means billions of dollars will be spent on test construction, validation, revision, etc. at a time when schools are already very short of funds, when many science classes have no lab equipment, school libraries (those that are left) have few books, many school bathrooms lack toilet paper, school years are being shortened, and teachers are losing their jobs.
>
> How can this increase in testing be justified, in light of the fact that schools are so short of money and the fact that there is no evidence that increasing testing increases learning?

Obama and Duncan have been outspoken supporters of the campaign to fire low-performing teachers. This approach also is advocated by household educational reform and mass media names: Bill Gates, Michelle Rhee, former New York City schools chancellor Joel Klein, Newt Gingrich, Al Sharpton, Nicholas Kristof, and Steven Brill (Brill, 2009; Kristof, 2009; Obama, 2009; Sharpton & Klein, 2009). The campaign peaked in February 2010, when Obama and Duncan applauded the mass firing of the entire teaching staff of Central Falls High School (Rhode Island). The Central High teachers were fired because they refused to accept district superintendent Frances Gallo's attempt to unilaterally increase their workday and workweek without increased compensation (Fletcher

& Anderson, 2010; Jordan, 2010). (Three months later, Gallo rescinded the firings, but only after teachers agreed to longer workdays, gave up seniority rights, and accepted a new evaluation system.)

Eli Broad (2009) has called the Obama presidency "our golden moment." After listening to Obama's March 2009 educational policy address, Tom Vander Ark, formerly executive director of the Bill and Melinda Gates Foundation, declared victory for Broad.

> But yesterday, Eli won. Obama's speech sounded like Eli wrote it. It was about choice and charter schools, human capital and performance pay. It was right on message from pre-school to college. We've never had a Republican president that so clearly articulated a Republican strategy. Only it's the new New Democrat strategy. It's Eli's strategy. He finally won. (Vander Ark, 2009)

WHERE WERE THE UNIONS?

Where were the nation's huge, affluent, and powerful teacher unions, the American Federation of Teachers and the 3-million-member National Education Association (the nation's largest union), when this program was being put in place?

Initially, teachers unions were resistant to the corporate campaign. However, teachers union leadership had a longstanding strategy of relying on Democratic politicians, and increasingly the Democrats joined Republicans in a bipartisan consensus around the neoliberal agenda generally, and around the corporate-driven educational reform program in particular.

The teachers unions' choice was clear: either break with reliance on the Democrats and resist, or find grounds for reaching an accommodation with the corporate reform program. They chose the latter. One compromise led to another, each a retreat. Now, they have led to accepting key parts of the corporate reform program, as we will see below.

When the Business Roundtable rolled out its campaign, starting in 1989, NEA and AFT were in a position to resist: Many Democratic candidates (and the party as a whole) owed their seats to funding from the teachers unions and campaigning by their members. Despite the corporate campaign, teachers still were viewed positively—often as heroes—by much of the public. But the teachers unions did not aggressively try to block the passage of NCLB, nor did they launch an alternative action, publicity, and electoral campaign.

Instead, in the early 1990s, NEA and AFT agreed to a compromise. In exchange for school site autonomy, the teachers unions would agree to take responsibility for increasing student achievement. At least on the surface, site autonomy seemed to promise greater academic freedom for teachers. But the unions' acceptance of adherence to state standards as the yardstick for measuring "student achievement" weakened their members' ability to resist the pressure to judge success or failure by student scores on the standards-based statewide tests. Emery and Ohanian (2004) capture this well:

> Under the pressure of a constant media barrage—editorials carping about teachers meddling in policy combined with editorials accusing teachers of caring only about money—NEA and AFT agreed to a division of labor: teachers are given the autonomy to make sure students meet goals established by outside forces. In the language of systemic reform, this is called site-based decision-management or site-based decision-making (SBDM). . . . At the local level some hoped that this autonomy, peculiar though it was, would finally allow teachers to have some say in what they taught. But this claim to autonomy, although sounding professionally high-minded, was, of course, a chimera. In agreeing to SBDM, the NEA leadership put its members in the position of accepting responsibility for increasing student achievement while relinquishing the very power that might help them do it. (p. 117)

In 1997, NEA President Bob Chase went further, arguing that "teacher unions need to be reinvented"—specifically, NEA needed to take responsibility for school quality, even in schools that were underfunded, under-resourced, and led by inept administrators.

> The fact is that while NEA does not control curriculum or set funding levels, or hire and fire, we cannot go on denying responsibility for school quality. (Emery & Ohanian, 2004, p. 117)

Similarly, in 1998 AFT President Sandra Feldman told that union's convention:

> Education reform is working! Academic standards and requirements are up, student attendance is up, dropout rates are down, and our students are achieving at much higher levels! (Emery & Ohanian, 2004, p. 118)

It should come as no surprise that in 2001 NEA did not actively oppose the NCLB legislation as it swept through Congress with overwhelming bipartisan support (Bracey, 2003). But the corporate reformers were not sitting back. They were escalating their attack, as the venture philanthropists arrived on the scene at almost the same time as the NCLB legislation was unveiled.

Some teacher leaders saw the danger and raised their voices, few more forcefully than Wayne Johnson, president of the 340,000-member California Teachers Association (NEA's largest state affiliate).

> American education is in crisis. It is a crisis of poverty. It is a crisis of under-funding. It is a crisis of poor kids not getting what they need. It is a crisis of administrative mismanagement. It is a crisis of huge teacher shortage.
>
> At the same time that the U.S. and California rank so low in educational funding, and the serious problems that face the children of our public schools, right wing advocacy groups and corporate leaders are demanding educational reform. They say our schools are failing—teachers are failing!
>
> Most of the reforms they advocate have nothing to do with the problems that face our schools. They only advocate reforming teachers and teacher contracts. I call it the phony reforms.
>
> To reform a public school system that is under-funded, overcrowded and running out of teachers, the pundits are demanding more teacher accountability, more testing, more punishment for kids and teachers in low performing or priority schools.
>
> As one of these advocates of phony reform, the Los Angeles billionaire Eli Broad told me in a one on one hour and a half meeting about three weeks ago, that public education needed merit pay and teacher transfer and seniority rights should be eliminated from teacher union contracts. He calls this progressive unionism. I call it sell out!
>
> Secretary of Education Rod Paige and Mr. Broad are proposing this concept of progressive unionism and the NEA and AFT have endorsed the plan. This is union and teacher bashing, not educational reform. (Johnson, 2001)

But the national AFT and NEA leaderships did not confront this new wave of "phony reforms," opting instead to maintain "a seat at the table." Several of the most influential teachers union officials found common ground with parts of the corporate program. Randi Weingarten, then-president of the New York City teachers union, the United Federation of Teachers, and currently president of the AFT, and Adam Urbanski, president of the Rochester Federation of Teachers, were among the 12 faculty members for the inaugural year of Eli Broad's Urban Superintendents Academy (class of 2002). Their faculty colleagues included outspoken architects of the corporate reform agenda, well known for their hostility to teachers unions: U.S. Secretary of Education Rod Paige, Fordham Institute president Chester Finn, Center for Reform of School Systems founder Don McAdams, and Education Trust principal partner Paul Ruiz (Broad Superintendents' Academy, 2002). This continued and deepened the "joint responsibility" partnership pioneered by Bob Chase and Sandra Feldman.

Broad and his foundation were clear about what kind of teachers unions they wanted. Dan Katzir, the Broad Foundation's managing director, and Broad Foundation policy analyst Wendy Hassett explained that:

> In labor, we have focused on new models of collective bargaining and union contracts, encouraging policies and practices that enable districts to place the most effective educators in the neediest schools, and supporting unions and districts with plans to use incentive-based, professional compensation. (Hassett & Katzir, 2005, p. 231)

Thus "progressive teacher unionism," Broad-style, means teachers unions that are willing to accept pay-for-performance and to dispense with seniority. Hassett and Katzir (2005) go on to specify which unions will get their dollars.

> The foundation seeks to work with those teacher unions that consider excellence in teaching and student achievement to be paramount. In 2002, we made a capstone investment in Denver's pay-for-performance pilot (ProComp), and in 2004 made a follow-on grant to support a critical phase of information-sharing and communication just prior to the teacher vote on ProComp, which helped yield a 59 percent margin for the proposal by the Denver Classroom Teachers Association. (pp. 233–234)

Eli Broad attempted to build on and spread his success in establishing pay-for-performance in Denver. Even some historically militant and independent-minded teachers locals attended Broad conferences aimed at establishing labor buy-in for school district labor/management collaboration around pay-for-performance. For example, in March 2004 local union and school district leaders from Houston, Milwaukee, New Orleans, Oakland, and Wichita attended a 2-day Broad Foundation Benchmarking Project "Knowledge Transfer Session" where teams from Columbus, Denver, and Douglas County (Colorado) promoted merit pay (Broad Foundation for Education, 2004).

By 2005, several other state and local teacher leaders (including Barbara Kerr, Wayne Johnson's successor as California Teachers Association president) joined Weingarten and Urbanski as participants in Broad's Strategic Retreat (other advisors included then-Chicago Public Schools CEO Arne Duncan and New York City schools chancellor Joel Klein) (Broad Foundations, 2006, p. 49). At approximately the same time, the Broad Foundation website announced funding for two new projects: a teachers union reform institute (Scholastic Administrator, 2009) and a biography of former UFT and AFT president Albert Shanker (Higgins, 2009).

RANDI WEINGARTEN
AND THE AMERICAN FEDERATION OF TEACHERS

In the movie "Waiting for Superman," AFT president Randi Weingarten is portrayed as the evil teachers union leader who almost single-handedly prevents heroic school principals from fixing public education by firing bad teachers. But in real life, Randi Weingarten is Eli Broad's kind of union leader. As already mentioned, she has been working with Broad for years (a trainer for his Superintendents' Academy, a frequent participant at his Strategic Retreats). Over the past 3 years, Weingarten has moved markedly farther by engineering a series of concessionary agreements, each of which accepts key parts of the corporate reform program, and each of which she hails.

In October 2007, when Weingarten was president of the AFT's New York local, she signed a pay-for-performance agreement funded by Broad and two other foundations.

In December 2009, she collaborated with Detroit's state-appointed school boss Robert Bobb on a contract that included a 2-year wage freeze (and a 1% raise in year 3), pay-for-performance, weakened seniority rights, and forced loans from teachers to the state via $250 per paycheck deductions *to be returned only when the teachers are no longer employed by Detroit Public Schools.* This contract was so unpopular that in March 2010 an opposition coalition swept all 20 Detroit Federation of Teachers delegate positions to the 2010 AFT national convention.

In May 2010, Weingarten reached agreement with notorious teacher-basher Michelle Rhee on a contract for Washington, DC, teachers, with a particularly insidious pay-for-performance clause that allows "better" teachers to trade job security for higher pay. Weingarten facilitated similar agreements in New Haven, Pittsburgh, and Hillsborough County, Florida (Tampa Bay). However, in October 2010 the members of the Baltimore Teacher Union rejected a similar Weingarten-negotiated contract.

Weingarten is now collaborating with the Gates Foundation on studying "teacher effectiveness." Shortly before the July 2010 AFT national convention, Gates gave AFT $3.4 million "to create and develop a teacher evaluation system." Gates was the keynote speaker at the AFT convention and made teacher effectiveness his main focus.

Studying teacher effectiveness is now the number one education priority of the Gates Foundation. In November 2009, Gates awarded $335 million in grants to measure and study teacher effectiveness in ten urban areas. The money is to be used to:

Develop and implement new approaches, strategies, and policies, including adopting better measures of teacher effectiveness that include growth in student achievement and college readiness; . . . tying tenure decisions more closely to teacher effectiveness measures and rewarding highly effective teachers through new career and compensation opportunities that keep them in the classroom. (Bill & Melinda Gates Foundation, 2009).

Sound familiar? "Growth in student achievement," "tying tenure decisions more closely to teacher effectiveness measures," and "rewarding highly effective teachers through new career and compensation opportunities" sound suspiciously like "test-based accountability, basing teacher pay and evaluations on student test scores" and "weakening tenure to facilitate firing veteran teachers." These phrases are also very similar to language written into the Detroit, Washington, DC, Pittsburgh, and Hillsborough County contracts, and rejected by the Baltimore Teachers Union membership.

Weingarten's increasingly warm embrace of the corporate educational reform agenda has not gone unnoticed. For example, consider the recent *New York Times* article, "Despite Image, Union Leader Backs School Change":

In the past year, for example, she has led her members—sometimes against internal resistance—to embrace innovations that were once unthinkable.

"She has shrewdly recognized that teachers' unions need to be part of the reform", said Richard D. Kahlenberg, a senior fellow at the Century Foundation.

Early this year, she delivered a major policy speech that embraced tying teachers' evaluations in part to students' scores on standardized test scores. (Gabriel, 2010, p. A1)

DENNIS VAN ROEKEL
AND THE NATIONAL EDUCATION ASSOCIATION

The NEA national leadership has been slower than Weingarten to come around to openly embracing the reform agenda. Until recently, NEA president Dennis Van Roekel, like Reg Weaver before him, maintained formal opposition to pay-for-performance. However, this opposition was generally passive. From 2002 through 2008, NEA's main message was: "We won't be able to get NCLB off our backs until we elect a Democratic President and a Democratic Congress." This was always a dubious proposition, since NCLB was passed with overwhelming bipartisan support.

Well, in 2009 and 2010 there was a Democratic President and a Democratic Congress. But Barack Obama and Arne Duncan promoted choice, competition, standards, and test-based accountability.

Despite stated opposition to Race to the Top, NEA's response in practice has been to praise the program:

- When in April 2010 Duncan announced the two winners of Phase 1 Race to the Top funding (Delaware and Tennessee), Van Roekel declared victory in a press release headed *NEA applauds selection of Race to the Top winners: Department of Education sends clear message that collaboration of all stakeholders is key* (National Education Association, 2010). Well, yes, the winners' proposals did call for collaboration of all stakeholders, but teachers collaborating with administration around pay-for-performance and test-based evaluation is the kind of labor–management collaboration that the Broad Foundation promotes and funds. It is a big part of the problem.
- When 3 months later Duncan announced Phase 2 RTTT winners, Van Roekel again applauded. Duncan, in his speech announcing the Phase 2 winners, described a "quiet revolution" taking place across a range of stakeholders in education and said his funding programs have "unleashed an avalanche of pent-up educational reform activity at the state and local level" (Duncan, 2010). Commenting on the speech, Van Roekel noted that "NEA members have been at the forefront of the 'quiet revolution' taking place in the nation's public schools for a long time," and commended the secretary "for urging so-called reformers to stop blaming educators for everything that ails public education" (NEA, 2010). However, the text of Duncan's speech makes clear what he meant by "quiet revolution" in education: "I was surprised to learn that some states had laws prohibiting the use of student achievement in teacher evaluation. Because of Race to the Top, those laws are gone." In addition, Duncan's speech effusively praised charter schools.

In his opening address at the July 2010 NEA national convention in New Orleans, Van Roekel verbally blasted Obama for his support of pay-for-performance and charter schools. He called this "the worst environment in his memory" for public education. He acknowledged that the Obama administration has put the needs of banks ahead of the needs of public education.

Such acknowledgment is not very meaningful. Two years ago, in his farewell address, outgoing NEA president Reg Weaver gave an eloquent speech about the moral, physical, and economic costs of war and military spending. The words said one thing, but NEA's deeds did not match the words. So too with Van Roekel, who ended his speech by warning that NEA has to maintain its strategy of lobbying the Democrats "because there's just no alternative." When his speech was done and the convention began in earnest, the NEA leadership succeeded in shelving or defeating every motion that called for taking action to stop the prioritization of banks and the military over jobs, education, and other vital services. It even opposed a mild motion calling for "a safe and orderly withdrawal" from Afghanistan, as well as a motion urging Obama to scuttle Race to the Top and fire Arne Duncan. Once more, NEA leadership displayed vagueness in message, passivity in action.

In October 2010 Van Roekel went further, joining with Arne Duncan to announce plans to convene "a national education reform conference on labor–management collaboration next year" (Buffenbarger & Maiers, 2010).

It has taken Van Roekel and NEA a bit longer than it took Weingarten and AFT, but they have arrived at the same place: public embrace of collaboration with the reform agenda.

CONCLUSION: WHAT CAN BE DONE?

What can we do? First of all, let's draw some lessons.

If we are serious about eliminating the "achievement gap," we must identify its source, and it's no mystery. It's social inequality. The deck is stacked against high-poverty schools and low-income families—especially low-income Black and Brown families. In other words, the "achievement gap" is rooted in class exploitation and racism. It is rooted in a system that sees the role of education as teaching kids that they must do what they're told if they don't want to be pushed out to the military, the streets, or the prisons.

Furthermore, we have seen that the educational reform campaign is part of a much larger austerity campaign by big business—an enormous mobilization dating to the late 1970s, as Hacker and Pierson (2010) demonstrate. This campaign continues to shift government policy more and more in favor of corporations and the very wealthy (i.e., in favor of big capital).

Will collaborating with this campaign make it go away? Will it make things better? To ask these questions is to answer them. Nevertheless, the NEA and AFT leaderships have moved far down that road. (This is not exactly a new approach. Anyone familiar with recent labor history knows that this is just what was done by the once-powerful private sector unions, and knows where that ended.)

Rather than putting their ample treasuries at the disposal of the Democratic Party, and instead of relying on the Democrats to be their salvation, NEA and AFT ought to take the lead in organizing a coalition of labor, community, and environmental groups to engage in mass action and political action (including, when feasible, running candidates) to fight for and implement the transformation of social priorities that is the only way forward for labor—indeed, for all working and poor people. However, saying that "NEA and AFT ought to take the lead in organizing mass action and political action" won't make it happen.

But it can happen nevertheless. There are beacons of light that point the way forward. One of these is the movement to restore and expand funding for public education and other essential public programs. That movement burst onto the scene suddenly and dramatically, on September 24, 2009, as 10,000 students, staff, faculty, and community members surged into Berkeley's Sproul Plaza and into the streets. Then the September 24 activists threw themselves into spreading the movement beyond the University of California, organizing the October 24, 2009, Mobilizing Conference to Save Public Education, where 800 representatives from more than 100 organizations came together to plan statewide actions. This led directly to the inspirational March 4, 2010, statewide Strike and Day of Action. Although this movement began as a fight to roll back tuition increases, it has developed into one that demands restoring and expanding all essential public services, rebuilding the infrastructure, and providing jobs for all. It has established a national network.

The CORE caucus in the Chicago Teachers Union is another encouraging development. Last spring, CORE threw out one of the most corrupt local AFT leaderships in the country. CORE understands and opposes the corporate educational reform agenda. It knows what Arne Duncan represents, having experienced him in his years as CEO of Chicago Public Schools.

Movements and groups like these show how quickly situations can change for the better. They can be the basis for a real fight forward. If that's going to happen, it will be because many other new movements and new groups spring up around the country and fight together around setting social priorities straight.

The priorities of neoliberalism—that is, the priorities of contemporary capitalism—need to be repudiated and turned upside down. These priorities revolve around profit and property and what it takes to ensure neoliberal social control—war, repression, police, and jails. Ours are the opposite: decent jobs and adequate income; healthcare; housing; education; and the democratic participation of all in deciding and implementing social priorities. The neoliberals want an education system that teaches working-class and poor students to accept their place in the world—to train students to obey instructions and accept hierarchical authority. We want an education system that helps students to develop their natural curiosity, to understand the world around them, and to work cooperatively to change it for the better. The counterposition is clear.

It won't be easy to build a mass movement-based political alternative to the pro-business Democrats and the "responsible" venture philanthropists—but that is what we need to do. And we should recall that many of the vital public programs and the institutions of the working-class that are now under attack were constructed in the worst of economic times—the Great Depression of the 1930s. They were forged by great mass movements that fought courageously for their visions. If those movements could be built in those times, then surely we can do so today.

REFERENCES

Berliner, D. (2006, June). Our impoverished view of educational research. *Teachers College Record, 108*(6), 949–995.

Berliner, D., & Biddle, B. (1995). *The manufactured crisis: Myths, fraud, and the attack on America's public schools.* New York: Basic Books.

Biddle, D., & Berliner, D. (2002). *What research says about small classes and their effects.* San Francisco: WestEd.

Bill & Melinda Gates Foundation. (2009, November 19). *Foundation commits $335 million to promote effective teaching and raise student achievement* [Press release]. Available at http://www.gatesfoundation.org/press-releases/Pages/intensive-partnership-for-effective-teaching-091119.aspx

Bracey, G. (2003). *What you should know about the war against America's public schools.* Boston: Allyn & Bacon.

Bracey, G. (2004). *Setting the record straight* (2nd Ed.). Portsmouth, NH: Heinemann.

Brill, S. (2009, August 31). Annals of education: The rubber room: The battle over New York City's worst teachers. *The New Yorker.* Available at www.newyorker.com/reporting/2009/08/31/090831fa_fact_brill

Broad, E. (Interviewer). (2009, July 5). *Transforming the system: An interview with Michelle Rhee* [video]. Available at http://fora.tv/2009/07/05/Transforming_the_System_An_Interview_with_Michelle_Rhee

Broad Foundation for Education. (2004, February 4-5). Improving and implementing differentiated compensation systems [Participant binder]. Broad Foundation Benchmarking Project Knowledge Transfer Session, Denver, CO.

Broad Foundations. (2006). Broad Foundations 2006: Entrepreneurship for the public good in education, science and the arts. Los Angeles: The Broad Foundations.

Broad Superintendents' Academy. (2002, November 21). *The Broad Center for Superintendents graduates inaugural class* [Press release]. Available at http://broadacademy.org/news/press/2002-1121.html

Buffenbarger, A., & Maiers, S. (2010, October 14). National summit on labor–management collaboration announced. Available at http://feaweb.org/ford-duncan-and-van-roekel-in-hillsborough

Center for Research on Education Outcomes. (2009). *Multiple choice: Charter school performance in 16 states.* Stanford: Stanford University.

Duncan, A. (2010, July 27). The quiet revolution: Secretary Arne Duncan's Remarks at the National Press Club. *U.S. Department of Education.* Available at http://www.ed.gov/speeches/quiet-revolution-secretary-arne-duncans-remarks-national-press-club

Emery, K., & Ohanian, S. (2004). *Why is corporate America bashing our public schools?* Portsmouth, NH: Heinemann.

Fletcher, M., & Anderson, N. (2010, March 2). Obama angers union officials with remarks in support of R.I. teacher firings. *Washington Post.* Available at http://www.washingtonpost.com/wp-dyn/content/article/2010/03/01/AR2010030103560.html

Futernik, K. (2010, October). Incompetent teachers or dysfunctional systems? *Phi Delta Kappan, 92*(2), 59–64.

Gabor, A. (2010, September 22). Why pay incentives are destined to fail. *Education Week, 30*(4), pp. 24, 28.

Gabriel, T. (2010, October 16). Despite image, union leader backs school change. *New York Times,* p. A1.

Hacker, J., & Pierson, P. (2010). *Winner-take-all politics.* New York: Simon & Schuster.

Hanushek, E. (2009). Teacher deselection. In D. Goldhaber & J. Hannaway (Eds.), *Creating a new teaching profession* (pp. 163–180). Washington, DC: Urban Institute Press.

Harvey, D. (2005). *A brief history of neoliberalism.* Oxford: Oxford University Press.

Hassett, W., & Katzir, D. (2005). Lessons learned from the inside. In F. M. Hess (Ed.), *With the best of intentions: How philanthropy is reshaping K–12 education* (pp. 227–252). Cambridge, MA: Harvard Education Press.

Herbert, B. (2010, November 2). Fast track to inequality. *New York Times,* p. A31.

Higgins, S. (2009). The politics of venture philanthropy in charter school politics. *Change. org.* Available at news.change.org/stories/the-politics-of-venture-philanthropy-in-charter-school-politics

Hudson, M. (2007, August 27). *Why the "miracle of compound interest" leads to financial crises.* Paper presented at the Financial Crises in Capitalism Conference, Oslo. Available at http://michael-hudson.com/2007/08/why-the-%E2%80%9Cmiracle-of-compound-interest%E2%80%9D-leads-to-financial-crises

Johnson, W. (2001, July 24). Speech at California Teachers Association Presidents' conference. Available at http://www.archive.cta.org/InsideCTA/GovernanceSupport/PresidentsConference_20010724.htm

Jordan, J. (2010, February 24). Every Central Falls teacher fired, labor outraged. *Providence Journal.* Available at http://www.projo.com/news/content/central_falls_trustees_vote_02-24-10_EOHI83C_v59.3c21342.html

Krashen, S. (2010, May 18). Four questions about ESEA and the blueprint. Email message posted to Education and Parents Against Testing Abuse listserve, http://interversity.org/lists/epata/subscribe.html

Kristof, N. (2009, October 15). Democrats and schools. *New York Times,* p. A35.

Lanchester, J. (2010). *I.O.U.: Why everyone owes everyone and no one can pay.* New York: Simon & Schuster.

National Education Association. (2010, March 30). *NEA applauds selection of Race to the Top winners: Department of Education sends clear message that collaboration of all stakeholders is key* [Press release]. Available at http://www.edweek.org/ew/articles/2010/04/21/29dccontract-2.h29.html

National Education Association. (2010, August 6). *ESEA/NCLB Update, 93*(6).

Obama, B. (2009, March 10). Speech to the U.S. Hispanic Chamber of Commerce. Available at http://www.nytimes.com/2009/03/10/us/politics/10text-obama.html

Ravitch, D. (2010). *The death and life of the great American school system.* New York: Basic Books.

Robertson, S. (2008). "Remaking the world": Neoliberalism and the transformation of education and teachers' labor. In M. Compton & L. Weiner (Eds.), *The global assault on teaching, teachers, and their unions* (pp. 11–27). New York: Palgrave Macmillan.

Rothstein, R. (2010, October 14). *How to fix our schools* [Economic Policy Institute issue brief No. 286]. Washington, DC: Economic Policy Institute.

Sawchuck, S. (2010, April 21). Foundations would help fund D.C. teachers' contract. *Education Week,* p. 11.

Scholastic Administrator (2009, August). Collaborating with the Enemy. *Scholastic Administrator.* Available at http://www2.scholastic.com/browse/article.jsp?id=3752506

Sharpton, A., & Klein, J. (2009, March 12). Teacher Rx: The perfect storm for reform. *Huffington Post.* Available at http://www.huffingtonpost.com/rev-al-sharpton-and-joel-klein/teacher-rx-the-perfect-st_b_174516.html

Springer, M., Ballou, D., Hamilton, L., Le, V., Lockwood, J., McCaffrey, D., Pepper, M., & Stecher, B. (2010). *Teacher pay for performance: Experimental evidence from the project on Incentives in Teaching.* Nashville, TN: National Center on Performance Initiatives at Vanderbilt University.

Stiglitz, J., & Bilmes, L. (2008). *The three trillion dollar war: The true cost of the Iraq conflict.* New York: Norton.

Vander Ark, T. (2009, March 11). Eli finally won. *Huffington Post.* Available at http://www.huffingtonpost.com/tom-vander-ark/eli-finally-won_b_174152.html

CHAPTER 6

The Role of the Religious Right in Restructuring Education

Malila N. Robinson
Catherine A. Lugg

The U.S. Protestant Right is a diverse group of competing religious and political people and organizations that support a broad social network of politically conservative ideas and policies that are loosely grounded in fundamentalist Protestant theology (i.e., the Bible is the literal and inherent word of God). Furthermore, these members are rooted firmly in a web of religious networks (Lugg, 1996, 2001; Lugg & Robinson, 2009; Regnerus, Sikkink, & Smith, 1999). Historically, there has been little national consensus across its membership, because like most large social groups, they represent different and competing religious and political perspectives (Diamond, 1995; Green, 1995; Regnerus et al., 1999). However, over the past 25 years, the social survey research with regard to its membership has been consistent—revealing it to be a White, Protestant, fundamentalist, generally southern, overwhelmingly Republican, and now *increasingly elderly* phenomenon (Detwiler, 2000; Lugg, 2001; Lugg & Robinson, 2009; Oldfield, 1996; Pew Forum on Religion & Public Life, 2008; Rosin, 2007; Shupe & Stacey, 1982; Wilcox, 1996).

The Black Church refers to the predominantly African American Protestant churches that serve a primarily Black congregation. It is often described as one of the most stable institutions in American society (Douglas & Hopson, 2001; Taylor, Thornton, & Chatters, 1999). When slaves were introduced to Protestant Christianity by White slave masters (Ahlstrom, 1972), the message of the church was clear to the slaves: Christian salvation depended upon obedience and hard work during their lifetimes. Yet, the Bible contains many verses extolling God's power, through Jesus Christ, to set the enslaved free. Thus, many free African Americans and even some slaves started their own congregations with a starkly different foundation for faith—from one of obedience and toil, to one of liberation and freedom (Fraser, 1999). Currently the Black Church is a mix of different Protestant denominations and doctrines. However, the desire for freedom and equality is still a major tenet of the Black Church, and despite its members' differences they share a common history and identity as Black Americans.

This chapter begins with a brief historical overview of U.S. Protestant conservatives, the Black Church, and the interaction—or lack thereof—between the two groups in an increasingly multicultural America. The chapter then moves to a discussion of a few of the shared educational policy goals of the Protestant Right and conservative African Americans, and how neoliberalism helps to tighten the links between these two groups. The chapter concludes with a discussion of why the Protestant Right generally fails to garner consistent political support from African Americans and how its shifting membership from the political far right to more moderate views may make the group more palatable to the population at large.

IN THE BEGINNING . . .

Why are issues such as when human life begins, and the authority of the state to protect it, religious freedom, the sexual activity of minors, and pornography political issues in the first place? These issues became political because liberal ideologues insisted on using the mechanisms of the state to impose their own values and policy goals on American society.

—Onalee McGraw, Heritage Foundation education scholar, in the *Moral Majority Report* (1981, pp. 4–5)

Early in its history, Protestant conservatives (who later would form the Protestant Right) learned to make strategic use of alliances across theologically diverse (as well as diffuse) individuals and organizations as it sought a host of policy changes in U.S. public schooling (Fraser, 1999). As time passed, this primarily White group also learned the value of seeking racially diverse allies to help to promote its causes. Whether the issue has involved vocal school prayer, vouchers, or a host of other curricular and noncurricular practices, Protestant Right activists, and their allies, have tended to cluster together (however temporarily) to advocate for their policy preferences as they relate to public schooling (Apple, 2001; Lugg, 2001; Vergari, 2000; Zimmerman, 2002).

Throughout America's history the links between public education, religion, and the Black Church are apparent. For example, in many parts of the south during Reconstruction, the only places that newly freed slaves were able to hold classes were in Black Church-based Sabbath schools (Anderson, 1988; Fraser, 1999). Additionally, at that time, Protestant Christianity was intertwined with lessons in reading and writing in both Black and White schools throughout America (Fraser, 1999). Clearly in situations such as these, it would be virtually impossible to separate religious instruction from public schools. Early on, Protestant conservatives might have had a number of allies in the Black Church had they not been hindered by their racist beliefs.

During the 1920s, once-dominant Protestant conservatives found that it was impossible to speak of a White Protestant America as it had existed over the previous century and a half (Fraser, 1999; Handy, 1971). Not only had "American Protestantism" fragmented into increasingly diverse theological and political camps (Ahlstrom, 1972), but the social composition of the "White America" was changing radically thanks to massive immigration of non-Anglos (largely Catholics and Jews) into the country. Thus, White Protestants increasingly took the defensive, fearing the "takeover" of other races during the late 19th and early 20th centuries. For example, the Imperial Wizard of the Ku Klux Klan spoke of three "great racial instincts" that were essential to the nation's future: "These are the instincts of loyalty to the white race, to the traditions of America, and to the spirit of Protestantism." They were condensed into the Klan slogan: "Native, white, Protestant supremacy" (Fraser, 1999, p. 130).

By the 1950s, despite Protestant conservatives' attempts to garner unity and strength, they found themselves in the midst of an America with ever-increasing religious and cultural diversity. This fear, that they were losing even more ground, coupled with a hefty dose of Cold War hysteria against the "godless communists," spurred the Protestant conservatives to insert God everywhere: The Pledge of Allegiance (under God), the dollar bill (In God We Trust), public schools (required prayer), and so on (Fraser, 1999). In an increasingly diverse population, it was their way of showing cultural outsiders (Jews and Catholics) exactly who was dominant— but, to paraphrase Shakespeare, the Protestant conservatives "doth protest too much, methinks" (Hamlet, Act 3, Scene 2). That said, beginning in the 1960s, some Protestant conservatives, particularly Protestant fundamentalists who largely were reacting against the African American Civil Rights Movement (see Balmer, 2008;

Lugg, 1996), re-examined their historic suspicion of overt political involvement and formed a nascent Protestant Right—a religious group that openly
aligned with avowedly conservative politics and politicians.

From the 1960s until the mid-1990s, the Protestant Right clearly embraced
neoliberal agendas, promoting their theology as public policy (school choice
in particular) as well as maintaining White racial privilege (Balmer, 2008; J.
Howard, 1992). The latter became a central feature of the national Republican
Party when the Protestant Right became a part of its political base in the late
1970s (Lugg, 1996; Phillips, 2006). While the Protestant Right had little success
in either banning abortion or promoting prayer in public schools (Blanchard,
1994; Lugg & Robinson, 2009), it did see the end of court-ordered busing for
school desegregation, and conservatives made the entire notion of governmental enforcement of racial equality increasingly suspect (Lugg, 1996). Clearly, this
desire to maintain the status quo of White racial privilege would be likely to
put a damper on a proposed alliance between the Protestant Right and African
Americans. Nevertheless, the following paragraphs detail a few of the policy
areas where the values of the Protestant Right and conservative African Americans often meet.

> For our movement to realize its full potential, we must reach beyond the white church
> to embrace the full racial diversity of America and make inroads among traditionally
> Democratic voters. (Ralph Reed, 1993, quoted in Diamond, 1998, pp. 96–97)

Historically, ethnicity and race have been critical factors in defining religious identity. This is particularly true for Black Protestants, who constitute
about 9% of the adult population. Although some Black Protestants belong to
denominations within the historically White Evangelical tradition, the overwhelming majority belong to congregations that are ethnically or racially ho-
mogenous. Integrated churches are rare among American Protestants, due to
the perceived and actual differences between the religious and political perspectives of African American and White Protestants (Green, 2004).

Until recently, the Protestant Right put very little effort into garnering African American supporters, even though many in the Black community largely
agree with the social conservative agenda of the Protestant Right (Robinson,
2006; Wilcox & Larson, 2006). Thus, Evangelical Blacks, who generally are mobilized politically around economic issues, largely side with the Democratic Party (Green, 2004; Robinson, 2006). In recent years, however, the Protestant Right,
which remains composed predominantly of White evangelicals (Pew Forum on
Religion & Public Life, 2008), has attempted to include African Americans in

many of its social policy initiatives (Diamond, 1998; Robinson, 2006). This effort has proved difficult because support for the Protestant Right from African Americans is largely unpredictable. For example, social conservatism does not predict support for the Protestant Right from African Americans to the degree it does for White Americans; however, Evangelical affiliation predicts support from both groups (Robinson, 2006). Additionally, Black women are more likely to support the Protestant Right than are Black men (Robinson, 2006), but membership in the Black Church is on average 70% female (Lincoln & Mamiya, 1990; Robinson, 2006).

In 1997, in an attempt to bring more African Americans into the Protestant Right, the Christian Coalition, a group founded by Pat Robertson out of the ashes of his failed 1988 presidential bid, developed the Samaritan Project. The goals of the Samaritan Project included working with Black communities on issues of school choice while providing scholarships to inner-city youth to attend the school they wished to attend—either public or private. However, in the same year, the funding that the Christian Coalition had promised was no longer feasible and the Samaritan Project quickly collapsed. Despite the failure of the Samaritan Project, the Christian Coalition still attracts some African American supporters, mainly Evangelicals, women, and those who have less formal education (Robinson, 2006).

Black voters generally favor agendas that include platforms popular with conservative Republicans, such as school vouchers, prayer in school, initiatives against gay marriage and expanded civil rights for lesbian, gay, bisexual, and transgendered people in general, abstinence-only education, and anti-abortion initiatives (Apple & Pedroni, 2005; Robinson, 2006). The Republican Party, whose political base overwhelmingly is part of the Protestant Right, has attempted to use religious sentiment and issues such as these to appeal to minority communities, yet we see little evidence that African Americans have responded to such appeals from the Republican Party or the Protestant Right (Robinson, 2006). Thus, come election day, Black voters tend to overwhelmingly support the Democratic ticket, largely because of that party's economic policies and recent history of promoting racial tolerance and justice (Diamond, 1998). The preference among African Americans for voting for Democrats was clear in the 2000 presidential election, when 90% of African American voters supported Al Gore, and in 2004, when John Kerry received 88% of the Black vote (Robinson, 2006). Barack Obama smashed all records by receiving 95% of the Black vote in the 2008 election (Pew Research Center Publications, 2008). That said, there are a few policy areas where both the Protestant Right and many conservative African Americans have shared common ground.

SCHOOL VOUCHERS AND MARKETIZATION

One day, I hope in the next ten years, I trust that we will have more
Christian day schools than there are public schools. I hope I will live to
see the day when, as in the early days of our country, we won't have
any public schools. The churches will have taken them over again and
Christians will be running them. What a happy day that will be!
             —Jerry Falwell, *America Can Be Saved* (1979, pp. 52–53)

In their zeal to return God to all of America's public institutions, the Protestant
Right stands firmly beside the goal of school choice in the form of vouchers
(Apple, 2001; Apple & Pedroni, 2005; Hall, 1980; Viteritti, 2002). Thus, since
the Constitution demands the separation of church and state in public schools,
the Protestant Right demands the taxpayer-funded option of sending their
children to schools where God still has a prominent role. The Protestant Right
claims that its desire for vouchers is based on such things as the belief in market
efficiency—the claim that all families will benefit when schools are forced to
compete—and the fear of a secularization of the beliefs and values they hold sacred (Apple & Pedroni, 2005; Howard, 1997). And, although their pro-voucher
argument is framed in terms of parental choice, they support vouchers largely
as a neoliberal attempt to "marketize" the public school system to allow students to go to religious private schools using public funds (Apple & Pedroni,
2005; Fowler, 2002; D. Howard, 1997; Viteritti, 2002). Thus, instead of fixing
the problems facing public schools through desegregating, reducing class size,
balancing school budgets, ensuring greater teacher competency, and raising low
test scores, vouchers avoid these issues entirely by letting families opt-out of
the public school system. Additionally, neither the economic nor the religious
elements of the pro-voucher argument can be divorced from the history of Protestant conservatives' efforts to avoid desegregation and from the loss of a federal tax exemption by conservative, segregated Protestant academies during the
1970s and 1980s (Apple & Pedroni, 2005; J. Howard, 1992; Lugg, 1996; Lugg &
Robinson, 2009).

The marketization of public schools began during what has been dubbed
by some scholars as the "neoliberal renaissance" of the 1980s (Bartlett, Fredrick, Gulbransen, & Murillo, 2002). During this time, the national discourse
moved from equity concerns to placing schools in the service of the economy
(Lugg, 1996). This rhetorical and policy shift allowed the White elite to further their class and race interests while excluding and disadvantaging poor

African American students and families (Bartlett et al., 2002; Lugg, 1996). While neoliberal theory is promoted as a neutral and efficient political theory that is beneficial to all, in practice it leads to economic and spatial separateness (Hursh & Lipman, 2008). The rhetoric of school choice in the form of vouchers, charter schools, and magnet schools situates parents and students as consumers of schooling and it misleadingly implies that all parents are equally well-informed, politically connected, and capable of securing the best education for their children (Bartlett et al., 2002). Yet, research shows that such policies often result in increased race and class stratification, which ultimately leads to low-performing and racially separate schools serving the poor and minority communities (Ball, 1993; Bartlett et al., 2002; Cookson, 1994; Dougherty & Sostre 1992; Gewirtz, Ball, & Bowe, 1995; Henig, 1994; Hursh & Lipman, 2008; Johanek, 1992; Molnar, 1996; Wells, Lopez, Scott, & Holme, 1999; Whitty, Power, & Halpin, 1998).

Despite this, there are many in the African American community who support vouchers because they live, and thus send their children to schools, in neighborhoods where largely segregated public schools have been struggling for generations (Kozol, 1991, 2005; McDonald, 2002). The emergence of African American support for this seemingly right-wing educational reform is itself a legacy of the failure of both the executive and legislative branches to enforce the *Brown v. Board of Education* decision to desegregate America's inner-city public schools (Apple & Pedroni, 2005). To date, efforts to desegregate urban public schools have proven nearly futile since most of the programs designed to equalize educational opportunity actually preserve the public schooling advantages White America enjoys and fights diligently to maintain (Apple & Pedroni, 2005; Lugg, 1996; Wells, Holme, Atanda, & Rivilla, 2005). Thus, organizations such as the Black Alliance for Educational Options (BAEO), which is known not only for aligning itself with the Protestant Right, but also for accepting funding from far-right sources like the Bradley Foundation, have mobilized around the issue of advocacy for urban working-class communities of color (Apple & Pedroni, 2005). The Bradley Foundation provided significant support for *The Bell Curve* (Herrnstein & Murray, 1994), which argued that since African Americans supposedly are genetically less intelligent than Whites, they should not be the target of governmental affirmative action programs (Apple & Pedroni, 2005). However, neither the BAEO nor the majority of African Americans who support the push for vouchers consider themselves to be politically aligned with the Protestant Right (Apple, 1996; Apple et al., 2003; Apple & Pedroni, 2005; Pedroni, 2004).

That said, President Obama's selection of Arne Duncan for secretary of education makes it unlikely that the marketization of public schools will cease anytime soon. Mr. Duncan has a history of enthusiastic neoliberalism, as can be seen by his leadership role in Renaissance 2010, the marketization of Chicago's public school system (Giroux & Saltman, 2008; Hursh & Lipman, 2008). Renaissance 2010 closed 100 public schools and reconstituted them as privatized charter schools, contract schools, and magnet schools. It has a heavy reliance on standardized testing as the ultimate measure of learning, and most of the new schools eliminated the teachers unions (Saltman, 2007). It was supposed to embrace competition in order to spur innovation in the schools in an effort to raise test scores. Yet, to date, there is absolutely no evidence that the efforts of Renaissance 2010 actually have improved student academic achievement—the stated goal of the effort. Nevertheless, with Duncan's appointment, it is clear that the longstanding neoliberal federal educational policies that embrace market solutions for underperforming public schools will continue unhindered (Giroux & Saltman, 2008).

VOCAL SCHOOL PRAYER

> The Supreme Court of the supposedly Christian United States guaranteed the moral collapse of this nation when it forbade children in the public schools to pray to the God of Jacob, to learn of His moral law or even view in their classrooms the heart of the law, the Ten Commandments, which children must obey for their own good or disobey at their peril.
>
> —Pat Robertson (1991, p. 233)

The Protestant Right has a long history of battling the U.S. court system in the attempt to reinstate state-sponsored prayer in public schools (Lugg & Robinson, 2009). In 1962, the Supreme Court considered for the first time the constitutionality of prayer in a public school and held that state-sponsored prayers in public schools violated the Constitution's Establishment Clause (*Engle v. Vitale*, 1962). One year later, the Supreme Court again invalidated government-sponsored daily religious devotionals in public schools—this time Bible readings—in *School District of Abington v. Schempp* (1963). In 1985, the Supreme Court held that an Alabama Statute that authorized a 1-minute period of silence in all public schools "for meditation or voluntary prayer" was unconstitutional because the primary purpose of the law was to advance religion (*Wallace v. Jaffree*, 1985). In 1992, the Supreme Court ruled that including clergy who offer prayers as part of an official public school graduation ceremony is forbidden by the Establishment Clause (*Lee v. Weisman*, 1992). At the turn of this century, the Supreme Court heard yet another case dealing with student prayer, *Santa Fe Independent School District v. Doe* (2000). In this case the Court ruled that the district's policy permitting student-led, student-initiated prayer, even if it was nonsectarian, at football games violates the Establishment Clause. Specifically, the Court concluded that the football game prayers were public speech authorized by a government policy of a student election and noted that they took place on government property at government-sponsored, school-related events and thus the district's policy involved both a perceived and actual government endorsement of the delivery of prayer at school events.

According to Robinson (2006), African Americans are even more likely than Whites to support mandatory Christian prayers in public school. They believe that having students recite prayers each day will restore a moral foundation to public schools. Because there are large numbers of African American children in dangerous inner-city schools, the argument is that if there are guns, drugs, sex, and violence in the schools already, why should prayer be the one thing the schools cannot legally include (Walsh, 1994). Furthermore, in many urban areas, the local public school is a critical part of the local Black community, as are the churches. Vocal school prayer is not seen as an oppressive governmentally imposed religious exercise but as a continuation of African American cultural traditions. Consequently, school prayer is considered to be a logical extension of community norms and values (Robinson, 2006).

That said, African American communities, like other racial and ethnic communities in the United States, are increasingly diverse theologically, although not to the same degree as other demographic groups (Pew Forum on Religion & Public Life, 2008). Currently, 78% of all African Americans are Protestant, with 92% of that figure belonging to historically Black Protestant churches (Pew Forum on Religion & Public Life, 2008). Another 5% are Catholic, 1% are Jehovah's Witness, 1% are Muslim, 2% are other (Jewish, Hindu, Buddhist, and other faith systems combined), and 12% are unaffiliated (Pew Forum on Religion & Public Life, 2008). While vocal school prayer in urban public schools might seem, at first blush, to be unproblematic, such exercises do violate the rights of religious minorities and the unaffiliated who often reside within a larger minority community.

ABSTINENCE-ONLY EDUCATION AND MARRIAGE INITIATIVES

The public schools have given us 25 years of SIECUS/Planned
Parenthood-style "comprehensive education about sexuality." The
results are rampant immorality, illegitimacy, abortions, venereal
diseases, infertility, and teenage emotional trauma that often follows
them through their entire life.

—Phyllis Schlafly (1999, para. 14)

Abstinence-only education is yet another policy area supported by the Protestant Right and a large number of conservative African Americans. Supporters
believe that sexuality education, which teaches students about safe sex methods,
encourages children to have sex, and thus they believe that schools should teach
only abstinence (Schlafly, 1999). Abstinence-only education programs promote
abstinence from sexual activity as the only acceptable option for adolescents
(Wiley, 2002).

An obvious issue that arises from the push for abstinence until marriage is
that it officially silences any mention of gayness. This curriculum extols sexual
celibacy until non-same-sex marriage, which is a neat mechanism to avoid dis-
cussing the politically volatile topics of gay sex and same-sex relationships.[1] As
PFLAG (Parents and Friends of Lesbians and Gays) spokeswoman Jean-Marie
Navetta observed, "Abstinence-only by definition sort of wrote any gay issues
out of the curriculum. . . . I mean, gays can't get married. It sounds like a ridicu-
lous premise, but it actually works" (see de Vise, 2007, p. C01).

This theological common ground for Black and White conservatives can
shape electoral outcomes. In May 2008, the California Supreme Court held that
laws excluding same-sex marriages were unconstitutional. Then on November
4, 2008, California voted on Proposition 8, a ballot initiative that changed the
state constitution to restrict the definition of marriage to a union between a
man and a woman and eliminated the right of same-sex couples to marry. According to CNN's (2008) exit poll, an unsurprising 82% of Republicans and 81%
of White Evangelicals voted for the measure. The surprise comes from the fact
that only 49% of White voters, the majority of whom were women, as compared
with 70% of Black voters, voted for the measure (CNN, 2008). This raises the
question of how African Americans can stand staunchly behind racial equality
while opposing gay equality (Brandt, 1999; Diamond, 1998; Douglas & Hopson,
2001). Reverend Jesse Jackson exemplified this dichotomy when he declared
that he supports equal protection to queer individuals under the law, but that
he does not agree with the comparison of queer equality to the fight for equality

that African Americans have struggled with. But many conservative leaders of the Black Church take a more hard-line approach to queer equality, such as African American Pastor Gregory Daniels of United Truth and Change Church in Chicago, who stated: "If the KKK opposes gay marriage I would ride with them" (Clemetson, 2004). This abhorrence of queer equality from both the Protestant Right and many conservative African Americans arises from the fact that they believe homosexuality is a sin, as defined by their theology (Diamond, 1998; Douglas & Hopson, 2001). Thus, the issues of abstinence-only education and same-sex marriage appear to have boosted the cooperation between White and Black religious leaders (Robinson, 2006). However, given the historic intolerance of most Christian sects toward queer people of all races, African Americans, like many other Americans, who oppose queer rights do so largely out of perceived religious obligation. And as in other demographic groups, this opposition wanes with younger voters (Pew Forum on Religion & Public Life, 2008). Consequently, even this opposition is softening and should fade with time, but for now it remains a unifying, if increasingly narrow, piece of common ground for the Protestant Right and conservative African Americans.

2008 AND BEYOND

We know that our patchwork heritage is a strength, not a weakness. We are a nation of Christians and Muslims, Jews and Hindus—and nonbelievers.

—President Barack Obama, Inaugural Address
(Chaddock, 2009, para. 3)

The historic 2008 election paved the way for the first biracial President to be elected in the United States on November 4, 2008. President Obama peeled away enough White Evangelicals and Catholics of all backgrounds to generate the largest win for a Democratic presidential candidate in over 40 years (Nolan, 2008). And he managed to raise enough questions about the economic competence of Republican candidate John McCain, and to successfully dampen many of the cultural concerns some conservative voters have with Democratic candidates, to secure a convincing national win (Nolan, 2008). While Obama's race was an "issue" for many voters, it was greatly overshadowed by the economic anxiety confronting the globe. Ironically for Protestant Right activists, in the 2008 election, the common ground for Black and White Protestants was just large enough to propel *the Democratic* candidate into the presidency.

Obama's election underscores the paradoxes facing the Protestant Right as it attempts to woo African American conservatives to its cause, particularly around those issues involving education. Early in its existence, the Protestant Right stood in staunch opposition to racial justice, particularly the desegregation of public schooling (Balmer, 2008; Lugg, 1996). Later on, many of its members retreated into silence, and as the former director of the Samaritan Project observed, "You cannot build trust with African-Americans when the white church is silent on racial issues" (Robinson, 2006, p. 600). Thus, it is likely that until the Protestant Right generates public, proactive, and consistent support for racial justice, it will not attract large and consistent numbers of African Americans (Robinson, 2006).

Furthermore, the Protestant Right is getting politically squeezed by some profound demographic changes. The United States is "less White" than at any point in its history (Pew Forum on Religion & Public Life, 2008) and is experiencing the "reign" of its first biracial president. Consequently, it is likely that any political movement or politician that embraces a highly racialized politics—like the Protestant Right did in its early history—will be treated by the general electorate as an anathema and will be trounced at the ballot box (Dionne, 2008; Lugg & Robinson, 2009). This is a reality that former Virginia governor George Allen, who was caught on camera hurling a racial slur at a minority cameraman during his failed 2006 U.S. Senate bid, knows only too well (Lugg & Robinson, 2009).

Additionally, in areas with large non-Protestant populations (the west, the northeast), if state and local Protestant Right groups do not moderate their tone and agenda, as well as seek political alliances with other concerned interest groups like the Black Church, they run the danger of political irrelevancy— at least in these regions. Recently the National Association of Evangelicals, a Protestant organization representing mostly White Evangelical churches across the United States, has begun to work on behalf of racial reconciliation. "Our churches have a special responsibility to model good race relations (Rom. 10:12). To correct the lingering effects of our racist history, Christians should support well-conceived efforts that foster dignity and responsibility" (National Association of Evangelicals, 2004, p. 22).

However, if the Protestant Right were to repackage some of its educational policy proposals in more neoliberal-sounding terms of "parental choice," it might find greater support, particularly at the presidential level. Obama clearly has not renounced the Bush educational agenda. Furthermore, his appointment of Arne Duncan as secretary of education indicates more than a passing sympathy for neoliberal educational ideals (Giroux & Saltman, 2008). Additionally, Obama's own experience as a professor at the University of Chicago—a bastion of neoliberalism for over 40 years— also should not be underestimated (Klein, 2007).

But perhaps the biggest stumbling block for the Protestant Right in its effort to court Black Protestants will remain to be theological. The theological orientation of the Protestant Right is toward "obedience and hard work," while the theological orientation of the Black Church is toward "liberation" (Fraser, 1999). While both groups share many of the foundational beliefs of Evangelical Christianity, these historic differences remain very salient and compelling, and are seemingly insurmountable. There may be instances where these two distinct groups might find common ground involving issues of public education, but this shared space will be quite fleeting. "Christ the master" and "Christ the liberator" remain two mutually exclusive understandings of a supposed common faith.

CONCLUSION

The U.S. public school system is far from perfect, but it guarantees all of America's youth a free education. Instead of bringing people together to work toward the common goal of ensuring that this free universal system continues to serve America's children, the neoliberal assault on public schools has the potential to bring together the Protestant Right and many Black conservatives to privatize and marketize the educational system. This privatized system will siphon funds from the already financially strained public education system, making reform efforts even more difficult. At the same time, the neoliberal marketizing agenda will ensure that those who can afford the best education will receive it, while also ensuring that those who cannot afford the best education will remain in dire educational straits. America's children should not be the ones to suffer from this unified attack on their schools.

Furthermore, the Obama administration's embrace of neoliberalism to shape national educational reform does not bode well for America's already struggling public school system. The recent federal proposal for educational reform, Race to the Top, allocates $4.35 billion in competitive grants (from the economic stimulus package) to states to promote specific forms of educational reform around economic competitiveness. Winning applications will focus on enhancing charter schools, rewarding teachers and principals who improve individual student academic achievement, and establishing measurable academic standards across the curriculum (U.S. Department of Education, 2009). Such a focus on choice and competitiveness is emblematic of a neoliberal approach. When schools compete for limited funds, they are less likely to share winning strategies with one another. And while these strategies will be in the public realm after the reward money is distributed, until then the children in schools without those strategies will be at a significant disadvantage.

America's public education system, and the children who seek to be educated within it, should not have to endure these incessant neoliberal attacks. There is no reason to believe that private/charter schools cannot continue to exist alongside public schools, and there is no need for one to dominate the other. The end goal of American education should be an equitably informed and democratic populace.

NOTE

1. The curriculum also focuses on the failure rates of contraception and the "risks" of premarital sex (see Sternberg, 2007).

REFERENCES

Ahlstrom, S. E. (1972). *A religious history of the American people.* New Haven, CT: Yale University Press.

Anderson, J. D. (1988). *The education of blacks in the South, 1865–1935.* Chapel Hill, NC: University of North Carolina Press.

Apple, M. W. (1996). *Cultural politics and education.* New York: Teachers College Press.

Apple, M. W. (2001). *Educating the "right" way: Markets, standards, God, and inequality.* New York: Routledge.

Apple, M. W., Aasen, P., Cho, M. K., Gandin, L. A., Oliver, A., & Sung, Y.-K. (2003). *The state and the politics of knowledge.* New York: Routledge.

Apple, M. W., & Pedroni, T. C. (2005). Conservative alliance building and African American support of vouchers: The end of *Brown's* promise or a new beginning? *Teachers College Record, 107*(9), 2068–2105.

Ball, S. (1993). Markets, choice and social class: The market as a class strategy in the UK and the USA. *British Journal of Sociology of Education, 14*(1), 3–19.

Balmer, R. (2008). *God in the White House, a history: How faith shaped the presidency from John F. Kennedy to George W. Bush.* New York: HarperCollins.

Bartlett, L., Fredrick, M., Gulbransen, T., & Murillo, E. (2002). The marketization of public education: Public schools for private ends. *Anthropology and Education Quarterly, 33*(1), 5–29.

Blanchard, D. A. (1994). *The anti-abortion movement and the rise of the religious right. From polite to firey protest.* New York: Twayne Publishers.

Brandt, E. (1999). *Dangerous liaisons: Blacks, gays and the struggle for equality.* New York: New Press.

Cable News Network (CNN). (2008). Exit polls, ballot measure California Proposition 8: Ban on gay marriage. Available at http://www.cnn.com/ELECTION/2008/results/polls/#val=CAI01p1

Chaddock, G. R. (2009, January 22). The role of religion under Obama. *The Christian Science Monitor.* Available at http://www.csmonitor.com/2009/0122/p01s02-usgn.html

Clemetson, L. (2004). Both sides court black churches in the debate over gay marriage. Available at http://www.nytimes.com/2004/03/01/national/01CHUR.html

Cookson, P. W. (1994). *School choice: The struggle for the soul of American education.* New Haven, CT: Yale University Press.

de Vise, D. (2007, March 18). The wide spectrum of sex-ed courses: Montgomery veers toward liberal end on homosexuality. *The Washington Post,* p. C01.

Detwiler, F. (2000). *Standing of the premises of God: The Christian right's fight to redefine American's public schools.* New York: New York University Press.

Diamond, S. (1995). *Roads to dominion: Right-wing movements and political power in the United States.* New York: Guilford Press.

Diamond, S. (1998). *Not by politics alone: The enduring influence of the Christian right.* New York: Guilford Press.

Dionne, E. J. (2008). *Souled out: Reclaiming faith and politics after the religious right.* Princeton, NJ: Princeton University Press.

Dougherty, K., & Sostre, L. (1992). Minerva and the market: The sources of the movement for school choice. *Educational Policy, 6*(2), 160–179.

Douglas, K. B., & Hopson, R. E. (2001). Understanding the black church: The dynamics of change. *Journal of Religious Thought, 56/57*(2/1), 95–113.

Engle v. Vitale, 370 U.S. 421 (1962).

Falwell, J. (1979). *America can be saved.* Murfreesboro, TN: Sword of the Lord Publishers.

Fowler, F. C. (2002). School choice. *The Clearing House, 76*(1), 4–38.

Fraser, J. (1999). *Between church and state: Religion & public education in a multicultural America.* New York: St. Martin's Press.

Gewirtz, S., Ball, S., & Bowe, R. (1995). *Markets, choice and equity in education.* Philadelphia: Open University Press.

Giroux, H. A., & Saltman, K. (2008, December 18). Obama's betrayal of public education? Arne Duncan and the corporate model of schooling. Available at http://pdamerica.org/articles/news/2008-12-18-09-39-22-news.php

Green, J. C. (1995). The Christian right and the 1994 elections: An overview. In M. J. Rozell & C. Wilcox (Eds.), *God at the grass roots* (pp. 1–18). Blue Ridge Summit, PA: Rowman & Littlefield.

Green, J. C. (2004). The American religious landscape and political attitudes: A baseline for 2004. Available at http://pewforum.org/publications/surveys/green-full.pdf

Hall, S. (1980). Popular democratic vs. authoritarian populism. In A. Hunt (Ed.), *Marxism and democracy* (pp. 150–170). London: Lawrence & Wishart.

Handy, R. T. (1971). *A Christian America: Protestant hopes and historical realities.* New York: Oxford University Press.

Henig, J. R. (1994). *Rethinking school choice: Limits of the market metaphor.* Princeton, NJ: Princeton University Press.

Herrnstein, R., & Murray, C. (1994). *The bell curve.* New York: Free Press.

Howard, D. (1997). Educational reform—return to the right!! *Contemporary Education, 68,* 246–249.

Howard, J. (1992, October 23). *Doing God's work: White church entanglement in the southern segregation academies.* Paper presented to the History of Education/ISCHE Conference, Boston.

Hursh, D., & Lipman, P. (2008). Renaissance 2010: The reassertion of ruling-class power through neoliberal policies in Chicago. In D. Hursh (Ed.), *High-stakes testing and the decline of teaching and learning* (pp. 97–120). Lanham, MD: Rowman & Littlefield.

Johanek, M. (1992). Private citizenship and school choice. *Educational Policy, 6*(2), 139–159.

Klein, N. (2007). *The shock doctrine: The rise of disaster capitalism.* New York: Metropolitan Books.

Kozol, J. (1991). *Savage inequalities.* New York: Crown.

Kozol, J. (2005). Still separate, still unequal: America's educational apartheid. *Harper's, 311*(1864), 1–30.

Lee v. Weisman, 505 U.S. 577 (1992).

Lincoln, C. E., & Mamiya, L. H. (1990). *The black church in the African American experience.* Durham, NC: Duke University Press.

Lugg, C. A. (1996). *For God and country: Conservatism and American school policy.* New York: Peter Lang.

Lugg, C. A. (2001, January & March). The Christian right: A cultivated collection of interest groups. *Educational Policy, 15*(1/2), 41–57.

Lugg, C. A., & Robinson, M. N. (2009). Religion, advocacy coalitions and the politics of U.S. public schools. *Educational Policy, 23*(1/2), 242–266.

McDonald, T. (2002). The false promise of vouchers. *Educational Leadership, 59*(7), 33–37.

McGraw, O. (1981, November 23). The Family Protection Act: Symbol and substance. *Moral Majority Report,* 4–5.

Molnar, A. (1996). *Giving kids the business: The commercialization of America's schools.* Boulder, CO: Westview Press.

National Association of Evangelicals. (2004). *For the health of the nation: An Evangelical call to civic responsibility.* Washington, DC: Author.

Nolan, B. (2008, November 14). Obama narrows, but doesn't end, electoral "God gap." *Religion News Service.* Available at http://pewforum.org/news/display.php?NewsID=16935

Oldfield, D. M. (1996). *The right and the righteous: The Christian right confronts the Republican Party.* Lanham, MD: Rowman & Littlefield.

Pedroni, T. C. (2004). Strange bedfellows in the Milwaukee "parental choice" debate: Participation among the dispossessed in conservative educational reform. *Dissertation Abstracts International, 64*(11), 3946A. (UMI No. 3113677)

Pew Forum on Religion & Public Life. (2008). *U.S. religious landscape survey.* Washington, DC: Author.

Pew Research Center Publications. (2008, November 5). Inside Obama's sweeping victory. Available at http://pewresearch.org/pubs/1023/exit-poll-analysis-2008

Phillips, K. (2006). *American theocracy: The peril and politics of radical religion, oil, and borrowed money into the 21st century.* New York: Viking Press.

Regnerus, M. D., Sikkink, D., & Smith, C. (1999). Voting with the Christian right: Contextual and individual patterns of electoral influence. *Social Forces, 77*(4), 1375–1401.

Robertson, P. (1991). *The new world order.* Dallas, TX: Word.

Robinson, C. (2006). From every tribe and nation? Blacks and the Christian right. *Social Science Quarterly, 87*(3), 591–601.

Rosin, H. (2007, May 16). For new generation of Evangelicals, Falwell was old news. *Washington Post,* p. A06.

Saltman, K. J. (2007). Schooling in disaster capitalism: How the political right is using disaster to privatize public schools. *Teacher Education Quarterly, 34*(2), 131–156.

Santa Fe Independent School District v. Doe, 530 U.S. 290 (2000).

Schlafly, P. (1999, July 21). The consequences of sex education. *The Eagle Forum.* Available at http://www.eagleforum.org/column/1999/july99/99-07-21.html

School District of Abington v. Schempp, 374 U.S. 203 (1963).

Shakespeare, W. (1994). *Hamlet.* New York: St. Martin's Press.

Shupe, A., & Stacey, W. A. (1982). *Born again politics and the moral majority: What social surveys really show.* New York: Edwin Mellon Press.

Sternberg, J. (2007, March 21). Lies we teach teenagers. *TomPaine.com.* Available at http://www.tompaine.com/articles/2007/03/21/lies_we_teach_teenagers.php

Taylor, R., Thornton, M., & Chatters, L. (1999). Subjective religiosity among African Americans: A synthesis of findings from five national samples. *Journal of Black Psychology, 25*(4), 524–543.

U.S. Department of Education. (2009). *Race to the top: Initial application for funding.* Washington, DC: U.S. Government Printing Office.

Vergari, S. (2000). Morality politics and educational policy: The abstinence-only sex education grant. *Education Policy, 14*(2), 290–310.

Viteritti, J. (2002). Coming around on school choice. *Educational Leadership, 59*(7), 44–47.

Wallace v. Jaffree, 472 U.S. 38 (1985).

Walsh, M. (1994, April 27). Big-city blacks join in push for prayer in school. *Education Week, 1*(8), 1, 8.

Wells, A. S., Lopez, A., Scott, J., & Holme, J. J. (1999). Charter schools as postmodern para-
dox: Rethinking social stratification in an age of deregulated school choice. *Harvard
Educational Review, 69*(2), 172–203.

Wells, A. S., Holme, J. J., Atanda, J. J., & Rivilla, A. T. (2005). *Teachers College Record, 107,*
(9), 2141–2177.

Whitty, G., Power, S., & Halpin, D. (1998). *Devolution and choice in education.* Philadelphia:
Open University Press.

Wilcox, C. (1996). *Onward Christian soldiers? The religious right in American politics* (1st
ed.). Boulder, CO: Westview Press.

Wilcox, C., & Larson, C. (2006). *Onward Christian soldiers? The religious right in American
politics* (3rd ed.). Boulder, CO: Westview Press.

Wiley, D. C. (2002). The ethics of abstinence-only and abstinence-plus sexuality education.
Journal of School Health, 72(4), 164–167.

Zimmerman, J. (2002). *Whose America? Culture wars in the public schools.* Cambridge, MA:
Harvard University Press.

CHAPTER 7

Resuscitating Bad Science
Eugenics Past and Present

Ann G. Winfield

One hundred years ago, the discourse among America's economic, political, and scientific elite focused on "weeding out" the "unfit" people of the nation in order to make way for "well-born," "superior" people to flourish and achieve the so-called "American Dream." Now, in the 21st century, we are witness to a modern version of the same agenda, an agenda that serves to devalue people. The push for privatization and corporate models of education provides structure around the assumption that some people are worth more than others (Kohn, 2004; Woods, 2004). Reformers who wave around international test score comparisons in support of their ever more draconian pursuit of test-driven mandates fail to see the irony: What those comparisons show is not that the United States is behind, but that the United States fails its poor, Black, and Brown children. If we compare American White, middle-class and wealthy students with similar students in other industrialized countries, the test scores are comparable, if not better (Berliner, 2005). Current school reform agendas do not seek to rectify this problem. Rather, these agendas show that profit margins now outweigh humanity in the public sphere (Gould, 1996; Iverson, 2005).

The message we hear today is less caustic than it was a century ago: We no longer talk about forced sterilization of the feebleminded, but the basic ideological rationale that allows us to live in a society that is so rewarding of the wealthy, and so punishing of the poor, remains intact (Winfield, 2007). Nineteenth-century Social Darwinism and 20th-century eugenics spell out in stark terms who among us is worthy and who among us is not (Haller, 1963; Hasian, 1996). The difference today is that the language is largely hidden in discourses of accountability, choice, and social justice (Darling-Hammond, 2004). Meanwhile, the fundamental assumption embedded in the national identity about terms like *equality* and *freedom* has been sucked out of the fabric of the way our nation operates. Instead, we live in a "brave new world" that enacts an ideological definition of basic human worth. This is evident in many places, none more starkly, or with more dire consequences for the future, than the current corporate school reform agenda.

IDEOLOGY AND REFORM

Public education is under siege. What we are witnessing is a modern manifestation of the same ideological opposition to the very idea of public education that existed a century ago. Using arbitrary measures of "standards" and "accountability," the majority of students, those with the least cultural capital, are cast as "at-risk" of failure, defective, and in need of remediation. These are the "unfit" of the modern era and are consistently characterized as lazy, parasitic, promiscuous, uneducable, and in need of surveillance and control. In what can only be described as a direct expression of eugenic ideology, these human beings are regarded not as a mere nuisance; rather, they represent a grave threat to the well-being of the "more deserving" among us. Neoliberal school reform quietly reaffirms the notion of societal worth at the same time as it harnesses this segment of the population to be in service to the capitalist imperative, that is, profit (Lipman, 2004).

The undercurrent of dissent toward the whole notion that all Americans are entitled to a free, quality public education, an undercurrent as old as the nation itself, is rooted in the decades of the early 20th century when the modern school system was being formed within a societal context of dominant eugenic ideology. During this period an ideological battle was waged, hinging on the argument that schools were a form of charity that disrupted natural law and that success in society was an expression of one's inherent, genetically endowed worth. Given that this battle has taken place at the expense of the well-being of generations of schoolchildren, a deeper understanding of the ideological roots of this hierarchy of human worth is needed.

Public education has seen many changes since the early 19th century when the country first considered the benefits of an educated citizenry. From the establishment of schools for domestic servitude for Black and Hispanic girls, schools for mechanical arts for boys, and boarding schools for Native American children, poor, Black, and Brown children have never been the beneficiaries of education's high aspirations (Anderson, 1988; Watkins, 2001). In fact, aside from the challenges to the status quo that occurred during the era of the Civil Rights Movement from 1950 to 1980, there has been little to disrupt the perpetuation of the oppression, segregation, experimentation, denigration, and disregard faced by all but the elite of American society.

Now we find ourselves, 30 years later, in an era characterized by unprecedented testing and accountability policies. Reformers have co-opted the language of social justice to declare that they will "leave no child behind" while at the same time schools are being closed, teachers fired, and students disregarded and displaced in a relentless subterfuge that has been percolating and building pressure for decades, beating down the hopes and aspirations of countless schoolchildren, their families, and teachers nationwide (Lipman, 2004).

The attack is now morphing into a new kind of "race" where the least powerful among us continue to be pathologized. Success in America is presented as the result of intelligence coupled with hard work and the right attitude. Never mind poverty and its attendant problems. Never mind that the most recent spate of "reforms," which slither in on gilded-tongue language like No Child Left Behind, Race to the Top, transformation, and turnaround, are models that attack schools predominantly populated with poor, Black, and Brown children (Kohn, 2010; Kozol, 2005). Never mind the inconvenient resemblance to past "utopian" visions that sought to sort, classify, and categorize students according to perceived racial purity—using tests as the mechanism to quantify and measure their "data." Never mind that the legislators and policymakers who dream up and implement these reforms typically choose for their own children to go to private schools where the specter of testing and all the state and federal mandates besieging schools are not required.

In May 2009, Secretary of Education Arne Duncan announced the Obama administration's intent to close 5,000 "underperforming" schools across the country. We know that this means the draconian firing of every teacher with no professional evaluation attached, continues the attack on communities of non-White, poor, and immigrant people—and we know this is something that would never be tolerated in wealthy, suburban White communities. Current proposed reforms don't come from the experience and research of professional educators, but are an expression of corporate ideology. In communities where wholesale firings have already taken place, veteran teachers have been replaced with often uncertified, certainly less qualified new teachers who are forced to work longer hours and for much-reduced pay (Ravitch, 2010). These new teachers are compliant; they tend to be fearful of standing up for themselves, are less likely to advocate for their students, and face tremendous pressure not to participate in unions or other forms of organized articulation of an alternative vision.

Twenty-first-century reforms, including No Child Left Behind and Race to the Top, are not far-removed policy mandates without real-world consequences, nor are they some gimmicky flash-in-the-pan political talking points that will fade away as so many have done before. What we are witnessing is a modern manifestation of ideological opposition to the very idea of public education altogether, founded on the notion that the majority of the students, teachers, and families with the least cultural capital are defective and in need of remediation.

This is nothing less than a form of ideological warfare, chipping away, weakening support over time, until the time to strike is upon us. It is upon us. For generations the majority of poor, Black, Brown, "socially deviant" children and adults have been targeted by policies and practices developed on an ideological foundation informed by eugenics. Just as racial purification was touted as society's best answer to poverty and disease 100 years ago, policymakers have long used arguments that ring of social justice to justify mandates that are decidedly unjust. This chapter will trace the influence of eugenic ideology for its role in creating a hierarchy of human worth (in schools and elsewhere) in this country and will conclude with implications for the present moment.

"RACE" TO THE TOP: HISTORIC FOUNDATIONS

It was prolific English scientist and statistician Sir Francis Galton (1822–1911), cousin of Charles Darwin, who developed the term *eugenics* in 1883 to explain his scheme to improve the human race through selective breeding (Black, 2003; Kevles, 1985). Basing his theory of relative human worth on the success of the long lines of wealthy Englishmen on both sides of his ancestral tree, Galton believed that "if a twentieth part of the cost and pains were spent in measures for the improvement of the human race that is spent on the improvement of the breed of horses and cattle, what a galaxy of genius might we not create" (Galton, 1865, cited in Spiro, 2009, p. 121). Indeed, one of the first formal groups in the United States to form a committee on eugenics was the American Breeders Association, which applied its knowledge of horse and cattle breeding to the improvement of "human stock." For reasons that will become clear, societal improvement through racial purification caught on quickly and it wasn't long before the phrase *blood tells* was firmly embedded in the common lexicon. Galton's epiphany that the success of his ancestral line was in his genes and, more importantly, not in the genes of the other 96% of the human race, served to expand and solidify the narrative of meritocracy and is reflected today in the nation's wealth distribution.

From this curious beginning at the turn of the 20th century, eugenicists during the 1910s and 1920s successfully pursued their goal of social betterment through forcible sterilization, anti-miscegenation laws, and immigration restriction, along with sorting, testing, and tracking policies implemented in schools across the country. This ideology of human worth was pushed by powerful legislators, philanthropists, social workers, and teachers on the front lines of the movement. Reformers targeted both urban and rural unwed mothers, young boys who masturbated, and anyone whose race, poverty, isolation, language, or habits rendered them unacceptable by "polite" society. These people were deemed mentally "unfit" and those who were not blind, deaf, epileptic, alcoholic, or paupers were labeled with the dubious term *feebleminded*.

The basic tenets of eugenic ideology have long supplied, either consciously or subconsciously, an explanation for the establishment, evolution, and perpetuation of inequality. One major spokesman for the eugenics movement was eminent psychologist and eugenicist Edward Thorndike. Thorndike, one of the "Fathers of Curriculum," played a leading role in the establishment and form of our modern system of education. The eugenic explanation for human inequality is captured in a *New York Times* article by Thorndike (1927b) that coincided with the release of his book *The Measurement of Intelligence* (1927a). Thorndike (1927b) wrote:

> Men are born unequal in intellect, character, and skill. It is impossible and undesirable to make them equal by education. The proper work of education is to improve all men according to their several possibilities, in ways consistent with the welfare of all. (para. 5)

Thorndike reflects a common belief that has persisted into the present, that social inequality is an expression of hereditary worth. This little nugget has served for nearly a century as justification for governmentally sanctioned and perpetuated racism, xenophobia, discrimination, and abuse for countless numbers of people. What today we identify as the racist fury of White supremacist extremists was, for the first 3 decades of the 20th century, the language of the dominant culture in the United States. Newspapers crowed about the winners of "fitter family" contests, and ministers extolled the virtues of eugenically harmonious life far from the crime, dirt, and degeneracy of the poor and immigrant "unfit" populations.

The common consensus was that American culture, defined as middle- and upper class White culture, was under grave threat from the throngs of overly fertile "dysgenic" poor, immigrant, and otherwise undesirable elements of the population. This consensus was the result of a clarion call of "progressive" rhetoric supplied by America's best known families, philanthropists, and top scientists, and carried out by the nation's teachers, social workers, and countless institutions and organizations that believed they were working for the "greater good" of society. Public education, which was largely formed during the height of the eugenics movement, has been a primary arena for the enactment of a publicly embraced hierarchy of human worth (Selden, 1999; Winfield, 2007).

THE BREEDING GROUND FOR EUGENIC IDEOLOGY

The notion that some humans are more worthy than others is nothing new. In fact, intellectual history has been saturated with it since Plato and Aristotle pontificated over 2,000 years ago, making early-20th-century eugenic ideology a mere blip in the grand scheme of things. Because of the way eugenicists were able to translate the deeply embedded racism that existed immediately prior to the 20th century into the newly minted progressive sentiment in the 1910s and 1920s, eugenic ideology is especially instructive of the way the past manifests itself in the present (Cremin, 1961; Kuhl, 1994; Pickens, 1968).

To understand the context of the times, we must go back to the end of the Civil War, when Charles Darwin introduced his theory of evolution in his magnum opus *On the Origin of Species* (1859). For the next 40 years, many scientists and policymakers used the *survival of the fittest* language of Darwin's theory to craft decades of oppressive social thought and policy in the form of Social Darwinism. It was commonly accepted that those who possessed wealth, power, and influence in America did so because they were more evolved: They were, to use Darwin's terminology, *fitter*. At the same time as this social Darwinist foundation was becoming entrenched in the public sphere, the industrial revolution was underway, capitalism was idolized, society was enamored with the promise of science, and public sentiment was becoming increasingly progressive. This combination of social phenomena provided a ripe new breeding ground for eugenic ideology to flourish and for the next generation to carry its tenets forward.

As is the case today, the early decades of the 20th century saw an incredible centralization of wealth and power in which a few families controlled the majority of industrial and economic capital. A vast separation between the rich and poor existed, with the rich filling their time with art, music, literature, theatre, education, and science. The modern environmental movement emerged during this period as eugenicists like Madison Grant (author of *The Passing of the Great Race* and longtime head of the Natural History Museum in Washington, DC), representing the purveyors of so-called "high culture," emphasized the importance of fresh air, clean water, and space in which to raise their large, vigorous families. These members of the economic and ideological elite were not subject, of course, to the squalid conditions the poor endured where poverty, abusive work conditions, and lack of sanitation led to disease and death.

Politicians and businessmen were focused on creating political and economic stability, while the working poor searched for reasoned answers to societal problems and vigorously protested the ravages of industrial working conditions and crowded cities. As Zinn (1980) notes, a fervor was created by a "sudden economic crises leading to high prices and lost jobs, the lack of food and water," spurred on by the daily reality of "the freezing winters, the hot tenements in the summer, the epidemics of disease, [and the] deaths of children" (p. 215). These uprisings occasionally were directed toward the rich, but just as often this anger was translated into "racial hatred for blacks, religious warfare against Catholics, [and] nativist fury against immigrants" (p. 216). Along both ends of the economic spectrum, racist hostility became an easy substitute for class frustration.

Finally, with these events and attitudes as a foundation, the late 19th century saw enormous economic growth and a level of corporatization that has continued into the present. Standard Oil, U.S. Steel Corporation, J.P. Morgan, Chase Manhattan Bank, and American Telephone and Telegraph all had profits in the millions by 1890. From the 1920s to the present, reformers and policymakers have sought to apply business practices to education, arguing that the efficiency innovations in industry that allowed the profit margins of giant corporate entities to swell also would deal effectively with the task of educating America's children most efficiently (Rury, 2005). These policies inevitably have led to perpetuation of the perception that some students are defective or not as likely to result in the best product. This ongoing belief and dedication to business practices and the idea of efficiency have had tremendous consequences for generations of children.

The 1930s witnessed profound change as the population, reeling from the 1929 stock market crash and ensuing economic depression, responded with a new questioning of the status quo. Thousands of banks and businesses closed within months and "the economy was stunned, barely moving" (Zinn, 1980, p. 378). Just before laying off 75,000 workers in 1931, Henry Ford explained that the problem was "the average man won't really do a day's work unless he is caught and cannot get out of it. There is plenty of work to do if people would just do it" (quoted in Zinn, 1980, p. 378). News clippings of the era provide a glimpse into the continued atmosphere of crisis and fear surrounding the poor and immigrant segments of the population.

Chicago, April 1, 1932. Five hundred schoolchildren, most with haggard faces and in tattered clothes, paraded through Chicago's downtown section to the Board of Education offices to demand that the school system provide them with food.

Boston, June 3, 1932. Twenty-five hungry children raided a buffet lunch set up for Spanish War veterans during a Boston parade. Two automobile-loads of police were called to drive them away. (Zinn, 1980, pp. 380–381)

Although they promoted the argument that hard work and attitude would lead to success and that America's best feature was that it was fundamentally a meritocracy, the wealthy didn't believe this themselves and needed a way to argue that grinding poverty was an expression of something else besides corporate greed. Enter genetics. The rediscovery of Gregor Mendel's theory of inheritance was prominent in early eugenic rhetoric and continued to have an enormous influence on public willingness to embrace the idea, even though the geneticists rather quickly (1915) disproved the specious claims of eugenics regarding the heritability of various behaviors and social positions (Paul, 1998).

One of the leading proselytizers of eugenic rhetoric in the United States was Charles Benedict Davenport (1866–1944), who is credited with giving form to the eugenics movement for decades (Spiro, 2009). In 1904, 30 miles from New York City on Long Island's North Shore, Charles Davenport set up the Cold Spring Harbor research station dedicated to the study of eugenics. Convinced that the explanation for human difference in society was an expression of heredity, Davenport dedicated his career to the study of inheritance, with a goal of having data on every man, woman, and child in America. Unable to experiment on human beings directly, Davenport set about collecting inheritance data by developing a "family records" form and distributing hundreds of copies to medical, mental, and educational institutions, as well as to individuals, college alumni lists, and scientists (Kevles, 1985).

The family records forms distributed by Davenport, and funded by the wealthy, eventually formed a large repository of data, which provided the basis of Davenport's book *Heredity in Relation to Eugenics* (1911). Davenport devoted over half the pages of his book to a discussion of the inheritance of dozens of human characteristics, including mental deficiency, pauperism, feeblemindedness, sexual deviance, and laziness. Additionally, Eugenics Record Office data served as "the source of bulletins, memoirs, and books, on such topics as sterilization, the exclusion from the United States of inferior germ plasm, and the inheritance of pellagra, multiple sclerosis, tuberculosis, goiter, nomadism, athletic ability, and temperament" (Kevles, 1985, p. 56). Cited by more than one-third of high school biology texts between World War I and World War II (Selden, 1999),

Davenport's book is considered by many to be the era's most important treatise on eugenics (Ludmerer, 1972). From 1920 to 1938, the Eugenics Record Office published the "avidly racist and restrictionist" tract *Eugenical News* (Haller, 1963, p. 149). Financially backed by the Carnegies, the movement mastered dissemination using an army of society's most highly regarded scientists, philanthropists, clergy, academics, social workers, and teachers. In short, the message was everywhere.

EUGENICS AND TESTING: ROOTED IN THE PAST

When we consider current research on, for example, the disproportion of Black and Hispanic students in special education, race, and graduation rates; race and incarceration rates; and race and college attendance, we see that the present is infused with the past. The reality for poor and non-White children in the United States seems to have been anticipated by Herbert Henry Goddard, the first American psychologist to recognize the potential of intelligence testing for furthering eugenic ideals. Differences in children required different educational responses, Goddard (1912) wrote, and, furthermore, the greatest threat to society was the "high grade," or "moron," type of feeble mind because although those individuals were unfit (but not unable) to reproduce, they nevertheless were able to function in society and thus were a threat to the gene pool.

> Here we have a group who, when children in school, cannot learn the things that are given them to learn, because through their mental defect, they are incapable of mastering abstractions. They never learn to read sufficiently well to make reading pleasurable or of practical use to them. Under our present compulsory school system and our present course of study, we compel these children . . . and thus they worry along through a few grades until they are fourteen and then leave school, not having learned anything of value or that can help them to make even a meager living in the world. (Goddard, 1912, p. 16)

This was the central dogma of eugenics, that "poverty and its pathologies, like affluence and its comforts, were in the blood—and not in the environment in which human beings were conceived, born, and developed" (Chase, 1975, p. 149).

The new field of psychology was a Petrie dish of eugenic invective. IQ psychologists were steeped in eugenic ideology and to a large extent it shaped their science (Gersh, 1981). The most prestigious psychology department was led by G. Stanley Hall at Clark University in Worcester, Massachusetts. Hall, long considered to be one of the "Fathers of Curriculum" (along with John Franklin Bobbitt, E. L. Thorndike, and James Cattell), is credited with developing one of the first applied forms of psychology known as scientific pedagogy. This is well documented in educational history—what is not documented is the extent to which Hall and his compatriots were steeped in eugenic ideology. Hall (1924) felt strongly that class divisions were inherited, writing that each child:

> will be not only tested from childhood on, but assigned his grade, and be assured the place that allows the freest scope for doing the best that is in him . . . some are born to be hewers of wood and drawers of water . . . and are fortunate if they can be made self-supporting; practical slavery under one name or another must always be their lot. . . . Ranks and classes are inherent in human nature . . . and each must accept the rating that consigns him his true and just place in the hierarchy of the world's work. (p. 465)

Hall trained a generation of educational psychologists who, it might be noted, were a very close group, often attending the same schools and joining the same organizations, and who were to become the nation's testers.

Psychologists, many of whom were part of the economic and cultural elite, were motivated to produce a measurement tool that would "prove" the intellectual superiority of Whites. Such superiority was, for them, evidenced by history; the "failure" of Reconstruction and the obvious "backwardness" of Africa, Asia, and Latin America showed that, beyond a doubt, Nordics were the only race capable of governing themselves (Gossett, 1963). The quest for a "normal distribution" infused decades of educational psychology research. The mission was twofold: to provide the public with a scientific understanding of heredity and to develop a test that would "prove" hierarchical inequity.

America had long clung to its meritocratic narrative, so it was a fairly easy task for prominent educational psychologists to convince the public that education and the nation's welfare would best be served by subjecting students to tests that would determine their rightful place in society. The motivation went beyond achieving the "natural order," however; elite Americans were afraid. Goddard reflected the national sentiment in a series of lectures at Princeton, where he explained that "the disturbing fear is that the masses—the seventy or even the eighty-six million [of 105 million U.S. population]—will take matters into their own hands" (quoted in Gersh, 1981, p. 49 n. 5). The solution, it was thought, according to Terman in his classic book *The Measurement of Intelligence* (1916), was that students ought to be "segregated in special classes [and] given instruction that is concrete and practical," because although they cannot master abstractions, "they can often be made efficient workers" (p. 92).

Here we begin to see the direct connection to present circumstances. In addition to the determination to test every child, Terman and other reformers often invoked monetary thrift in their rhetoric about education, explaining, for example, that "between a third and a half of the school children fail to progress," and that the United States is spending more than 10% of the $400 million education budget for instruction that is "devoted to re-teaching children what they have already been taught but have failed to learn" (Terman, 1916, p. 3). Much was made of the "waste" of energy and money put into teaching unteachable students and, in particular, students who were termed "high-grade defectives," meaning they could function (and procreate) but otherwise were destined for "practical slavery."

In light of the general consensus regarding the "unteachability" of so many schoolchildren, the field of psychology and the general public who read Terman's book must have been very relieved when they read the following:

> It is safe to predict that in the near future intelligence tests will bring tens of thousands of these high-grade defectives under the surveillance and protection of society. This will ultimately result in curtailing the reproduction of feeble-mindedness and in the elimination of an enormous amount of crime, pauperism, and industrial inefficiency. It is hardly necessary to emphasize that the high-grade cases, the type now so frequently overlooked, are precisely the ones whose guardianship it is most important for the State to assume. (p. 7)

In light of the present widespread use of testing to sort and categorize students, not to mention the demographic makeup of the prison industrial complex, the dropout rate, and the nation's wealth distribution, it seems as if Terman and the eugenicists got their wish.

EUGENIC IDEOLOGY AND PRESENT-DAY SCHOOL REFORM

The story we tell ourselves is the reflection we want to see and is framed largely by the collective memory of the generations that preceded us. Take, for example, the 1954 United States Supreme Court decision *Brown v. Board of Education of Topeka, KS*, which targeted legal segregation in schools. This was, there is no doubt, a monumental moment in our nation's history, but to focus solely on this moment is to lose the avalanche of additional information that is needed to understand the present. From post-World War II racist housing and banking policies that led to present-day demographic segregation (Rury, 2005) and

wealth disparity, to the most restrictive and punishing educational reforms being aimed at urban schools (Lipman, 2004), there is no shortage of ways to trace
ideological power in American life. However, the historical dividing line that
marks the starting point for the present era, few would argue, is the election of
Ronald Reagan to the presidency in 1980.

During the 1980 presidential election cycle, the nation was close to bursting
with pent-up racist hostility and resentment in response to civil rights gains of
the previous decades (Rury, 2005). The discontent was global and launched what
is now referred to as the "conservative restoration" orchestrated by Reagan and
British Prime Minister Margaret Thatcher (Harvey, 2005). The consequences
were, and continue to be, dire for education, representing a substantially qualitative shift in the arenas of policy and reform. Starting with the 1983 *A Nation
at Risk* report on the state of public education issued by a Reagan-appointed
presidential commission, it effectively was communicated to the public that the
reforms (put in place for poor, non-White, immigrant and disabled children)
of the past 2 decades had weakened us as a country and that we needed to be
fearful of a *rising tide of mediocrity* (echoing the *rising tide of feeblemindedness*
of earlier decades). All this led to generations of labeling "at-risk" children and
ever-thickening layers of so-called standards and accountability in education
purportedly set up to achieve equity. School reform ever since has been consumed by the business of tracking, testing, and sorting students just as before,
yet with a new veneer of the language of social justice.

The re-establishment of a nearly impermeable funnel (schools) for poor
and non-White children to be kept in what eugenicists called their rightful
place, on the lowest rungs of the economic ladder, has been effective. Since 1980
we have seen the re-establishment of the pre-Keynesian wealth distribution
charts of the 1920s and 1930s, where the top 5% of the population control over
50% of the wealth and the bottom 50% of the population control less than 3%
of the wealth (Harvey, 2005). During the 1960s and 1970s, wealth distribution
actually evened out some, and we know that even the slightest elevation in socioeconomic status can have a tremendous positive effect on the lives of millions
and is reflected in school "success" (Berliner, 2005). And of course, we continue
to fund schools primarily through property tax, as we have done since the early
1800s, which in itself is a built-in system of inequity.

Almost everything we recognize about public schools today was developed and conceived by educational psychologists, scientists, and legislators
who were wholly wedded to the idea that society could be made better by defining, identifying, and controlling who was worthy (Selden, 1999; Winfield,

2007). In other words, eugenic ideology is ubiquitous in American public education. Although the infusion has been there all along, and saw tremendous challenge between 1950 and 1980, reforms of the post-1980 era have served to institutionalize stratified society in ways previously unseen in America. It is possible to find the effects in multiple places, many of which have already been mentioned, but it is within testing and the curriculum (both hidden and overt) that the social philosophy of biological determinism (i.e., eugenics) is most evident.

A survey of current trends reveals that testing requires of practitioners the same emphasis on "efficiency" that characterized the application of eugenic ideology to school reform during the 1920s and 1930s. Teaching is reduced to piecemeal curriculum, bite-sized chunks of decontextualized information delivered in a fashion most suitable for memorization and regurgitation (Gould, 1995). When we think of the transformative possibilities inherent in more progressive, student-centered approaches to the craft, we can see that the kind of curriculum required by testing is perfect for maintaining the status quo. Students who are perceived as failures, and who too often internalize that message, are less likely to be a threat to the current system.

The deep mistrust embedded in current reform agendas for students, their families, and communities has been expressed by an increasingly Panoptic model of surveillance in schools (Kohl, 2009). From cameras in every hallway and classroom, to practices that require elementary students to march from place to place in school with their wrists behind them as if they have handcuffs on, school administrators are expressing their unexamined fear and contempt in ever more controlling and suggestive ways. Besides the fact that they can't touch one another or "fool around," students are lined up this way because "it's also good education for their future," according to a school principal (cited in Kohl, 2009, p. 1). Couched in a liberal desire to "help," to address the needs of "at-risk" youth, there is an abiding blindness to the extent to which we create what we expect to see.

Embedded eugenic ideology exists, too, in the scripted, proscriptive, curriculum encased in slick packaging by textbook monopolies like McGraw Hill (Kohn, 2002). Teachers in "failing schools," and, by default, their students, are subject to manuals that dictate what they say, and when and to whom they say it, all timed and monitored by emissaries from the front office with little variation in form, severity, or implementation. Underlying contempt for public education, and educational theory altogether, is expressed as well in the dramatic rise in slipshod teacher certification programs. Presumably, the

thinking is: Since teachers are told what to do, timed to the second, and sur-
veilled anyway, who needs teachers who think, or who have a grasp of the
historical, sociological, and philosophical realities of their chosen profession?
Over half a century has passed since the Supreme Court ruling in *Brown v.
Board of Education of Topeka* and yet we have created a school system that is
more segregated than it was during the 1950s when the *Brown* decision was
handed down (Kozol, 2005).

The human hierarchy created by eugenic ideology is evident in the very solutions we seek to dismantle seemingly intractable problems like the impact of
poverty. Take, for example, the Ruby Payne phenomenon as an example of both
corporate profit-mongering and pathologization. Despite decades of research
that has discredited the "deficit approach" to explaining opportunity and access
in education, Ruby Payne is indoctrinating a generation of teachers with a series
of books that contain "a stream of stereotypes, providing perfect illustrations for
how deficit-model scholars frame poverty" (Gorski, 2006, p. 8). District superintendents intent on solving the "poverty problem" in their schools are paying
millions of dollars to Payne's company, Aha!, Inc., for textbooks and workshop
trainings for thousands of teachers nationwide.

Payne's overall message is that poor people are slow processors, that they
can't be made to think critically, and that the best way to teach them is to know
their "culture," which she presents as the most stereotyped imaginable, steeped
in historic drivel. Payne sounds like a eugenicist right out of the 1920s as she explains that "the typical pattern in poverty for discipline is to verbally chastise the
child, or physically beat the child, then forgive and feed him/her . . . individuals
in poverty are seldom going to call the police. . . . [because] the police may be
looking for them" (quoted in Gorski, 2006, p. 37). Poverty in this conception, a
conception that is being delivered en masse to teachers today, is a problem that
needs to be fixed not systemically or through social policy, but by fixing the
people themselves.

This ability to avert the gaze of the public from systemic analysis and instead to emphasize personal weakness or lack of gratitude as an explanation for
school failure has been a hallmark of educational reform for over a century. It
is entwined within the stories we tell ourselves as a nation: Our national identity narratives are rife with rags-to-riches stories—the implication always being
that anyone can succeed, one only has to work hard, avoid making excuses of
any kind, and follow the rules (Kohn, 2010). This is a formula that has worked
very well to institutionalize deterministic/status-confirming policies in education and elsewhere.

CONCLUSION: WHAT WE ARE UP AGAINST

Governmental uses of eugenically rooted ideology have imposed on the underclass what Nancy Ordover (2003) has called the "technofix," wherein policies and practices routinely have served to protect elite interests and prevent mobility for everyone else. Indeed, as the current economic meltdown reveals, the same arguments that focus on moral failings are brought to bear, while the unadulterated greed and exploitation practiced by the economic elite continue despite publicly expressed outrage (and even, in the case of the so-called "Tea Party" activists, because of it). The ruse of unprecedented testing, national standards, student control, and surveillance in our nation's schools, which has been foisted on the American public using the language of social justice, must be revealed for the ideological Trojan Horse that it is.

Systemic inequality may be inherently at odds with democracy but it nevertheless has co-opted the public sphere (Iverson, 2005). The elite in society are reliant on the status quo, including the underlying assumptions that define eugenic ideology, and they effectively have defined, regulated, and enforced access in society for generations. They have done this by institutionalizing the notion that fairness and equity are found through the opportunity to prove one's worth—in other words, that we are a meritocracy. As we have seen, a look at the history that is left out of the official narrative reveals that meritocracy is a myth that has resulted in direct harm to generations of American people.

The current assault on public education is a push toward a larger ideological agenda that will serve to substantially deepen the degree to which capital gain outweighs human solidarity (Lipman, 2004). The assumption that some are more worthy than others, or that access to wealth and privilege is indicative of moral stature, is a premise that needs to be immediately exposed and resoundingly rejected. We are witness to a profound qualitative reordering of American society, the genesis of which is occurring in American schools. Present reform agendas are not about making schools better, nor are they about tidying things up and becoming more efficient at what we do. Make no mistake; what is happening now is about institutionalizing human worth.

The pathologization and corporatization of humanity go on. A profound co-optation of public knowledge is in operation not just about people, institutions, and corporations, but also about representations of the past, harnessed by a deeply rooted racialized scientism known as eugenics. Eugenic ideology is insidiously intertwined in fabric of the nation, yet the thread is invisible. Progressives on the left opine about whether the pre-eminent issue is race or capitalism, while the ideology of the empire, which is firmly rooted in both, chugs on. Eugenic ideology hasn't re-emerged; it never left, and it should be considered as the foundational root for much of the current school reform agenda and the deepening corporatization of the public sphere.

REFERENCES

Anderson, J. (1988). *The education of black folks in the south.* Chapel Hill: University of North Carolina Press.

Berliner, D. C. (2005, August 2). Our impoverished view of educational reform. *Teachers College Record.*

Black, E. (2003). *War against the weak: Eugenics and America's campaign to create a master race.* New York: Four Walls Eight Windows.

Chase, A. (1975). *The legacy of Malthus: The social costs of the new scientific racism.* New York: Knopf.

Cremin, L. A. (1961). *The transformation of the school: Progressivism in American education 1876–1957.* New York: Vintage Books.

Darling-Hammond, L. (2004). From "separate but equal" to "No Child Left Behind." In D. Meier & G. Woods (Eds.), *Many children left behind: How the No Child Left Behind Act is damaging our children and our schools.* Boston: Beacon Press.

Darwin, C. (1859). *On the origin of species by means of natural selection.* London: J. Murray.

Davenport, C. (1911). *Heredity in relation to eugenics.* New York: Henry Holt.

Gersh, D. A. (1981). *The development and use of IQ tests in the United States from 1900–1930.* Doctoral dissertation, State University of New York, Stony Brook.

Goddard, H. H. (1912). *The Kallikak family: A study in the heredity of feeblemindedness.* New York: Macmillan.

Gorski, P. (2006). Savage unrealities: Classism and racism abound in Ruby Payne's framework. *Rethinking Schools, 21*(2).

Gossett, T. F. (1963). *Race: The history of an idea in America.* New York: Schocken Books.

Gould, S. J. (1995). Curveball. In S. Fraser (Ed.), *The bell curve wars.* New York: Basic Books.

Gould, S. J. (1996). *The mismeasure of man.* New York: Norton.

Hall, G. S. (1924). Can the masses rule the world? *Scientific Monthly, 18,* 456–466.

Haller, M. (1963). *Eugenics: Hereditarian attitudes in American thought.* New Brunswick, NJ: Rutgers University Press.

Harvey, D. (2005). *A brief history of neoliberalism.* New York: Oxford University Press.

Hasian, M. A., Jr. (1996). *The rhetoric of eugenics in Anglo-American thought.* Athens: University of Georgia Press.

Iverson, T. (2005). *Capitalism, democracy, and welfare.* New York: Cambridge University Press.

Kevles, D. J. (1985). *In the name of eugenics: Genetics and the uses of human heredity.* Berkeley: University of California Press.

Kohl, H. (2009, January). The educational panopticon. *Teachers College Record.*

Kohn, A. (2002). The 500 lb. gorilla. *Phi Delta Kappan.*

Kohn, A. (2004). NCLB and the effort to privatize public education. In D. Meier & G. Woods (Eds.), *Many children left behind: How the No Child Left Behind Act is damaging our children and our schools.* Boston: Beacon Press.

Kohn, A. (2010, October 20). How to sell conservatism: Lesson 1—Pretend you're a reformer. *Huffington Post.* Available at http://www.huffingtonpost.com/alfie-kohn/how-to-sell-conservatism-_b_767040.html

Kozol, J. (2005). *The shame of the nation: The restoration of apartheid schooling in America.* New York: Crown.

Kuhl, S. (1994). *The Nazi connection: Eugenics, American racism, and German national socialism.* New York: Oxford University Press.

Lipman, P. (2004). *High stakes education: Inequality, globalization, and urban school reform.* New York: Routledge.

Ludmerer, K. M. (1972). *Genetics and American society: A historical appraisal.* Baltimore, MD: Johns Hopkins University Press.

Ordover, N. (2003). *American eugenics: Race, queer anatomy, and the science of nationalism.* Minneapolis: University of Minnesota Press.

Paul, D. B. (1998). *The politics of heredity: Essays on eugenics, biomedicine, and the nature–nurture debate.* Albany: State University of New York Press.

Pickens, D. (1968). *Eugenics and the progressives.* Nashville, TN: Vanderbilt University Press.

Ravitch, D. (2010). *The death and life of the great American school system: How testing and choice are undermining American education.* New York: Basic Books.

Rury, J. L. (2005). *Education and social change: Themes in the history of American education.* Mahwah, NJ: Erlbaum.

Selden, S. (1999). *Inheriting shame: The story of eugenics and racism in America.* New York: Teachers College Press.

Spiro, J. P. (2009). *Defending the master race: Conservation, eugenics, and the legacy of Madison Grant.* Burlington: University of Vermont Press.

Terman, L. (1916). *The measurement of intelligence: An explanation of and a complete guide for the use of the Stanford revision and extension of the Binet-Simon intelligence scale.* Boston: Houghton Mifflin.

Thorndike, E. L. (1927a). *The measurement of intelligence.* New York: Teachers College Press.

Thorndike, E. L. (1927b, August 27). The new psychology sheds light on man. *New York Times.* Available at http://query.nytimes.com/mem/archive/pdf?res=F7061FFE395D1 3728DDDA80A94D0405B878EF1D3

Watkins, W. H. (2001). *The white architects of Black education: Ideology and power in America, 1865–1954.* New York: Teachers College Press.

Winfield, A. G. (2007). *Eugenics and education in America: Institutionalized racism and the implications of history, ideology, and memory.* New York: Peter Lang.

Woods, G. (2004). A view from the field: NCLB's effects on classrooms and schools. In D. Meier & G. Woods (Eds.), *Many children left behind: How the No Child Left Behind Act is damaging our children and our schools.* Boston: Beacon Press.

Zinn, H. (1980). *A people's history of the United States.* New York: Harper Perennial.

CHAPTER 8

"It's All About the Dollars"

Charter Schools, Educational Policy, and
the Racial Market in New Orleans

Kristen L. Buras

The auditorium of McDonogh 35 High School in New Orleans was packed with hundreds of people on October 14, 2010. Five years earlier the state-run Recovery School District (RSD) assumed control of the majority of public schools in Orleans Parish, leaving only a handful of schools to be governed by the locally elected Orleans Parish School Board (OPSB). The schoolchildren of New Orleans would be part of a grand experiment: Educational reformers and their state allies set out to create the first all-charter school system in the nation (Bring New Orleans Back Commission, 2006a; Buras, 2011a, forthcoming). By 2009–10, the majority of schools were charters (51 of 88 schools, enrolling 61% of students), with more than 30 charter school operators in two different school districts (Cowen Institute, 2010; see also Figure 8.1).

On this October evening, students, teachers, principals, parents, and community members gathered for a public hearing before the Louisiana Board of Elementary and Secondary Education (BESE), which governs RSD schools from the capital in Baton Rouge. The future of RSD schools was under consideration. How would they be governed in the years to come? Would presumably "successful" charter schools opt to be governed by OPSB instead? And if so, under what conditions would they be transferred? In short, would or should the educational market be sustained and whose interests would be served? Perhaps most important, who would decide?

The Assault on Public Education: Confronting the Politics of Corporate School Reform, edited by William H. Watkins. Copyright © 2012 by Teachers College, Columbia University. All rights reserved. Prior to photocopying items for classroom use, please contact the Copyright Clearance Center, Customer Service, 222 Rosewood Dr., Danvers, MA 01923, USA, tel. (978) 750-8400, www.copyright.com.

Figure 8.1. Public Schools in New Orleans, 2009–10

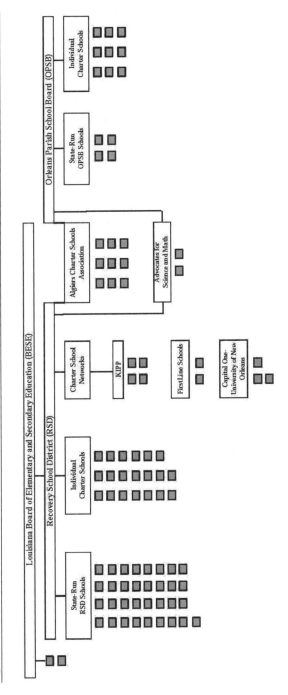

Just a few weeks before, Louisiana State Superintendent of Education Paul Pastorek and RSD Superintendent Paul Vallas (2010) had issued a set of recommendations addressing the above questions. They clearly stipulated that OPSB would be expected to maintain the "autonomy" and "innovation" enabled by RSD governance of charter schools; in short, the plan imposed a host of rigid conditions on OPSB for reacquiring schools—all intended to ensure that the educational market would persist despite substantial local opposition. It was sure to be a heated public hearing, as many African American parents, veteran teachers, and longstanding community members had grave concerns regarding the so-called reforms implemented since 2005, conceiving them to be an assault on public education and Black self-determination rather than a sign of social and educational progress (Buras, 2009; Buras, Randels, Salaam, & Students at the Center, 2010). Of course, not all agreed and at the outset of the hearing this was evident.

The BESE members, who were largely White, were seated on stage in the auditorium. Community members, mostly African American, meandered through the crowd greeting one another and taking their seats. Some held posters expressing their views—"Discrimination is NOT innovation" and "Equal Education Access for ALL children"—referring to both the formal and informal selective admissions policies of many charter schools. Some wore t-shirts, with one reading, "We are ready! Orleans Parish School Board," indicating a desire for public schools governed by locally elected officials. Stickers with slash marks through RSD (meaning "no more RSD") conveyed opposition to the state takeover. Stirring the humid southern air and the tension, others waved handheld fans printed with the words, "I [heart] my charter school," while the reverse side listed perceived benefits, including, "I support parents having a CHOICE in deciding the best school to educate their child" (field notes, 2010).

The hearing was called to order by Chas Roemer, BESE member and son of former Republican governor Buddy Roemer; his sister, Caroline Roemer Shirley, is executive director of the Louisiana Association of Public Charter Schools. State and local officials were introduced and Senator Mary Landrieu, charter school advocate and designated "hero" of the market-oriented political action committee Democrats for Education Reform, was one of the first to speak (e.g., see Democrats for Education Reform, 2010). She mispronounced the OPSB superintendent's name (calling him Darryl *G*ilbert rather than *K*ilbert), which prompted corrective shouts from local community members, and then went on to tout New Orleans as an educational "model" of "choice" and "opportunity" both nationally and internationally. Landrieu characterized the grand experiment as a form of *coopetition* (a hybrid of cooperation and competition) in which school officials, school management organizations, and communities "work together" to build an unprecedented marketplace of possibility. Red t-shirts worn by teachers, students, and parents associated with specific charter schools created bright clusters in the auditorium and reflected similar sentiments, reading "MY CHILD, MY SCHOOL, MY CHOICE" (field notes, 2010).

One particular RSD charter school had organized its supporters. A stream of affiliated students and parents offered testimony about the school and their desire for ongoing support of charter schools governed by the RSD. One Black parent emphasized:

> I am here to support charter schools, especially Sophie B. Wright. If you look to my left [where members of Wright were seated], you're going to find the best of the best right here in the house. I support what it is right now and I don't want it changed. If you look on the back of my shirt, it says it's *my choice*. My choice is to leave it as is [in the RSD]. . . . About a year ago I was worried about where to send my child when it came time to leave Wright Middle School. . . . We asked that Wright be allowed to become a high school. The BESE Board approved that amendment. This could not have happened if we were not a charter school. *My* son would not be getting the education that he's getting from that charter school. (field notes, 2010)

Queries issued from elsewhere in the auditorium, however, portrayed a very different understanding of school choice and the educational market. One woman, for example, projected her concerns, asking, "What about your neighbor's child?" The parent from Wright defensively responded: "Let's speak about the neighbor's child! . . . I am an educator at New Orleans Job Corps Center. At my center there's 80% of failures from the Orleans Parish School Board. So let's talk about my neighbor. If you think the charter school can't do it [educate successfully], [then] send [your child] to the people who do." Gasps of disapproval echoed around the auditorium (field notes, 2010).

Indeed, despite the organized testimony of individual parents-turned-charter school advocates, much of the public testimony revolved around serious critiques of the effects of decentralization and the educational market on community well-being as a whole. An African American woman presenting herself as a concerned citizen issued the following warning:

> I would like to go back to *Brown v. Board of Education* . . . [which] simply said that separate was not equal. What I'm seeing now in this room as I listen to people talk today—we are more separated today than we have ever been. I hear people talk charter, I hear people talk RSD, I hear people talk about all

types of other schools, but the bottom line is we are a community, we are *one* community. . . . Our children have the right to be educated—be it charter, be it RSD, be it Orleans Parish—they have the right to be educated. They all have the right to the *same* education and I'm not finding it. And I'm listening to too many people talk about *my* school, *our* school, *their* school. All of the schools should be equal . . . and it's not happening. (field notes, 2010)

This commentary and similar ones throughout the evening reflected the distinct and divisive ethos defining educational markets—possessive individualism— even if partly rooted in the "good sense" (Gramsci, 1971; Apple & Buras, 2006) of Black parents frustrated by a long history of educational neglect and disinvestment and who understandably hope to shape the destiny of their own children by exercising "choice" (Pedroni, 2007) and seeking access to a curriculum promising high-status knowledge and upward mobility (Buras, 2008).

The apparent tensions around charter schools and educational equity in New Orleans take on added significance when one considers the history of the high school where the public hearing occurred. Until 1917, the state didn't provide a publicly funded high school education, not even an unequally funded one, for African American students in New Orleans; McDonogh 35 was the city's first Black public high school (DeVore & Logsdon, 1991). It is telling that almost 100 years later community members would gather there to debate the effects of current reforms on educational access and the role of the state in either advancing or undermining racial justice.

This history, combined with persistent and current school inequities, illuminates a fundamental point: The confluence of race, markets, and state power has never been neutral (e.g., see Mills, 1997; Watkins, 2005). Rather, African Americans specifically and communities of color more generally have themselves been viewed as useful but disposable material assets for White exploitation and benefit. At the present time, a more elaborate understanding of neoliberalism as not simply an economic but also a *racial* project is greatly needed. That is, we cannot adequately grasp the current assault on public education without a critical racial analysis of political economy.

In this chapter, I will trouble the neoliberal assertion that by allowing individual choice and entrepreneurial innovation to reign as policy, educational markets produce greater equity. Drawing on data gathered over the past 5 years on charter school reform in New Orleans (e.g., state education reports, documents of school reform organizations, local and national newspapers, school and community observations, stakeholder interviews, and participant-observation in public forums) as well as critical theories of political economy

(Apple, 2006; Harvey, 2006) and race (Crenshaw, Gotanda, Peller, & Thomas, 1995; Taylor, Gillborn, & Ladson-Billings, 2009), I reveal the "invisible hand" in living color. More specifically, I argue that educational markets are raced and thus have differential racial effects. In the interest of coherence, testimony from the aforementioned public hearing will be a primary source and point of reference throughout the chapter. Perhaps more than any other gathering, this hearing represents the culmination of 5 years of reform and exemplifies the key concerns and views I have encountered through my ongoing research (Buras, 2005, 2007, 2009, 2011a, 2011b, forthcoming; Buras et al., 2010).

Moreover, in the short span of this chapter, the central components of the neoliberal project will be charted through an analysis of school reform in New Orleans, rendering transparent a multifaceted and interlocking policy regime that includes: (1) a managerial state that provides the legislative infrastructure necessary for venture philanthropists and education entrepreneurs to capitalize and privatize public education; (2) private management, contracting, and decision making over public schools and a corresponding marketization of schoolchildren; (3) an attack on veteran educators and teachers unions, accompanied by alternative teacher recruitment on the cheap; and (4) the use, abuse, and outright manipulation of standardized testing to validate allegedly evidence-based market reforms. In the case of each component, racial dynamics and effects will be underscored. It is my hope this framework will assist critical scholars and activists in a more thorough analysis of reforms unfolding in other cities and contexts.

In sum, I will show that educational *coopetition* is far from benevolent but rather is divisive and productive of gross racial and economic inequities.

THE RACIAL MARKET IN NEW ORLEANS: PAST AND PRESENT

Charter school proponents say that educational markets are neutral and generally self-correcting, driven by informed consumer choice and mediated by individuals acting in self-interested ways that ultimately produce wider social good. Ineffective, inefficient, and inequitable schools will be disciplined by the "invisible hand," which ensures that substandard products and services don't survive. At the very least, they claim, the negative consequences of such schools may be curtailed by adopting minimal structural constraints that guard against market imperfections (Hill, 2002; Hill et al., 2009).

In reality, however, the hand of the market has never been neutral or invisible, or limited in its consequences for communities of color. Just the opposite: The market exists and persists in living color, reflecting and more often than not

166The Assault on Public Education

166The Assault on Public Education

perpetuating unequal relations of racial power. The institution of slavery is the most brutal example, with Blacks in the South treated as property and subjected to White ownership, unspeakable abuses, myriad forms of exploitation, and market exchanges beyond their immediate control (Blassingame, 1977). Even after the abolition of slavery, state-sanctioned forms of violence and segregation in labor markets, schools, and other public and private venues curtailed the choices available to African Americans and perpetuated racial, economic, and cultural subjugation (Du Bois, 1935/1992; Roediger, 1991). The market never corrected this, but was instead a key instrument in sustaining such oppression. Historian Robin D. G. Kelley (1997) challenges the myth of the color-blind market, arguing that even contemporary advocates of Black capitalism as the most effective self-help strategy "take for granted that the 'free market' actually operates free of racism and that the playing field is even." He continues, "Their arguments betray an incredibly naïve faith in the free market to do the work of creating equality" (p. 91). Equally important, Kelley emphasizes state culpability.

> Calls for color blindness and laissez-faire economic strategies also camouflage the critical role the state has played in reproducing inequality and creating an *uneven* playing field. Tax laws and social welfare, retirement, and housing policies have impaired the ability of African Americans to accumulate assets while facilitating white access to wealth. (p. 92)

The same may be said of state education policies, particularly ones that rely on the free market to provide equitable access to schools.

Historically, the racial structure and market in New Orleans were more complex than in other southern cities. The city had one of the largest free Black communities in the United States, which meant that some level of cultural and economic power—albeit relative, constrained, and always under threat—was exercised by Afro-Creole professionals and tradesmen and women who created markets to meet community needs (Desdunes, 1911/1973; Gehman, 1994). At the same time, a portion of enslaved Blacks in antebellum New Orleans, unlike those on plantations in rural Louisiana, were skilled and unskilled laborers—carpenters, bricklayers, painters, blacksmiths, bakers, barbers, dock workers, seamstresses, nurses, and street vendors. While their labor power was largely controlled by White owners, their involvement in a range of occupations meant they experienced relatively more mobility and the chance to develop a richer social life. In New Orleans, enslaved Blacks were released from work on Sundays. Gathering in local Black establishments and marketplaces to sell the products of their labor, generate income, and purchase needed goods, they generally ended their day at Congo Square, where they reinvented the music and dance of Africa, ultimately developing rich cultural forms indigenous to New Orleans (Blassingame, 1973; Sublette, 2008). While this constituted a mode of enjoyment, it likewise fostered solidarity and resistance. Demonstrating the hyper-exploitive and racially inflected tendencies of the market, however, Black cultural forms ultimately became the focus of marketization and White profiteering.

The present-day economy of New Orleans revolves largely around cultural tourism in the French Quarter (Bring New Orleans Back Commission, 2006b; Souther, 2006). Although the French Quarter is the place where White business leaders, local White consumers, and White visitors invest themselves, the entire "industry" is based on cultural forms produced in Black spaces, whether in historic Congo Square or later in Black working-class neighborhoods. More to the point, Black producers' culture and labor have been extracted, commodified, and expropriated by White owners and consumers: the Creole food, brass bands and jazz music, the accent and patois ("Who *dat* say . . . ?"), the festivities surrounding Mardi Gras, and southern services that are both sophisticated and profane. Writing about the cultural and racial dynamics of the market in New Orleans, Souther (2006) explains:

> If tourist dollars enriched businessmen who could profit from the popularity of the French Quarter, only low wages went to most of the many African Americans who worked [there]. . . . African American cultural contributions underlay most aspects of the tourist experience in New Orleans, but in the French Quarter, white promoters cast blacks merely as supporting actors who furnished services and amusement to a tourist-oriented tableau. . . . Although much of the city's peculiar charm sprang from Afro-Caribbean roots, blacks were seldom beneficiaries of their own contributions. . . . Tourism . . . rested to a great extent on white exploitation of African Americans. (p. 28)

Kalamu ya Salaam, an educator and respected poet in New Orleans's Black Arts Movement, goes even further, describing the interconnections between education and political economy, race, and culture.

> Education is ground zero in the systemic exploitation of black people in New Orleans—ground zero because public schools are the direct feeder for the necessary, albeit unskilled, labor needed for the tourist-oriented economy. . . . It is enough to note that in New Orleans they are building more hotels everyday. Where will the bellhops and maids come from? . . . Our schools are the way they are because the economy . . . continues to require a labor force to clean, cook, and serve. (Buras et al., 2010, pp. 66–67)

It should be clear by now that such exploitation has a long history (see also Hall, 1992).

One reasonably might ask: What does all this have to do with charter schools? The fact is this—the cultural and economic exploitation of African Americans within markets has an educational correlate. Under current reforms in New Orleans, the public schools attended by African American schoolchildren have been rapaciously commodified by White entrepreneurs (and their Black allies), who care much less about improving the life chances of Black youth and much more about capitalizing schools, obtaining contracts, and lining their pockets with public and private monies. In light of the preceding history, there is little reason to believe that African Americans will fare well in an educational market or that the market itself is even intended to advance their interests. For education entrepreneurs, as I will show, Black children and Black schools *constitute* the market.

I want to recognize upfront that charter schools sometimes have enabled racially oppressed communities to create culturally relevant spaces that nurture self-determination and achievement. But these spaces are too few and far between and do not reflect the agenda of the wider charter school movement, which is defined and controlled by market-inspired reformers who share a very different set of commitments, even as they strategically attempt to wed their own agenda to the concerns of oppressed communities. Knowledge may be power according to the KIPP charter school network (Mathews, 2009). But *whose knowledge* counts and *whose power* is bolstered as well-funded White reformers selectively groom a minority of "at-risk" children to "work hard" and "be nice," while undermining the cultural and economic fabric of public schools and the communities in which they are situated? In New Orleans, where charter school reform has been instituted at a scale unheard of elsewhere, the effects have been devastating.

CHARTER SCHOOLS, RACE, AND THE NEOLIBERAL POLICY REGIME

In what follows, I chart the central dynamics propelling charter school reform in New Orleans and underscore the racial effects of this project. To provide a more textured account, I highlight the views and actions of elite policymakers as well as the voices of community members, periodically revisiting the public hearing that occurred at McDonogh 35 High School.

The Managerial State and Legal Infrastructure
of Charter School Ventures

The neoliberal project depends on the managerial state. While prevailing educational reforms, such as charter schools, rely on decentralization and a "weak" noninterventionist state, they simultaneously require the state to actively create a climate hospitable to capital accumulation and the leveraging of public assets for private interests (Clarke & Newman, 1997; Harvey, 2006). Very often this climate is created through state law.

When Hurricane Katrina struck New Orleans in late August 2005, a vacuum was created and Louisiana's governor and legislators, prompted partly by federal pressure, immediately stepped in to renovate state law and prepare the ground for mass experimentation with charter schools. By October, Governor Kathleen Blanco had already signed Executive Orders 58 and 79, suspending certain provisions of charter school law, such as the need to consult and obtain the votes of affected faculty, staff, and parents before converting an existing public school into a charter school (Louisiana Federation of Teachers & American Federation of Teachers, 2007). In early November, Blanco called a special legislative session. This became the occasion for passing Act 35, which redefined what constituted a "failing" school so that most of New Orleans Public Schools could be deemed failing and placed in the state-run RSD. Act 35 enabled 107 of 128 schools to be folded into the RSD; only 13 schools could have been assumed before the legislation was passed (United Teachers of New Orleans et al., 2006). Notably, the definition of failure shifted from a state test score cutoff of 60 to just below the state average of 87.4. At the local level, White business leaders on the Bring New Orleans Back Commission (2006a) developed plans for an all-charter school system. Laws were changed and passed and corresponding plans were made while the residents of New Orleans, largely African American, remained displaced.

The law, generally depicted as apolitical and color-blind and based on well-established legal reasoning, is malleable and often reshaped to converge with the interests of Whites. Critical race theorists contend the law does more than simply reflect existing forms of racial power—it *produces* them. This is possible because the law is indeterminate and subject to constant redefinition regardless of precedent (Crenshaw et al., 1995). In the case of New Orleans, state law shifted quickly and capriciously without regard for even the most basic tenets of democratic governance. While poor and working-class African American communities were in utter disarray and families remained far from

home, public schools were abruptly taken over by charter school operators—
a point I will soon address. For now, it is essential to underscore the role
of the state in establishing the legislative infrastructure necessary for such
"ventures."

With the legal infrastructure for mass decentralization set in place and state
assumption of the vast majority of public schools in New Orleans, so-called
education entrepreneurs and venture philanthropists were able to more easily
access community assets and capitalize them. A number of local charter school
reform organizations emerged, such as New Schools for New Orleans (NSNO),
which "incubates" charter schools. Although local, NSNO, along with some
of its partner organizations, received national funding from foundations such
as Broad, Gates, Fisher, and Walton (for more on the role of foundations, see
Saltman, 2010; Scott, 2009). More specifically, NSNO and its partners received
$17.5 million in December 2007 (Maxwell, 2007) and another $28 million from
the federal government in September 2010, with the latter grant dependent on
an additional $5.6 million in private funds (Chang, 2010). In this way, the state
creates the legal apparatus necessary for charter school expansion and venture
philanthropy, and even subsidizes venture capitalists who leverage public assets
for their own profit.

The racial dimensions of this project have not gone unnoticed by community members, and the effects of such legislative maneuvering were the focus
of commentary at the public hearing with BESE. One longtime volunteer in
the public schools of New Orleans expressed her disgust over venture-driven
reform enabled by such governance:

> I resent the fact that Paul Vallas came here from out of town and he brought
> all of his crew from out of town. He said to the New Orleans residents: You
> cannot take care of your community or your schools. So we're bringing people
> from out of town to come here and charter your schools and run your schools
> and you sit down and shut up because you do not have the capacity to run
> your schools. And that I resent because there are a lot of intelligent people
> here that are indigenous to this community. . . . I understand Mr. Vallas still
> has residency in Chicago, Illinois. . . . How can you come here? We can't come
> to Chicago and just say we want to set up a charter school there. . . . We all
> need to fight for local governance and input, so that we can properly educate
> our children and not let them be experiments. (field notes, 2010)

Another well-known community activist shared an equally damning critique of the legal assault on Black schools, stating:

What we're talking about here tonight is a simple question of democracy. We want in Orleans Parish what every other parish has in this state and that's the right to control our own schools. High crimes and misdemeanors have been carried out against the people of New Orleans . . . by the RSD and the people who run these charter operations. We don't believe that these schools have served the best interests of the majority of our African American students. (field notes, 2010)

Here again, there is a palpable sense that education entrepreneurs in New Orleans, assisted by White lawmakers in Baton Rouge, have been the real beneficiaries.

Perhaps most striking, Harry Rosenberg—former U.S. attorney, New Orleans lawyer, and graduate of New Orleans Public Schools—stressed that ongoing control of schools by the RSD, essentially advocated in Pastorek and Vallas's recommendations to BESE, violates the Louisiana State Constitution (Louisiana State Senate, 1974/2009). In Article 8, Section 9, for example, the constitution addresses the role of local school boards and superintendents:

(A) Boards. The legislature shall create parish school boards and provide for the election of their members.

(B) Superintendents. Each parish board shall elect a superintendent of parish schools. (p. 66)

Clearly, the state-run RSD is not vested with the power to run local schools in perpetuity; this violates the tenet of locally elected representation and community input. According to Rosenberg, the RSD's attempt to indefinitely control the city's public schools "directly contravenes 92 years of state constitutional law." "The RSD has kidnapped local control," Rosenberg proclaimed to loud applause, "and local control of schools is the cornerstone of the constitution" (field notes, 2010).

In this way, state law has enabled ongoing experimentation on Black children and Black communities, disenfranchising parents and citizens in the name of school choice and innovation.

Private Management, Contracting, and Decision Making Over Public Schools—and the Marketization of Schoolchildren

Assisted by state law, charter operators seized public schools in New Orleans in the months following Hurricane Katrina. Take, for example, the formation of the Algiers Charter Schools Association (ACSA) in January 2006, which foreshadowed the RSD's perverse commitment to charter schools. On the west bank of the Mississippi River in Algiers ("across the river from the city"), there's high ground and schools were largely spared damage. Brian Reidlinger, who advised the Bring New Orleans Back Commission's education committee, headed the ACSA that abruptly took over 13 public schools. With similar precision, the state legislature virtually eliminated the central office. In turn, each school was given its own operating budget and ability to autonomously hire and fire teachers; some 400 veteran teachers were fired (Mirón, 2008). One veteran educator of more than 20 years who returned home to teach discovered her school had been taken over by a charter management organization without teacher or parent input; upon arrival, she was commanded to remove her belongings by a principal she'd never met (Louisiana Federation of Teachers, n.d.). Such conditions spurred the People's Hurricane Relief Fund to file a lawsuit challenging the legitimacy of the ACSA. Additionally, the class action suit charged the charter association with failing to enroll students who did not satisfy school requirements for admission (Mirón, 2008). Conflict over rightful control of the schools was intense and "the first public meeting of the newly created [ACSA] had to be guarded by armed National Guardsmen" (Cowen Institute, 2009, p. 10).

Examples of this abound. At the historic Frederick Douglass High School in the Upper 9th Ward, community members had real concerns about the school's future. Despite its rank as one of the lowest performing schools prior to 2005, Douglass was one of only a few remaining open-access high schools in the neighborhood. The school had many dedicated alumni and the support of the Frederick Douglass Community Coalition (2007), which sought to make the school the center of community life. In May 2008 the community organized a public meeting with RSD officials, who promised the community would have input regarding the school's future (field notes, 2008; Buras et al., 2010). Nonetheless, Douglass was closed and the building was annexed by KIPP charter school network, which needed space to accommodate a high school.

At the BESE hearing, the president of one high school alumni association articulated his opposition to the private seizure and management of public schools by charter operators and the so-called autonomy they had in excluding unwanted students. He used Douglass as an example, announcing: "Before the school year began, KIPP took over the whole school without including any students from Douglass. As a result, those students were scattered throughout the city and forced to attend other RSD schools." He went on to trouble such exclusionary practices:

Without an open door enrollment policy, after the cherry-picking, many students who were rejected from the charter schools would not have had the opportunity and right to an education. . . . We are afraid the countless number of children who do not fit into the scheme of the charter will walk the streets and a new generation of unemployed and uneducated youth will fill our streets with crime and violence. . . . Charters are not friendly to students presenting with special needs and the concern is that they get rejected. . . . [This] will further exacerbate problems for students with special needs, thus instituting discrimination. (field notes, 2010)

Not only did he highlight the thin line between autonomy and the liberty to discriminate—and the inequitable consequences for students when private operators mediate "risky" market transactions through processes of direct exclusion—he simultaneously criticized the actions of operators who dump particular students after acquiring state funds to serve them. In this case, he spoke of charter schools collecting and retaining Minimum Foundation Program (MFP) money (Louisiana Department of Education, 2009), which is distributed by the state on a per-pupil basis: "When students are removed from the charter schools after the October MFP, they are not accepted into another charter school, but are found on the doorsteps of [open-access, state-run] public schools. . . . And the money does not follow those students. It stays with the charter school" (field notes, 2010). Charter school operators, in other words, are in the business of cutting costs, minimizing risk, and maximizing income without regard for the well-being of children.

Importantly, schools are not simply managed by charter operators according to market imperatives. They are governed by boards exercising virtually unregulated authority over contracts for accounting services, food provision, transportation, and a host of other needs once met by the central office. The wasteful use of public resources remains to be calculated, as countless individual charter schools lack the economy of scale to secure essential services at reduced cost. Put another way, running schools as businesses generates business, while the real business of educating all students is forgotten. Another issue that merits attention is the possibility that MFP money, intended to support the instruction of students, is instead being used on lucrative contracts that provide fellow entrepreneurs and business allies with a share of the public education market. This, of course, diverts financial resources from children of color.

It should be mentioned that although Louisiana law disallows the granting of charters to for-profit management organizations, there is nothing in the law that prohibits *subcontracting* with for-profit management organizations. Here again, the marketization of children and schools can be quite extreme in its consequences. In the case of RSD charter Lafayette Academy, for instance, the governing board actually canceled its contract with the for-profit charter operator Mosaica. In the first year of its 5-year contract, Mosaica was paid $773,000. Nonetheless, according to Lafayette's board, it failed to provide copy machines, clean the school building, follow state curriculum standards, create education plans for students, organize transportation, secure school insurance, and establish a requested after-school program for students below grade level. Canceling the contract cost the board an additional $100,000 (Simon, 2007). Clearly, every penny of that money should have gone toward providing support and resources for students.

Aside from contracts, charter school boards govern major decisions on curriculum, faculty, and educational policy without any requirement to consult teachers, parents, or community members. New Leaders for New Schools, affiliated with the charter incubator New Schools for New Orleans, recruits and trains principals and charter school board members. It maintains a "board bank" including the names and resumes of interested parties and makes them available to schools seeking board members. The raced and classed character of the required qualifications says a great deal about the private nature of school management and governance (New Schools for New Orleans, 2010):

- Expertise in law, real estate, financial management, governance, marketing, fund raising, community organizing/outreach, education, or strategic planning
- Personal experience with entrepreneurship
- Willingness to leverage personal and professional networks on behalf of the school

It is safe to say that very few poor and working-class parents—most of whom in New Orleans are African American—command the social, economic, and political capital to participate on such a board. This, of course, implies a very serious question: Who is managing the schools of New Orleans? Who has a voice in their governance?

The plan formulated by Pastorek and Vallas for the future of RSD schools (2010)—the one at the center of the public hearing—reflects the state's ongoing disregard for democratic management and governance. On one hand, it states that "community input is essential" in determining the future governance of public schools. But there are deeper contradictions. The *vast majority* of RSD schools are charter schools. In the case of charter schools, the plan states that the school's *governing board* is to decide which district governs the school—the state-run RSD or local OPSB. Only state-run schools require a majority vote by staff and parents. This means that in most cases the central stakeholders—teachers and parents—will have no say whatsoever regarding whether a school remains in the RSD or rejoins OPSB. In short, the proposed process for making future governance decisions remains anti-democratic: Charter school boards will decide the fate of public schools in New Orleans. This is decidedly not "self-determination," to use Pastorek and Vallas's strategic term for site-based autonomy. It is another attempt to control public assets in the absence of community input and to shield the education market from "interference." It is autonomy without accountability.

A representative from the Louisiana Association of Public Charter Schools shared its view at the public hearing and began by querying, "So why are parents of 20,000 children [in New Orleans] choosing charter schools?" They provide "new opportunities," he explained, opportunities made possible "because of the autonomy and accountability that charters have in our state." He moved on to forthrightly deny the legitimacy of concerns over the power of charter school boards in privately steering public schools, claiming:

> There is no more local control than the immediate accountability that the parents of 20,000 students provide on a daily basis when they entrust us, charter schools, with their students. *When you talk to parents of 5-year-olds or a 5th-grader or a 9th-grader, they do not care what board governs their school.* They care about whether the school can deliver on the promise of individualized education and the promise of college readiness. Charter schools are doing this and we ask that you preserve their ability to deliver. (field notes, 2010, emphasis added)

Parents don't care about the board that governs their school? For the majority of parents, this clearly isn't the case—they care very much about who is making the decisions that affect their children. What's noteworthy is how the Louisiana Association of Public Charter Schools manages to frame private management as local control.

The move to dismiss grievances over lack of representation was passionately challenged by a community elder and veteran of New Orleans' civil rights movement, who also spoke at the hearing: "Let's keep this real, it's been twisted *all night long* 'cause the real issue here, brother—where that little man at?—I got you, Paul [Vallas]. Inalienable rights, inalienable rights, we have the vote! We didn't vote for him!" Drawing inspiration from past civil rights activists, she continued: "We went to jail. A lot of people died for us to *have the right to vote for who we want to represent us.* This governance mess is like this other real word: R-A-C-I-S-M. Vicious, it's malicious, and it's got to stop." Most poignantly, she addressed charter school parents whose "I need mine" discourse seemed disconnected from collective sacrifices and past struggles for representation and racial equity: "These two people [Pastorek and Vallas] don't have no right to control us as a people. We're the only group of people in America that was denied an education *by law.* . . . They're [charter school parents] too young to know this. That's why I forgive my babies back here talking crazy." It was no small irony that several hundred people were locked out of the public hearing, unable to participate and be heard. In closing, this elder warned education officials: "Can I tell you something? Don't do this like this no more. Because if I had really been in my right mind today, they would've had more people outside than in here. I'm from an era where we don't allow people to have meetings without us in the room" (field notes, 2010). The message? Although the neoliberal policy regime depends on privatized decision making, especially by White state and local reformers, it isn't color-blind and it certainly isn't democratic.

The Attack on Veteran Teachers
and Alternative Teacher Recruitment on the Cheap

The marketization of students isn't an isolated matter. Under the neoliberal policy regime veteran teachers have been subjected to market imperatives as well. For charter school operators, teachers constitute a form of "human capital." This perspective should cause pause, especially in light of the racial market's history. In this case, Black veteran teachers in New Orleans, who were unionized and entitled to various benefits (accrued sick leave, laddered pay, health insurance, retirement), were framed as deficient, disposable, a drain on limited public resources, and simply not worth the cost. In turn, the search for "more qualified" teachers—White, transient, and thus ultimately cheaper—acquired the air of legitimacy. This would have serious implications for the Black middle class of New Orleans, as a notable segment was constituted by veteran teachers.

In November 2005, the announcement went out: 7,500 New Orleans teachers and school employees were informed they'd be fired and lose health insurance on January 31, 2006 (Louisiana Federation of Teachers & American Federation of Teachers, 2007; United Teachers of New Orleans et al., 2007). At the time, BESE President Linda Johnson stated positively on congressional record that the state takeover "was the only way to . . . eliminate the collective bargaining agreement and leverage the opportunity to start anew" (Tisserand,

2007, para. 27). BESE member Chas Roemer, who chaired the aforementioned public hearing, affirmably said that "charter schools are now a threat to a jobs program called public education," a statement pivoting on the notion that existing teachers—Black teachers—are lazy, unproductive, and on the government dole (Sentell, 2009, para. 2). Paul Vallas has touted charter schools without unionized teachers, announcing: "I don't want the majority of my teaching staff to work for more than 10 years. The cost of sustaining those individuals [with healthcare and retirement] becomes so enormous" (Conway, 2010, para. 21).

Black veteran teachers were fired en masse without due process and without any regard for either their contributions as educators or their hard-won rights and entitlements. For decades they had taught in horrendously underfunded schools—a legacy of segregation and White flight—and had more than earned their pensions. New Orleans had one of the strongest Black teachers unions in the nation, United Teachers of New Orleans (UTNO), with a long history of struggle for equal pay for Black and White teachers, for adequate educational resources, and for ongoing professional development (Randels, 2010). When the New Orleans public school system was dissolved and reorganized as a mere shadow of itself, and the state-run RSD was installed, veteran teachers who had worked for 20 to 30 years effectively lost all protections and entitlements guaranteed by UTNO's collective bargaining agreement. That is to say, the agreement was nullified because the district with which it was negotiated no longer existed.

The city simultaneously became the site of one of the most comprehensive alternative teacher recruitment initiatives in the nation. TeachNOLA, a teacher recruitment project organized by the RSD and New Schools for New Orleans, assumed a "no experience necessary" posture for hiring (Robelen, 2007; United Teachers of New Orleans et al., 2007). Before 2005 only 10% of the city's teachers were in their first or second year of teaching; in 2008, 33% met that description (Nelson, 2010; United Teachers of New Orleans, 2010). In 2006–07, the year immediately following Hurricane Katrina, the bulk of teachers in both RSD schools and OPSB schools were veterans. As time proceeded, however, the assault became more organized and progressed. In 2007–08 and 2008–09, veteran teachers declined in percentage, especially in the RSD where their presence plummeted to 46% (Nelson, 2010). In his study on teacher quality and distribution in New Orleans, Nelson reports, "Both the RSD and many charters decided to hire new teachers enrolled in alternative certification [programs] and some teachers with no certification at all" (p. 11). He goes on to explain:

> The central issue, however, is that New Orleans' low-achieving poor and minority students attend schools with the least experienced teachers. In 2008–2009, in the

state-run RSD schools—the poorest, highest minority and lowest scoring in New Orleans . . . and the only schools required to admit any student at any time—virtually
half (49 percent) of teachers were in their first- and second-year. (p. 12)

The same goes for RSD charter schools, especially those that subcontracted with
school management organizations, which barely hired any veteran teachers. It
also should be mentioned that new teachers on temporary licenses have been
largely affiliated with Teach for America and teachNOLA and trained through
the New Teacher Project, the leading alternative teacher recruitment initiative
in the nation. Even more significant, while traditional schools under RSD and
OPSB had substantial portions of African American teachers (roughly 70%),
Nelson explains that "charter school governance is associated with a disproportionately white teacher population" (2010, p. 19). In both RSD and OPSB charter
schools, less than half of the teaching force was African American in 2009–10.
The reality is that 73% of public school teachers were African American in
2004–05—that is, before charter school reform was thrust on New Orleans. In
2009–10, only 56% were African American and 40% were White (Nelson, 2010,
pp. 18–19).

At the public hearing with BESE, one educator commented on the troubling
dismissal of veteran teachers, proclaiming:

I am here to address RSD instability. I'm an RSD teacher . . . I'm certified, I'm
highly qualified, and yet I've been surplused every year with all my other co-
workers and teachers across the whole district. Surplused *every* year, which
means I have to reapply, I have to get out resumes, phone calls, set up appoint-
ments, in order to be rehired. . . .

For students that no one wants to deal with, there's too much instability
among teachers, which also leads to instability for our students, *our* students.
There's instability that then goes into the community. We need stable communities. Stable schools will give us stable communities. I'm afraid that these
students will be lost in the shuffle. What will happen to them? Where will
they go? Our students [and teachers] need stability. Give our schools back to
OPSB. (field notes, 2010, italics indicate emphasis in original speech)

Indeed, veteran teachers have been systematically dismissed as charter
schools take over traditional public schools. During focus group interviews
I completed with veteran teachers, this was a universal concern. One veteran
teacher shared the following account regarding one of the RSD's "transformation" schools, where a newly chartered school was set to push out an existing

traditional school grade-by-grade: "Evidently, there's an unwritten memo that says, 'Anyone making over $50,000, don't hire them.' I have an excellent teaching record. I've been teaching for 30 years. And no one would hire me." This included the incoming charter school that made hiring promises to veteran teachers (group interview, 2009). Another veteran pondered the racial dynamics of New Orleans' neoliberal policy regime:

> It's all about the dollars. . . . Our rights as teachers have been trampled upon. . . . They are saying that they are revamping the schools or whatever. They get rid of everyone . . . and they rehire whoever they want to rehire. In many cases, they replace veteran teachers with first-, second-, and third-year teachers. (group interview, 2009)

Novice White teachers assume jobs that many evacuate within several years (see Heilig & Jez, 2010; Nelson, 2010) and don't demand laddered pay or health and retirement benefits. In addition, charter school operators reportedly threaten new teachers, instructing them not to speak with union organizers or to disclose information about their salaries (group interview, 2009). When new teachers depart, they in turn utilize the "capital" of this so-called urban experience to launch into graduate programs and other lucrative positions at the expense of largely Black veteran teachers and poor Black students.

All of this has cultural and racial implications for African American schoolchildren, who make up 95% of public school enrollment in New Orleans (Nelson, 2010). Black veteran teachers possess intimate knowledge of the city's history, its culture, and its communities. For example, in the case of indigenous musical traditions, which admittedly have been commercialized in the French Quarter but are also deeply tied to identity, resistance, and community building in Black neighborhoods, veteran teachers have mentored generations of students in the jazz tradition (Kennedy, 2005).

All the while, the rights and benefits of remaining teachers have been substantially undermined, if not eliminated (Southern Education Foundation, 2009; United Teachers of New Orleans, 2010). One teacher's experience illustrates the vacuum that's been created and the gross injustice that longtime teachers have confronted with respect to health insurance premiums and vesting. This teacher dedicated 35 years of her life to a New Orleans public high school and had plans to retire after her return in 2005, but not before she assisted with reopening schools and teaching for another year or two. At the end of 2006–07, she was informed: "You have 60 days to enroll in the state's benefit plan for retirees." Promptly driving to Baton Rouge to enroll, she learned that "Orleans Parish teachers are not eligible for the state retirement insurance." "You have to go through Orleans Parish to get your retirement insurance," she was told, "but just go there and everything will be fine." In Orleans she learned yet more: "We're sorry. Orleans Parish isn't responsible for you either. You're [now] retiring from a charter school so you can't get insurance from us either. Your charter school will have to help you." The charter indicated it didn't provide insurance for retirees. Echoing the concerns of many veteran educators, this teacher explains: "So I cannot retire until I die because I cannot get insurance," which was estimated at $1,400 per month (group interview, 2009). What's more, if veteran teachers are hired in RSD schools, including charters, they are treated as first-year teachers in terms of vesting; despite 20 or 30 years of teaching, they start all over in accumulating long-term health insurance benefits.

In the end, the accumulative desires and market-driven actions of charter school operators really constitute a form of state-sanctioned theft. The president of the Louisiana Federation of Teachers challenges this regime, proclaiming, "If [the] idea is to lower the wages for educators, to deprive them of benefits, then we are definitely going to oppose those kinds of initiatives" (Sentell, 2009, para. 16).

Use, Abuse, and Outright Manipulation of Standardized Testing

In order for the neoliberal policy regime to persist, it must be "effective" in producing results. Higher standardized test scores have been cast as the hallmark of school improvement. Pastorek and Vallas's (2010) plan for the future of RSD schools is premised on the *alleged* improved performance of charter schools. The plan asserts:

> Just as BESE made the determination to place schools in the RSD for the past five years, it must ensure that those schools choosing to return [to OPSB] are afforded the conditions [autonomy over programming, staffing, finance, and operations] . . . that provide support and oversight similar to their experiences in the RSD, which led to their improved performance. (p. 6)

It is more accurate to say that charter school "success" has been legislatively contrived through outright manipulation of standardized testing. The RSD has capriciously shifted its definition of academic "success" and "failure" since assuming control of public schools in Orleans Parish.

Recall that in November 2005, Act 35 redefined what counted as a failing school, raising the bar from a test score cutoff of 60 to just below the state average of 87.4. Under these terms, most of the public schools in New Orleans were designated as failing, taken over by the RSD, and ultimately chartered. In 2009 the standard shifted downward to 75. Despite the claim that the "vast majority of RSD schools are making steady progress in student academic performance," the plan itself contains a footnote that reads: "At SPS [School Performance Score] 60, approximately 66% of students are performing below grade level. At SPS 65, roughly 63% are below grade level; at SPS 75, roughly 54% are below grade level" (Pastorek & Vallas, 2010, p. 3). Perhaps most telling, by Act 35 standards (SPS 87.4), all but a handful of schools *continue to fail*; this includes state-run schools as well as charter schools in the RSD. This is evident upon reviewing the performance data provided in Pastorek and Vallas's own plan (attachment A of plan). When this is brought to light, the question arises: Is the educational market actually generating success? Clearly not, but it's been quite successful at privatizing public schools for profit and undermining the best interests of African American children.

The aforementioned president of a public high school alumni association, whose own alma mater was being threatened with closure and charter takeover, had the following to say at the public hearing about the contrivance of charter school "success":

> We stand in opposition of changing our school into a charter. The public was told the charter school was needed to take over failing schools. However, they forgot to tell the public that was a lie. Those entities who were granted charters for so-called failing schools only took over failing school buildings. The students who were attending the so-called failing schools were not the same students admitted when the school became a charter. (field notes, 2010)

This prompted loud applause. He continued: "Success is only based on a newer and smaller population of students, which is false reporting if the same population has not been measured" (field notes, 2010). What's more, some charters have strategically opted to open their doors without offering seats in tested grade levels. They begin a few years before or after the state LEAP (Louisiana Educational Assessment Program) test given in grades 4, 8, 10, and 11. Thus, one KIPP school began with kindergarten and 5th grade.

By combining new teachers and the lowest performing students in open-access, state-run RSD schools, which have become known as the "dumping ground" for students not admitted or retained by charter schools, the state effectively orchestrates the failure of traditional public schools; it is well known that less experienced teachers are generally less effective in producing higher student achievement (Wilson, 2009). The low performance of traditional schools is then used to legitimize their takeover and chartering by reformers who claim that "autonomy" will improve them. Meanwhile, the very same charter schools that claim success operate under both formal and informal selective admissions policies, accepting and retaining only the highest performing students (e.g., see Ferguson & Harper Royal, 2010).

A prime example of neoliberal reformers' disregard for improving school performance is Thurgood Marshall Middle School. Prior to August 2005, Marshall was one of the top public middle schools in New Orleans. Without Act 35, Marshall would never have qualified for takeover by the RSD. The school was only minimally damaged, but upon assumption by the RSD it remained closed from 2005 to 2007. During this time, millions were spent on renovation and the school was slated to reopen for the 2007–08 school year. The first day of school stunned the community.

> Parents brought their children to the newly renovated Marshall building only to find that two [RSD] charter schools . . . were in the building. The Marshall students were to be bused to modular buildings in the Lower Ninth Ward on the site of the damaged and abandoned Holy Cross Catholic High School. . . . There was no one from RSD to explain to parents and students why they were being moved or why their school was being occupied by two charter schools. The only explanation . . . received through the principal was that the charter schools' buildings were not ready. (Sanders, n.d., p. 2)

The conditions at Holy Cross were terrible and to make matters worse the principal was assigned a teaching staff by the RSD, with 100% first-year teachers who came from teachNOLA and Teach for America; within 2 months, 70% had quit. In May 2008 Vallas agreed that Marshall would return to its original site, but at the start of the next school year it was given access only to the third floor, while Pierre Capdau, a school in the Capital One–University of New Orleans charter network, continued to occupy the first and second floors. But that wasn't all. In March 2009, Marshall's principal met with Vallas and was informed that the school would be closed—not the school building, clearly, but the school community itself. Indeed:

> One would think that given [RSD's] mission to improve schools, it would at least make every effort to replicate the academic achievement that occurred at Marshall before [August 2005]. Instead, the RSD has made a very concerted effort to destroy the school and give the building to a charter operator, who has not demonstrated success. . . . [This state of affairs] calls into question the stated reason for the state takeover, allegedly to improve academic achievement. (Sanders, n.d., p. 5)

What, then, is the reason? One veteran teacher explains that the state takeover is ultimately about business, reflecting: "In charter schools, it's test scores and checkbooks. It's no longer people. . . . Now in the charter schools, it [the test score] is held over your head every breathing moment that you have to do this or we're not going to exist." Ultimately she warns that test scores and checkbooks are numbers, "not people," and "when you stop treating teachers and students like people, you have an ultimate breakdown in your education system" (group interview, 2009). Yet isn't this the tragedy and injustice of the racial market— schools don't treat Black teachers and students as people but instead treat them as material assets to be bartered for White financial gain.

Equally tragic, the discussion around test scores does not account for the narrow definition of what counts as "success" irrespective of the scores produced. That is, knowledge is presumed to be neutral rather than culturally situated and wedded to issues of identity and power (Buras, 2008). As one young spoken-word poet eloquently shared at the public hearing:

> I come here to talk about the death of a generation
> from the cradle to the grave
> and how the Recovery School District
> contributes to its causes and effects. . . .
>
> It's not the students failing in our schools,
> rather it's our schools failing our students.
> Anytime the RSD fails to make Black history studies
> a part of the school curriculum in order to instill Black pride.
> Y'all contributing to D-O-G: Death of a Generation.

CONCLUSION:
THE SACRIFICED BLACK SCHOOLCHILDREN

Long before the reforms of 2005 in New Orleans, critical race scholar Derrick Bell authored a counterstory entitled "The Chronicle of the Sacrificed Black Schoolchildren." In the tradition of critical race theory, counterstories are intended to illuminate the perspectives and experiences of communities of color and to shed light on the racial interests underlying majoritarian (i.e., White-washed) narratives and policies. In Bell's chronicle, which takes place during the era of school desegregation, Black students suddenly disappear on their way to school. The story unfolds:

At first, the white people, both in town and around the country, were generous in their support and sincere in the sympathy they extended to the black parents. It was sometime before anyone mentioned publicly what, early on, many had whispered privately: that while the loss was tragic, perhaps it was all for the best. (Bell, 2005, pp. 268–269)

While the White community welcomed the chance to avoid desegregation and took comfort in Black students' disappearance—this was all to Whites' benefit—a "new shock" suddenly emerged. Since more than 55% of the public school attendees had been Black and because state funding of schools was based on daily attendance, the school system now faced serious financial challenges. As a result, a substantial number of White teachers would have to be fired; bus drivers would be laid off; federal desegregation funds would be forfeited; and so forth. All of this would have dire consequences for Whites. These harms prompted government officials to allocate "a large sum [of money] to conduct a massive search for the missing black children" (p. 272). Evidently desegregation, although often discussed in terms of presumed benefits for Black children, ultimately hinged on the degree to which it benefitted Whites. Only when White interests converged with Black ones did the White community seek to find the missing Black children who were needed for their own financial benefit. Bell concludes, "In the monumental school desegregation struggle, the intended beneficiaries had been forgotten long before they were lost" (p. 272).

Is this not the case of charter school reform in New Orleans? The displacement and removal of Black communities from the city as a result of Hurricane Katrina were viewed in positive terms by many Whites in New Orleans. At the same time, however, monies associated with largely Black public schools in New Orleans would be lost. So would the necessary and exploitable Black labor force needed for New Orleans's profitable tourist-oriented economy. It seems it was more beneficial to foster the return of Black schoolchildren—at least a portion of them—and subject the schools to marketization and the control of White entrepreneurs. This would ensure federal and state funding of public schools while generating economic opportunities for new White teachers, charter school operators, RSD personnel, and a host of businesses needed to provide private services (food, transportation, etc.) to charter schools in a decentralized system no longer served by a central office.

As it turns out, under neoliberal reforms presumably intended to help Black schoolchildren in New Orleans, they had been forgotten long before they returned to their newly chartered schools. (See Buras, 2009, 2011b, forthcoming, and Buras et al., 2010, for a more thorough discussion of organized grassroots resistance to neoliberal educational reform in New Orleans.)

REFERENCES

Apple, M. W. (2006). *Educating the "right" way: Markets, standards, God, and inequality* (2nd ed.). New York: Routledge.

Apple, M. W., & Buras, K. L. (Eds.). (2006). *The subaltern speak: Curriculum, power, and educational struggles.* New York: Routledge.

Bell, D. (2005). The chronicle of the sacrificed black schoolchildren. In R. Delgado & J. Stefancic (Eds.), *The Derrick Bell reader* (pp. 268–272). New York: New York University Press.

Blassingame, J. W. (1973). *Black New Orleans, 1860–1880.* Chicago: University of Chicago Press.

Blassingame, J. W. (1977). *Slave testimony: Two centuries of letters, speeches, interviews, and autobiographies.* Baton Rouge: Louisiana State University.

Bring New Orleans Back Commission. (2006a, January 17). *Rebuilding and transforming: A plan for world-class public education in New Orleans.* New Orleans, LA: Author.

Bring New Orleans Back Commission. (2006b, January 17). *Report of the cultural committee.* New Orleans, LA: Author.

Buras, K. L. (2005). Katrina's early landfall: Exclusionary politics behind the restoration of New Orleans. *Z Magazine, 18*(12), 26–31.

Buras, K. L. (2007). Benign neglect? Drowning yellow buses, racism, and disinvestment in the city that Bush forgot. In K. Saltman (Ed.), *Schooling and the politics of disaster* (pp. 103–122). New York: Routledge.

Buras, K. L. (2008). *Rightist multiculturalism: Core lessons on neoconservative school reform.* New York: Routledge.

Buras, K. L. (2009). "We have to tell our story": Neo-Griots, racial resistance, and schooling in the other south. *Race, Ethnicity and Education, 12*(4), 427–453.

Buras, K. L. (2011a). Race, charter schools, and conscious capitalism: On the spatial politics of whiteness as property (and the unconscionable assault on black New Orleans). *Harvard Educational Review, 81*(2).

Buras, K. L. (2011b). "We're not going nowhere": Urban space, race, and the struggle for King Elementary School in New Orleans. Submitted to *Race, Ethnicity and Education.*

Buras, K. L. (forthcoming). *Charter schools, race, and southern urban space: Where the market meets grassroots resistance.* New York: Routledge.

Buras, K. L., Randels, J., Salaam, K. Y., & Students at the Center. (2010). *Pedagogy, policy, and the privatized city: Stories of dispossession and defiance from New Orleans.* New York: Teachers College Press.

Chang, C. (2010, August 26). $1.8 billion from FEMA for Hurricane Katrina school rebuilding is "worth the wait," Sen. Mary Landrieu says. Available at http://www.nola.com/katrina/index.ssf/2010/08/18_billion_from_fema_for_hurri.html

Clarke, J., & Newman, J. (1997). *The managerial state: Power, politics, and ideology in the remaking of social welfare.* London: Sage.

Conway, Z. (2010, April 8). Education "revolution" in New Orleans. *BBC News.* Available at http://news.bbc.co.uk/go/pr/fr/-/2/hi/americas/8608960.stm

Cowen Institute. (2009, November). *Creating a governing framework for public education in New Orleans: Charter school authorizers and charter school governance.* New Orleans, LA: Author.

Cowen Institute. (2010). *The state of public education in New Orleans: 2010 report.* New Orleans, LA: Author.

Crenshaw, K., Gotanda, N., Peller, G., & Thomas, K. (Eds.). (1995). *Critical race theory: The key writings that formed the movement.* New York: New Press.

Democrats for Education Reform. (2010, September 13). *Bursting the dam: Why the next 24 months are critical for education reform politics.* Washington, DC: Author.

Desdunes, R. L. (1973). *Our people and our history: Fifty Creole portraits* (D. O. McCants, Ed.). Baton Rouge: Louisiana State University Press. (Original work published 1911)

DeVore, D. E., & Logsdon, J. (1991). *Crescent City schools: Public education in New Orleans, 1841–1991.* Lafayette: Center for Louisiana Studies at the University of Southwestern Louisiana.

Du Bois, W. E. B. (1992). *Black reconstruction in America, 1860–1880.* New York: Free Press. (Original work published 1935)

Ferguson, B., & Harper Royal, K. (2010, April). *Fewer special education students in charter schools.* New Orleans, LA: Research on Reforms.

Frederick Douglass Community Coalition. (2007, June). Plans and principles for rebuilding community schools in New Orleans: Douglass Community Coalition model. In Students at the Center (Ed.), *Katrina and me* (pp. 191–197). New Orleans, LA: Students at the Center.

Gehman, M. (1994). *The free people of color: An introduction.* New Orleans, LA: Margaret Media.

Gramsci, A. (1971). *Selections from the prison notebooks* (Q. Hoare & G. Nowell Smith, Eds.). New York: International Publishers.

Hall, G. M. (1992). *Africans in colonial Louisiana: The development of Afro-Creole culture in the eighteenth century.* Baton Rouge: Louisiana State University Press.

Harvey, D. (2006). *Spaces of global capitalism: Towards a theory of uneven geographical development.* New York: Verso.

Heilig, J. V., & Jez, S. J. (2010). *Teach for America: A review of the evidence* [Policy brief]. Boulder, CO, & Tempe, AZ: Education and the Public Interest Center and Education Policy Research Unit. Available at http://epicpolicy.org/publication/teach-for-america

Hill, P. T. (Ed.). (2002). *Choice with equity.* Stanford, CA: Hoover Institution Press.

Hill, P., Campbell, C., Menefee-Libery, D., Dusseault, B., DeArmond, M., & Gross, B. (2009, October). *Portfolio school districts for big cities: An interim report.* Seattle, WA: Center on Reinventing Public Education.

Kelley, R. D. G. (1997). *Yo' mama's disfunktional! Fighting the culture wars in urban America.* Boston: Beacon Press.

Kennedy, A. (2005). *Chord changes on the chalkboard: How public school teachers shaped jazz and the music of New Orleans.* Lanham, MD: Scarecrow Press.

Louisiana Department of Education. (2009, December). *Minimum Foundation Program, 2009–2010 handbook.* Baton Rouge: Author.

Louisiana Federation of Teachers. (n.d.). *Imagine just for a moment.* Baton Rouge: Author.

Louisiana Federation of Teachers & American Federation of Teachers. (2007, January). *The chronology: Scenario of a nightmare.* Baton Rouge: Author.

Louisiana State Senate. (2009). *Louisiana Constitution of 1974.* Baton Rouge: Author. (Original work published 1974)

Mathews, J. (2009). *Work hard, be nice: How two inspired teachers created the most promising schools in America.* Chapel Hill, NC: Algonquin Books of Chapel Hill.

Maxwell, L. A. (2007, December 13). Foundations donate millions to help New Orleans schools' recovery. *Education Week.* Available at http://www.edweek.org/ew/articles/2007/12/13/16nola.h27.html?qs=Foundations+donate+millions+to+help+New+Orleans+schools+recovery

Mills, C. W. (1997). *The racial contract.* Ithaca, NY: Cornell University Press.

Mirón, L. (2008). The urban school crisis in New Orleans: Pre- and post-Katrina perspectives. *Journal of Education for Students Placed at Risk, 13*, 238–258.

Nelson, F. H. (2010, September). *Teacher quality and distribution in post-Katrina New Orleans* [Draft]. Washington, DC: American Federation of Teachers.

New Schools for New Orleans. (2010). Charter board member qualifications. New Orleans, LA: Author. Available at http://newschoolsforneworleans.org/serve_boardmember.php

Pastorek, P. G., & Vallas, P. (2010, September 14). *Conditioning for success: A process to transfer schools placed in the Recovery School District.* Baton Rouge: Louisiana Department of Education.

Pedroni, T. C. (2007). *Market movements: African American involvement in school voucher reform.* New York: Routledge.

Randels, J. (2010). Passing on a torch. In K. L. Buras, J. Randels, K. Y. Salaam, & Students at the Center (Eds.), *Pedagogy, policy, and the privatized city: Stories of dispossession and defiance from New Orleans* (pp. 101–103). New York: Teachers College Press.

Robelen, E. W. (2007, November 12). New teachers are New Orleans norm. *Education Week.* Available at http://www.edweek.org/ew/articles/2007/11/14/12nola-human.h27.html?qs=New+teachers+are+New+Orleans+norm

Roediger, D. (1991). *The wages of whiteness: Race and the making of the American working class.* New York: Verso.

Saltman, K. J. (2010). *The gift of education: Public education and venture philanthropy.* New York: Palgrave Macmillan.

Sanders, R. (n.d.). The Louisiana Recovery School District: The post-Katrina saga of Thurgood Marshall School. Available at www.researchonreforms.org

Scott, J. (2009). The politics of venture philanthropy in charter school policy and advocacy. *Educational Policy, 23*(1), 106–136.

Sentell, W. (2009, September 12). Charter schools praised: BESE member Chas Roemer calls them shape of future. *The Advocate*, p. 9A.

Simon, D. (2007, September 14). Charter school wins lawsuit against management company. Available at http://blog.nola.com/times-picayune/2007/09/charter_school_wins_lawsuit_ag.html

Souther, J. M. (2006). *New Orleans on parade: Tourism and the transformation of the Crescent City.* Baton Rouge: Louisiana State University Press.

Southern Education Foundation. (2009, November). *New Orleans schools four years after Katrina: A lingering federal responsibility.* Atlanta, GA: Author.

Sublette, N. (2008). *The world that made New Orleans: From Spanish silver to Congo Square.* Chicago: Lawrence Hill Books.

Taylor, E., Gillborn, D., & Ladson-Billings, G. (Eds.). (2009). *Foundations of critical race theory in education.* New York: Routledge.

Tisserand, M. (2007, August 23). The charter school flood. *The Nation.*

United Teachers of New Orleans. (2010, March). *The New Orleans model: Shortchanging poor and minority students by over-relying on new teachers* [Issue brief]. New Orleans, LA: Author.

United Teachers of New Orleans, Louisiana Federation of Teachers, & American Federation of Teachers. (2006, November). *"National model" or flawed approach? The post-Katrina New Orleans public schools.* New Orleans, LA: Authors.

United Teachers of New Orleans, Louisiana Federation of Teachers, & American Federation of Teachers. (2007, June). *No experience necessary: How the New Orleans school takeover experiment devalues experienced teachers.* New Orleans, LA: Authors.

Watkins, W. H. (2005). A Marxian and radical reconstructionist critique of American education: Searching out black voices. In W. H. Watkins (Ed.), *Black protest thought in education* (pp. 107–135). New York: Peter Lang.

Wilson, S. (Ed.). (2009, November). *Teacher quality* [Education policy white paper]. Washington, DC: National Academy of Education.

CHAPTER 9

Re-Imagining Public Education

William H. Watkins

Contrary to fairy tale telling, important contradictions in American society, and in the world, are not disappearing but rather are increasing. Concentrations of wealth have created an elite unlike the world has ever seen, even in feudal times. The gap between the educated and uneducated is pronounced and alarming. The ongoing battle for ideas and groceries rages on.

Corporate, privatizer, free-marketeer, "bankster" neoliberals are working feverishly to create a narrative for 21st-century education. Theirs is a story of competition, power, and profit. For them America must produce a layer of high-ly educated people to operate the new technocracy. Such people must be better educated than any in previous generations because the demands are greater. In their story, America is in a life or death battle to maintain its competitive edge in an increasingly competitive world where it is losing ground to emergent coun-tries. The bogeymen BRICS, that is, Brazil, Russia, India, and China, are closing in on us in the world horse race. For the corporatists, America's very survival is at stake. The corporate media and other means of information regularly pro-mote this story.

The corporatists are challenged at every turn as ordinary people understand the importance of accessible education for both individual and social advance-ment. The (organized) resistance to corporate education is expanding as people gain understanding of the corporate agenda.

Education is the enemy of ignorance and autocracy. Uneducated people cannot understand or participate in the governance of their own lives. People are social animals in a constant state of development and inquiry. Learning is as natural as eating. Education opens up the world of our mind. Knowledge is power and powerful. Knowledge is enabling. Knowledge is our vehicle to understand nature, ourselves, and others. Knowledge helps us put the jigsaw puzzle of life together. All actions begin with ideas. Ideas are powerful things. The pen is indeed mightier than the sword.

Another view of public education must be advanced in opposition to the "competition" model. That view must place people above profit and power. Notions of humanity and civil society must be elevated. Civil society is a major weapon in the quest for understanding, tolerance, and the equitable distribution of wealth and power. No society can endure where a small percentage of the population usurp and expropriate the substance of others. Authentic education is one of society's most valuable assets.

This book should not be received as a call to retreat to status quo ante. Returning to the old model, the pre-corporate "neighborhood" school, is not acceptable. Even prior to the triumph of neoliberalism, school governance, curriculum, and inequity were abhorrent. Among the most egregious were the models of funding, over-reliance on testing, the use of Fordist/Taylorist models, and the embrace of Perennialist curriculum theorizing.

By now all are familiar with the savage inequalities (Kozol, 1991) in school funding. Despite ongoing legal challenges and community protest, the property tax multiplier most often governs dollar allotments to schools. Affluent communities draw from large financial resources, providing higher teacher salaries, enhanced honors and compensatory programs, modern computer and language labs, state of the art athletic facilities, and a variety of enrichment programs. Despite decades of a carefully crafted assertion that we cannot throw money at problems, we all know money counts. An equitable system of funding public education must be high on any education agenda.

The testing movement, first embraced by behavioral psychologists around the time of World War I, has now become the tail that wags the dog. Bestowing life or death entitlement, the standardized test has become an instrument of social engineering. It is a killer of dreams for some and a ticket to the promised land for others. No civilized society should exclude and distribute people on the basis of tests.

Scientific management provided a boost to both industry and public schooling. Large numbers of products could be turned out with efficiency and economy. In the early 20th century, the assembly line model of schooling allowed millions of children to receive the necessary rudimentary education for the new industrial order. Modern technology now allows us to privilege quality over quantity. Research on small classrooms, advances in learning theory, and a host of electronic resources allow the opportunity to create a new classroom.

Finally, the Perennialist and Essentialist curricula, the master narrative, must be relegated to a museum for school knowledge. We now know that the world is larger than Europe, capitalism is not eternal, Columbus did not "discover" anything, and other music besides that composed by Beethoven and Mozart exists. The new curriculum must explore beyond the Western world. The histories of Kemet, the Aztecs, and the great Han peoples must be presented. American students need to be exposed to labor history, peace studies, alternative economic systems, and non-Christian religious beliefs.

The "common school" movement pointed us in the right direction. Education must be made available to all, free of charge. Our recommitment to public education must take into account society's vast resources now wasted on war and conquest.

Much work remains to be done in the realm of ideas and goals. Education is for the public good, not a feast for profiteers. The notion of education as a right must be reasserted. Every human being has a right to be informed and literate. Citizens of the 21st century require both technical skills for the digitized world and social knowledge for the sociopolitical world. The Universal Declaration of Human Rights adopted by the General Assembly of the United Nations on December 10, 1948, eloquently stated in Article 26:

> (1) Everyone has the right to education. Education shall be free, at least in the elementary and fundamental stages. Elementary education shall be compulsory. Technical and professional education shall be made generally available and higher education shall be equally accessible to all on the basis of merit.
>
> (2) Education shall be directed to the full development of the human personality and to the strengthening of respect for human rights and fundamental freedoms. It shall promote understanding, tolerance and friendship among all nations, racial or religious groups, and shall further the activities of the United Nations for the maintenance of peace.
>
> (3) Parents have a prior right to choose the kind of education that shall be given to their children.

Finally, our hearts cry as we hoped new and powerful forces for "change" would rescue us from the swamp. Instead, suffering people have been thrust into a competitive lottery called Race to the Top, better known as "Race to the Flop," where already-meager resources are dangled to the states that promise to link merit pay to test score increases. Et tu, Brute!!!

Just as our government has taught us in foreign policy, we the people can have no permanent friends or permanent interests—only permanent interests!!!

We are going to have to do this ourselves. We choose education no matter who is in the big house. We citizens, educators, and students demand a WORLD CLASS school in every neighborhood!!!

REFERENCES

Kozol, J. (1991). *Savage inequalities: Children in America's schools.* New York: Crown.
United Nations. (1948). *Universal declaration of human rights.* Available at http://www.un.org/en/documents/udhr/index.shtml

About the Editor
and the Contributors

William H. "Bill" Watkins, Ph.D., is Professor, College of Education, Department of Curriculum and Instruction, University of Illinois at Chicago. Bill is the author of *The White Architects of Black Education* (2001), lead editor/contributor to *Race and Education* (2001), and editor/contributor to *Black Protest Thought and Education* (2005). His numerous articles, chapters, essays, and reviews have appeared in scholarly journals, books, encyclopedias, and the popular press. He has served on numerous editorial boards and held leadership positions in professional organizations. His life's work is dedicated to equality, social justice, and peace.

Kristen L. Buras is an assistant professor of urban educational policy at Georgia State University. She is coauthor of *Pedagogy, Policy, and the Privatized City: Stories of Dispossession and Defiance from New Orleans* (2010), which received recognition for its outstanding contribution to the field from the Curriculum Studies Division of the American Educational Research Association (AERA). She is also the author of *Rightist Multiculturalism: Core Lessons on Neoconservative School Reform* (2008) and coeditor of *The Subaltern Speak: Curriculum, Power, and Educational Struggles* (2006). She has worked extensively with teachers, public schools, and grassroots organizations in New Orleans, where she was born and raised. She is cofounder and director of the Urban South Grassroots Research Collective for Public Education and was granted the Distinguished Scholar-Activist Award by Critical Educators for Social Justice of AERA. Her next book is entitled *Charter Schools, Race, and Southern Urban Space: Where the Market Meets Grassroots Resistance*.

Jack Gerson taught high school math at Oakland's Castlemont High School until his retirement in June 2010. He remains active in the Oakland Education Association, where he has served on the Executive Board, Bargaining Team, and as a delegate to the state council of the California Teachers Association. He was an antiwar and anti-draft activist in the 1960s, and remains active today in the fight against austerity and for a just society. Gerson has a B.S. in mathematics from Brooklyn College, an M.S. in mathematics from Stanford, and a Ph.D. in biostatistics from University of California, Berkeley.

Alfie Kohn is the author of 12 books on education, parenting, and human behavior, including *Punished by Rewards* (1993), *Beyond Discipline* (1996), *The Schools Our Children Deserve* (1999), *Unconditional Parenting* (2005), *The Homework Myth* (2006), and *Feel-Bad Education* (2011). He has written for most of the leading education periodicals and has been described by *Time* magazine as "perhaps the country's most outspoken critic of education's fixation on grades [and] test scores." Kohn speaks to educators, researchers, and parents across the country; he lives (actually) in the Boston area and (virtually) at www. alfiekohn.org.

Pauline Lipman is Professor of Educational Policy Studies at University of Illinois at Chicago. Her research focuses on race and class inequality in schools, globalization, and the political economy and politics of race in urban education. Her newest book is *The New Political Economy of Urban Education: Neoliberalism, Race, and the Right to the City*. She is a founder and active member of Teachers for Social Justice and is active in coalitions of teachers and community organizations challenging neoliberal education policies in Chicago.

Catherine A. Lugg is a professor of education in the Department of Theory, Policy and Administration, Graduate School of Education, at Rutgers, the State University of New Jersey. Her research interests include educational politics and history, and the influences that social movements and political ideology have on educational politics and policy. Her research has appeared in *Educational Policy, Educational Administration Quarterly, The Journal of School Leadership, The Journal of Educational Administration, School Leadership and Management, The Journal of Curriculum and Practice, The American Journal of Semiotics, Pennsylvania History,* and *Education and Urban Society.* She is also the author of two books, *For God & Country: Conservatism and American School Policy,* and *Kitsch: From Education to Public Policy.* Dr. Lugg also maintains the blog Thinking Queerly: Schools, Politics and Culture. In addition to her faculty position,

Dr. Lugg is currently the President of the Politics of Education Association, member of the Executive Committee for the University Council for Educational Administration, and serves as Treasurer for Rutgers AAUP/AFT.

Malila N. Robinson is a Ph.D. student in Educational Policy at The Graduate School of Education at Rutgers, the State University of New Jersey. She received a JD from Rutgers School of Law in 2002. Her research interests include educational law and policy and issues of equity. Her research has appeared in *Educational Policy, Journal of LGBT Youth,* and *Leadership and Policy in Schools.*

Kenneth Saltman is an associate professor of Social and Cultural Foundations in Education at DePaul University. His interests include the political economy and cultural politics of public school privatization. His work also explains how the privatization movement in education is part of the broader movement to undermine public democratic power and expand global corporate power.

Ann G. Winfield has a Ph.D. in Educational Research and Policy Analysis with a concentration in Curriculum Studies. An educational historian, Dr. Winfield's book, entitled *Eugenics and Education in America: Institutionalized Racism and the Implications of History, Ideology, and Memory* (2007) reflects her concern with the role of eugenic ideology in the establishment of our modern form of education as well as its manifestation in present educational policy. Dr. Winfield is an associate professor of Philosophical and Social Foundations of Education at Roger Williams University in Bristol, Rhode Island where, in addition to teaching both undergraduate and graduate Foundations of Education classes, she also teaches courses in Issues in Multicultural Education and Social Studies Methodology.

Index

Aasen, P., xiii, 131
Abbot Laboratories, 11
Abstinence-only education, 134–135
Accountability, 5
  connection with privatization, 87–90
  test-based, 82–87, 100, 104, 109–110, 145,
    151–153, 190
Accountability Express, 89
Achieve Inc., 73–74
Achievement gap, 67, 74, 98, 103–104, 120
Adequate yearly progress (AYP), 85
Adhockery (Ball), 34–35
Afghanistan, 18, 99, 101, 120
African Americans. *See* Blacks
Agrarianism, 9
Aha!, Inc., 156
Ahlstrom, S. E., 125, 127
Alabama, 132–133
Alger, Horatio, 28
Algiers Charter Schools Association (ACSA;
    Louisiana), 171–172
Allegretto, L., 11
Allen, George, 136
Alliance for the Separation of School and
    State, 93–94 n. 3
Allstate Insurance, 11
America Can Be Saved (Falwell), 130
American Breeders Association, 146
American Dream, 143
American Enterprise Institute, 59, 65
American Federation of Teachers (AFT), 97,
    102, 113–118, 120–121, 169, 176
American Telephone and Telegraph, 149
America's Choice (NCEE), 26
Anderson, J. D., 127, 144
Anderson, N., 112–113
Annenberg Foundation, 25–26
Apple, Michael W., ix–xiv, 29, 42, 77 n. 3,
    127, 129–131, 164–165

Applied Research Center, 21
Archer Daniels Midland, 11
Arendt, Hannah, 73
Aristotle, 148
Arizona, 88
Arkansas, 87
Arnove, R., 28
Aronowitz, Stanley, 72–73
Assessment, in public education, 28
Associated Press (AP), 71
Atanda, J. J., 131
Audit culture (Apple), xi
Authoritarianism, 15

Bacevich, A., 9, 18
Ball, Stephen J., 34–35, 131
Ballou, D., 105
Balmer, R., 127–128, 136
Baltimore, Maryland, 91
Banana Republic, 65
Barlow, Andrew L., 38
Barnes, Brenda C., 11
Bartlett, L., 130–131
Bath and Body Works, 65
Bauman, Zygmunt, 72
Bear Stearns, 99–100
Bell, Derrick, 183–184
Bell Curve, The (Herrnstein & Murray), 131
Bennett, L., 33–34, 39, 43, 44
Bennett, William, 84–87, 92
Berlin Conference (1885–1886), 16
Berliner, D. C., 80, 103, 106, 108, 143, 154
Bernanke, Ben, 99
Bernstein, J., 11
Biddle, B. J., 80
Biddle, D., 106, 108
Bill and Melinda Gates Foundation, 2, 10,
    25–26, 46, 55, 57, 59, 70–71, 76, 77 n. 2,
    109–110, 113, 117–118, 170

Bill of Rights, 8
Bilmes, Linda, 101
Black, E., 146
Black Alliance for Educational Options
    (BAEO), 131
BlackAmericaWeb.com, 23
Black bourgeoisie (Frazier), 22
Black Independent Schools, 48
Blacks. *See also* Protestant Right
  Civil Rights Movement, 22, 127–128,
      144–145, 175–176
  living in poverty, 11
  middle class, 21–23
  neoliberal urbanism in Chicago and,
      33–42
  wealth gap and, 10–12, 20–21
Blanchard, D. A., 128
Blanco, Kathleen, 169
Blassingame, J. W., 166, 167
Bloomberg, Michael, 102
Blueprint for Reform, 102, 112
Bobb, Robert, 117
Bobbitt, John Franklin, 151–152
Boeing, 11
Bonilla-Silva, E., 44
Boston College, 91–92
Boston Globe, 83
Bourdieu, P., xiii
Bowe, R., 131
Bowman, D. H., 94 n. 5
BP, 98
Bracey, Gerald, 80, 85, 103, 105, 114
Bradley Foundation, 131
Brandt, E., 134
Braun, Carol Moseley, 85
Brazil, 189
Brenner, N., 35, 46
BRICS (Brazil, Russia, China, India), 189
Brill, Steven, 112
Bring New Orleans Back Commission, 160,
    167, 169, 172
Broad, Eli, 4–5, 57, 59, 62–73, 102, 109–111,
    113, 115–117
Broad Foundation Benchmarking Project,
    116
Broad Foundation for Education, 25–26, 55,
    57, 58–77, 109–111, 116, 117, 119, 170
Broad Prize for Urban Education, 69–73

Broad Urban Superintendents' Academy, 66,
    111, 115, 117
Brookings Institution, 44
Brooks, David, 79–80
Brophy, P. C., 43
Brown, J., 42
Brown v. Board of Education of Topeka, 131,
    153–154, 156, 163–164
Buffenbarger, A., 120
Buffett, Warren, 10
Bullock, H., 21
Bullying, 91
Buras, Kristen L., xi, xiii, 6, 160–188, 162,
    164, 165, 167, 172, 183, 184
Bush, George W., 18, 21, 23, 57, 58, 77 n. 4,
    85–89, 98, 99, 102, 136
Bush Doctrine, 18
Business Roundtable (BRT), 56, 108, 113

Cable News Network (CNN), 23, 134
California, 5, 90, 104, 110–111, 115, 116, 134
California Teachers Association, 115, 116
Campbell, C., 165
Capdau, Pierre, 182
Capitalism
  emergence of speculative, 11–12, 24
  stages of, 9
Capital One–University of New Orleans, 182
Carlyle Group, 17
Carnegie Corporation, 26, 45, 56, 68, 77 n. 4
Carter, Jimmy, 101
Castlemont High School (East Oakland,
    California), 104
Catalyst Chicago, 44
Catholic schools, 89
Cattell, James, 151–152
Celimli, I., 34, 40–41
CELT Corp., 73–75
Center for Education Reform (Washington,
    D.C.), 89
Center for Reform of School Systems, 115
Center for Research on Education Outcomes,
    105
Central Falls High School (Rhode Island),
    112–113
Central Intelligence Agency (CIA), 17
Century Foundation, 118
Chaddock, G. R., 135

Chang, C., 170
Change
  consolidation of social power, 18–19
  impact of, 1
Charter schools, 39, 45–49, 56–57, 66, 70–71,
    81, 100, 105, 109–110, 131, 160–184
Charter Schools Growth Fund, 56–57
Chase, A., 151
Chase, Bob, 114, 115
Chase Manhattan Bank, 149
Chatters, L., 125
Chicago
  Chicago Public Schools (CPS), 4, 15, 17,
    33–35, 38–51, 91, 111–112, 116, 121,
    132, 170
  Chicago Teachers Union, 121
  Commercial Club of Chicago (CCC), 25,
    38–39, 46, 56
  Plan for Transformation, 33–34, 40–41,
    43–45
  Renaissance 2010 (Ren2010), 25, 33–35,
    38–51, 57, 132
  tax increment financing (TIF), 37, 51 n.
    2–3
Chicago Defender, 46
Chicago Tribune, 11
China, 26, 188
Cho, M. K., xiii, 131
Chou, V., 20
Christian Coalition, 129
Christianity, xi. *See also* Protestant Right
  Catholic schools, 89
Christie, H. K., 77 n. 2
Citizens of the 21st Century, 191
Civil Rights Movement, 22, 127–128, 144–
    145, 175–176
Clarke, J., 169
Clark University, 151–152
Clemetson, L., 135
Clinton, Bill, 94–95 n. 14
Clowes, G., 38–39
CNN.com, 23, 134
Cohen, Rick, 77 n. 2
Cold Spring Harbor research station, 150
Cold War, 127
Coleman Report, 103
Collective bargaining, 5
Colorado, 83–84, 116

Columbus, Christopher, 191
Commercial Club of Chicago (CCC), 25,
    38–39, 46, 56
Common school movement, 191
Computer chip, impact of, 1, 10
Conservative modernization (Apple), x, xi
Conservative restoration, 14, 154
Contract schools, 39
Conway, Z., 177
Cookson, P. W., 131
CORE, 121
Corporate reform, 2
  consolidation of corporate power, 18–19
  corporatization of humanity, 157–158
Council of Chief State School Officers
    (CCSSO), 87–88
Cowen Institute, 160, 172
Cremin, L. A., 148
Cremmenos, D., 50
Crenshaw, K., 165, 169
Critical race theory (CRT), 169–171,
    183–184
Critical social theory (CST), 2–3
C-SPAN, 29
Cultural deficit theories, 44
Culture of poverty, in Chicago, 43–45
Cypher, James, 17

Dale, Roger, 49
Daley, Richard M., 51 n. 2, 102
Daniels, Gregory, 135
Darling-Hammond, L., 143–144
Darwin, Charles, 146, 148
Data Partnership, 73–76
Davenport, Charles Benedict, 150–151
Davies, J. B., 10
Davis, J., 20
DeArmond, M., 165
Deficit approach to education, 156
Deficit-spending program, 99
Delaware, 119
Delhi, K., 81
Dell, Inc., 66
Demissie, F., 34
Democracy
  reduction to consumption practices, x
  Ren2010 (Chicago) and, 39
Democratic deficits (Smith), 36, 39

Democratic Party, 22–23, 58, 79–80, 84, 97, 101–102, 113, 118–122, 128–129, 135–136, 162
Democrats for Education Reform, 162
Denson, L. R., 43, 44
Denver Classroom Teachers Association, 116
Desdunes, R. L., 166
Detroit Public Schools, 117
Detwiler, F., 125
de Vise, D., 134
DeVore, D. E., 164
Dewey, John, 72
Diamond, S., 125, 128–129, 134, 135
Dionne, E. J., 136
Displacement, in Chicago, 24, 36–38, 40, 42, 43–45
Dixiecrats, 22
Dobbs, M., 88
Dougherty, K., 131
Douglas, K. B., 125, 134–135
Douglass, Frederick, 22
Dowd, D., 17
Driscoll, David, 83
Du Bois, W. E. B., 166
Dumke, M., 51 n. 2
Duncan, Arne, 45, 98, 100, 102, 111–113, 116, 119–121, 132, 136, 145
Dussault, B., 165

Educational Management Organizations (EMOs), 46, 56–57
Educational Policy, 65
Education Leaders Council (ELC), 87–88
Education Trust, 115
Education Week, 105
Eli and Edythe Broad Foundation, 25–26, 55, 57, 58–77, 109–111, 116, 117, 119, 170
Emergency Banking Act, 99
Emery, K., 108, 114
Engle v. Vitale, 132
English, Fenwick W., 67–69
Entrepreneurial university, 37–38
Essentialist curricula, 191
Ethnic cleansing, 24
Eugenical News, 151
Eugenics, 6, 143–158
    historic foundations of, 146–148
    nature of, 146

school reform and, 144–146, 153–156
Social Darwinism and, 143–144, 148–151
testing and, 145, 151–153
Eugenics Record Office, 150
European Union (EU), 18
Evans, D., 76
ExxonMobil Foundation, 56

Failing schools, 107–108, 155–156, 169–171, 181
Fainstein, S., 36, 42
FairTest, 85
Falwell, Jerry, 130
"Fathers of Curriculum," 147, 151–152
Federal Deposit Insurance Corporation (FDIC), 99
Federal Reserve Bank, 99–101
FedEx, 65
Feldman, Sandra, 114, 115
Ferguson, B., 182
Financial speculation, 12–13
Finn, Chester, 59, 65, 84–87, 92, 115
Fisher Foundation, 57, 65, 70–71, 170
Fletcher, M., 112–113
Flexible production, 13–14
Florida, 71, 91, 117
Foner, E., x
Forbes, 11
Ford, B., 46
Ford, Henry, 149
Ford Foundation, 26, 55
Fordham Foundation, 56, 59, 88
Fordism, 13, 190
Fowler, F. C., 130
France, 89
Fraser, J., 126, 127, 137
Frazier, E. F., 22
Frederick Douglass Community Coalition, 172
Frederick Douglass High School (New Orleans), 172
Fredrick, M., 130–131
Freeman, J., 79–80
Fuentes, A., 94 n. 11
Fukuyama, Francis, 28–29
Fuller, B., 90
Futernik, K., 106

Gabbard, D., 61
Gabor, A., 105
Gabriel, T., 118
Gallo, Frances, 112–113
Galton, Francis, 146
Gandin, L. A., xiii, 131
Gannett Foundation, 26
Gap, 65
Gates, Bill, 2, 4–5, 10, 112
Gates Foundation, 2, 10, 25–26, 46, 55, 57,
    59, 70–71, 76, 77 n. 2, 109–110, 113,
    117–118, 170
Gatewood, W., 22
Gatto, John Taylor, 81–82, 93–94 n. 3
Gehman, M., 166
Geithner, Timothy, 99
General Electric, 62
Gentrification, 24, 36–38, 40, 42, 57
Georgia, 65
Gersh, D. A., 151, 152
Gerson, Jack, 5, 97–124
Gewirtz, S., 131
GI Bill, 88–89
Giddens, Anthony, 15
Gillborn, D., xi, 165
Gingrich, Newt, 112
Giroux, Henry A., 61–62, 73, 77 n. 3, 132,
    136–137
Giroux, Susan Searls, 62
Glass-Steagall Act, 99–100
Globalization
    defining as social architecture, 14
    techno-globalization, 10–14
Goddard, Herbert Henry, 151, 152
Goldman Sachs, 15
Gorbachev, Mikhail, 14
Gore, Al, 129
Gorski, P., 156
Gossett, T. F., 152
Gotanda, N., 165, 169
Gould, S. J., 143, 155
Gramsci, A., 35, 42–43, 47, 164
Granholm, Jennifer, 102
Grant, Madison, 148–149
Great Britain, 49, 81, 93 n. 2
Great Depression, 122, 149–150
Great Recession, 1, 62–64, 98–99
Green, J. C., 125, 128

Greenlee, A., 39, 41
Greenspan, Alan, 62
Gross, B., 165
Grossberg, Lawrence, 61–62
Gulbransen, T., 130–131
Gutstein, E., 42

Haas School of Business, 65
Hacker, Jacob, 101, 120
Hackworth, J., 36–37, 42
Haines, N., 34, 41, 42
Haiti, 18
Hall, G. M., 167–168
Hall, G. Stanley, 151–152
Hall, S., 130
Haller, M., 143, 151
Halliburton, 17
Halpin, D., 131
Hamilton, L., 105
Handy, R. T., 127
Haney, Walt, 91–92, 94–95 n. 13–14
Hanushek, Eric, 105–107
Hargrove, T., 90
Harper Royal, K., 182
Harper's, 93–94 n. 3
Harvey, David, 14, 35–37, 55, 62, 77 n. 1, 98,
    99, 154, 164–165, 169
Hasian, M. A., Jr., 143
Hassett, Wendy, 116
Hayes, Tracy, 46
Haymes, S. N., 45
Head Start, 17
Heilig, J. V., 179
Henig, J. R., 131
Herbert, Bob, 101
Heredity in Relation to Eugenics (Davenport),
    150–151
Heritage Foundation, 25–26, 56, 70, 89–90
Herrnstein, R., 131
Hess, Frederick, 59, 65, 77 n. 2
Heubert, J. P., 91
Hickok, Eugene W., 87–88
Higgins, S., 116
High culture, 148–149
High-stakes testing, 82–87, 100, 109–110
Hill, P. T., 165
Hirschl, T. A., 20
Hispanic Americans. *See* Latinos

Holme, J. J., 48, 131
Holy Cross Catholic High School (New Orleans), 182
Homeland Security Act, 100
Home Owners' Loan Corporation, 99
Hoogvelt, A. M. M., 13, 14
Hoover Institution, 56, 59
HOPE VI public housing redevelopment plan, 33–34, 43–44
Hopson, R. E., 125, 134–135
Howard, D., 128, 130
Howard, J., 130
Hudson, M., 100
Hudspeth, N., 39, 41, 44
Humanitarianism, 15
Hurricane Katrina, 6, 70–71, 169, 171–172, 177, 184
Hursh, D., 131, 132
Hurst, M., 71
Hutson, W., 46

Ideological racism, 38
Illinois. *See also* Chicago
Illinois Institute of Technology, 38
Illinois Network of Charter Schools, 46
Imbroscio, D., 44
India, 26, 188
Individuality, 28
Industrialization, 9, 10, 13–14, 20, 24
Institute for Assets and Social Policy, 23
International Monetary Fund (IMF), 14
Iraq, 17, 18, 89, 99, 101
Iron triangle of milex (Cypher), 17
ISLLC/ELCC standards, 67–68
Iverson, T., 143, 157

Jackson, Jesse, 134–135
Jacobson, L., 90
Jeffords, James, 85, 94 n. 6
Jez, S. J., 179
Johanek, M., 131
John Paul II, Pope, 14
Johnson, Linda, 176–177
Johnson, S. W., 94 n. 6
Johnson, Wayne, 115, 116
Johnston, R. C., 88
Joint Center for Political and Economic Studies (JCPES), 23

Jones, B. D., 90
Jones, M. G., 90
Joravsky, B., 51 n. 2
Jordan, J., 112–113
J.P. Morgan, 149
Juvenile justice, 91

K12, 87
Kahlenberg, Richard D., 43, 45, 118
Kaplan, 87
Karp, Stan, 85, 88
Katz, Bruce, 44
Katz, Michael B., 39, 44
Katzir, Dan, 66, 116
Keegan, Lisa Graham, 88
Kelley, Robin D. G., 166
Kelly, Andrew, 65
Kennedy, A., 179
Kennedy, Ted, 102
Kenwood Oakland Community Organization, 35, 40
Kerr, Barbara, 116
Kerry, John, 23, 129
Kevles, D. J., 146, 150
Keynesian welfare state, 36–37, 97–99, 101, 154
Kilbert, Darryl, 162
King, Martin Luther, Jr., 20–21
KIPP, 60, 65–66, 172–173, 181
Klein, Joel, 112, 116
Klein, N., 136–137
Klonsky, Michael, 77
Klonsky, Susan, 77, 77 n. 2
Kodak Foundation, 26
Kohl, H., 155
Kohn, Alfie, 5, 79–96, 82, 85, 143, 145, 155, 156
Kovacs, Philip, 77 n. 2
Kozol, J., 131, 156, 190
Kraft Foods, 11
Krashen, Stephen, 112
Kristof, Nicholas, 112
Kronholz, J., 87
Kuhl, S., 148
Ku Klux Klan (KKK), 127, 135

Lacy, K. R., 22
Ladson-Billings, G., 165

Lafayette Academy, 174
Lanchester, J., 98
Landrieu, Mary, 162
Landry, B., 22
Larson, C., 128
Latinos
    browning of America, 23–24
    middle class, 22
    neoliberal urbanism in Chicago and, 33–51
Le, V., 105
LEAP (Louisiana Educational Assessment
    Program), 181
Lee v. Weisman, 133
Lehman Brothers, 99–100
Lenin, V. I., 9
Leonardo, Z., xi, 3
Lewis, J., 20
Leys, C., xi
Liberation (Fraser), 137
Lincoln, C. E., 129
Linn, R. L., 85
Lipman, Pauline, x, xi, 4, 14, 33–54, 34, 35,
    36, 39–43, 47–48, 131, 132, 144, 145,
    153–154, 157
Lipsitz, G., 38
Local School Councils (LSCs), 39, 49, 50
Lockwood, J., 105
Logsdon, J., 164
Lopez, A., 48, 131
Louisiana, 160–184
Louisiana Association of Public Charter
    Schools, 175
Louisiana Board of Elementary and
    Secondary Education (BESE), 160, 162–
    163, 170–172, 176–178, 180
Louisiana Department of Education, 173
Louisiana Federation of Teachers, 169, 172,
    176, 180
Louisiana State Senate, 171
Low-performing schools, 107–108, 155–156,
    169–171, 181
Ludmerer, K. M., 151
Lugg, Catherine A., 5–6, 125–142, 127–128,
    130–132, 136

MacArthur Foundation, 26, 40
Macedo, Donaldo, 75
Magdoff, H., 9

Magnet schools, 45, 131
Maiers, S., 120
Males, Mike, 61–62
Mamiya, L. H., 129
Marginalization, xiii
Marketization, xii, 1, 4, 34
    Renaissance 2010 (Ren2010; Chicago), 25,
        33–35, 38–51, 57, 132
    of schools in New Orleans, 171–176
    vouchers in, 84, 88, 130–132
Marx, Karl, 20
Maryland, 91
Massachusetts, 83
Mathews, J., 168
Maxwell, L. A., 66, 170
McAdams, Don, 115
McCaffrey, D., 105
McCain, John, 135
McDonald, T., 131
McDonald's, 11
McDonogh 35 High School (New Orleans),
    160, 164, 168
McGraw, Onalee, 126
McGraw-Hill, 155
McGuire, William W., 11
McKenna, Andrew J., 38
McKenzie, Jamie, 85, 94 n. 6
McNerney, W. James, Jr., 11
Measurement of Intelligence, The (Terman),
    152–153
Measurement of Intelligence, The (Thorndike),
    147
Mendel, Gregor, 150
Menefee-Libery, D., 165
Merit pay, 105, 110
Michigan, 64, 117
Middle class, xi
    Black, 21–23
Midsouth Plan (Chicago), 40–41
Miles Davis Elementary School (Chicago),
    46–47
Military-industrial complex, 16–18, 61–62,
    99
Miller, D., 34, 40–41
Miller, George, 102
Mills, C. W., 164
Milton and Rose Friedman Foundation,
    83–84

Minimum Foundation Program (MFP), 173
Mirón, L., 172
Mishel, L., 11
Mobilizing Conference to Save Public Education, 121
Modernization theory, 16
Molnar, A., 131
Montessori schools, 40
Moral Majority Report, 126
Mosaica, 174
MPR Associates, Inc., 71
Murillo, E., 130–131
Murphy, A., 34, 40–41
Murray, C., 131

Nader, Ralph, 23
NAEP, 91–92
National Association of Evangelicals, 136
National Center for Educational Accountability, 75–76
National Center on Performance Initiatives (Vanderbilt University), 105
National Commission on Education and the Economy (NCEE), 25–28
National Education Association (NEA), 94 n. 9, 97, 102, 111, 113–116, 118–121
National Priorities Project, 17
Nation at Risk, A, 102–103, 108, 154
Navetta, Jean-Marie, 134
Nayak, R. D., 34, 40–41
NCATE/National Policy Board for Educational Administration, 67–68
NCEE (New Commission on the Skills of the American Workforce), 26–28
Neill, Monty, 85
Nelson, F. H., 177–179
Neoconservatism, x–xi, xii–xiii
Neoliberalism, x, xii, xiii, 1, 4, 5, 77 n. 1
  agenda of, 98–100
  corporate intrusion in public schools, 25–28
  corporate war against public education, 108
  crisis in education and, 102–108
  defined, 98
  economic prosperity and, 22–23
  in economic restructuring process, 14–16

impact of choice in education markets, 164–165, 168–183
  in neoliberal urbanism, 35–42
  Protestant Right and, 128
  and teachers' unions, 113–122
  in venture philanthropy, 58–59, 62–69
Neoliberal renaissance, 130–131
Neuman, Susan, 85
New Commission on the Skills of the American Workforce (NCEE), 26–28
New Deal, 22
New Deal Agency, 99
New Leaders for New Schools (NLNS), 60, 66, 174
Newman, J., 169
New Orleans Black Arts Movement, 167–168
New Orleans Public Schools, xiii, 6, 70–71, 160–184
New Schools Expo (Chicago, 2008), 46
New Schools for New Orleans (NSNO), 170, 174, 177
New Schools Venture Fund, 56–57
Newsday, 83
New social order, 4, 7–30
  corporate role in, 18–19, 25–28
  costs of, 17
  militarism in, 16–18
  neoliberalism in restructuring, 14–16
  overview of transition to, 8–9
  plutocracy in, 29–30
  political economy in, 7–8, 20–25, 29
  race in, 20–25
  techno-globalization in, 10–14
  wealth gap in, 19–21
New Teacher Project, 106–107, 111, 178
New Visions for Public Schools (New York), 57
New York City schools, 57, 112, 115–117
New York state, 83, 115
New York Times, 79–80, 118, 147
Ng, J., 44
NLNS (New Leaders New Schools), 60, 66, 174
No Child Left Behind (NCLB), ix, 5, 47–48, 61, 73–74, 84–93, 94 n. 9, 94 n. 10, 94–95 n. 14, 100, 102, 108–109, 112–114, 118, 145–146
NoChildLeft.com, 85

Nolan, B., 135
North Carolina, 91–92
Novak, J. R., 90

Oakland Unified School District (OUSD), 5,
    104, 110–111
Obama, Barack, 57, 58, 98–100, 102, 111–
    113, 119–120, 129, 132, 135–137, 145
Ohanian, S., 108, 114
Ohio, 65
Ohio Principals Leadership Academy, 65
Oldfield, D. M., 125
Old Navy, 65
Oliver, A., xiii, 131
Olson, L., 75
Olszewski, L., 40
On the Origin of Species (Darwin), 148
Ordover, Nancy, 157
Orleans Parish School Board (OPSB),
    160–184
Others, xi
Ottoman Empire, 16
Owens, Bill, 83–84

Paige, Rod, 88–89, 94 n. 8, 94 n. 9, 115
Panoptic model of surveillance (Kohl), 155
Pappano, L., 94 n. 10
Parents for School Choice, 46, 48–50
Passing of the Great Race, The (Grant),
    148–149
Pastorek, Paul G., 162, 171, 174–176,
    180–181
PATCO, 101
Patillo-McCoy, M., 22
Patriot Act, 8
Paul, D. B., 150
Paulsen, Pat, 99
Pay-for-performance, 105, 110, 116, 117
Payne, Ruby, 44, 156
Pear, R., 94 n. 9
Peck, J., 35–36
Pedagogy, Policy, and the Privatized City
    (Buras et al.), xiii
Pedroni, T. C., 35, 47, 129–131, 164
Peller, G., 165, 169
Pennsylvania, 87–88
People for the American Way, 87, 94 n. 7
People's Hurricane Relief Fund, 172

Pepper, M., 105
Perennialist curricula, 190–191
Permanent war (Bacevich), 9
Person, A., 35, 40
Pew Forum on Religion and Public Life, 125,
    128–129, 133, 135, 136
Pew Foundation, 26
Pew Research Center Publications, 23, 129
Peyser, James, 83–84
PFLAG (Parents and Friends of Lesbians and
    Gays), 134
Phillips, K., 128
Pickens, D., 148
Pierson, Paul, 101, 120
Pinzur, M., 71
Pioneer Institute, 83
Plan for Transformation (PFT; Chicago),
    33–34, 40–41, 43–45
Plato, 148
Poland, Scott, 94 n. 12
Political economy, 3
    changes in, 7–8
    defined, 29
    multidisciplinary approach to, 35
    in new social order, 7–8, 20–25, 29
    of race, 20–25
    study of, 29
Politics of exclusion, 15
Popkin, S. J., 43
Poverty
    children living in, xiii, 10–12
    impact on student achievement, 103–104,
        106, 110
    as social pathology, 44–45
Powell, Colin, 22–23
Power, S., 131
Prayer, in schools, 132–133
Presley, Elvis, 5
Princeton Review Inc., 87
Privatization, ix, xii, 1, 4–5, 5, 79–95. *See also*
    School choice
    collateral damage from, 90–92
    connection with accountability, 87–90
    expanding wealth gap, 19–20
    and "freedom" from public education,
        82–84
    in globalization process, 14
    in neoliberal urbanism, 35–38

No Child Left Behind (NCLB) and, 84–93
in venture philanthropy, 56–57, 73–74
ProComp, 116
Progressive educational policy, 47, 72–73, 116
Protestant Right, 5–6, 23, 125–138
Black Church in, 125–129, 134–137
evolution of, 126–129
same-sex marriage and, 129, 134–135
school vouchers and, 130–132
vocal school prayers, 132–133
White Evangelical tradition, 128–129, 134–137

Race, 6
in defining religious identity, 128
political economy of, 20–25
wealth gap based on, 10–12, 20–21
Race to the Top (RTTT), 57, 100, 102, 112, 119–120, 137–138, 145–146, 191
Raffel, J. A., 41, 43, 44
Randels, J., xiii, 162, 177
Ravitch, D., 109–110, 145
Reagan, Ronald, 14, 101, 108, 154
Reconstruction, 22, 127, 152
Recovery School District (RSD; New Orleans), 160–184
Redd, C. K., 83
Reed, Ralph, 128
Rees, Nina Shokraii, 89
Regnerus, M. D., 125
Reidlinger, Brian, 172
Religious Right. *See* Protestant Right
Renaissance 2010 (Ren2010; Chicago), 25, 33–35, 38–51, 57, 132
Renaissance Schools Fund, 46
Republican Party, 22–23, 79–80, 83–84, 97, 101–102, 113, 125–126, 128–129, 134–135
Reyes, Augustina, 91, 94 n. 11
Rhee, Michelle, 112, 117
Rhode Island, 112–113
Rice, Condoleezza, 22–23
Rimer, S., 91
Riordan, Richard, 102
Rivilla, A. T., 131
Robbins, C. G., 61
Robelen, E. W., 86, 177

Robertson, Pat, 129, 132
Robertson, S., 100
Robinson, C., 128–129, 133, 135, 136
Robinson, Malila N., 5–6, 125–142, 128, 130, 132, 136
Rochester Federation of Teachers, 115
Rockefeller Foundation, 26, 55, 56
Roediger, D., 166
Roemer, Buddy, 162
Roemer, Chas, 162, 177
Roll back neoliberalism, 36
Roll out neoliberalism, 36
Roosevelt, Franklin D., 22
Rosenberg, Harry, 171
Rosenfeld, Irene, 11
Rosin, H., 125
Rothstein, R., 80, 103–104
Ruiz, Paul, 115
Rury, J. L., 44, 149, 153–154
Russia, 189

Sabbath schools, 127
Sack, J. L., 88
Sadovi, C., 40
Salaam, Kalamu ya, 162, 167
Saltman, Kenneth J., 4, 55–78, 61, 70, 73, 77 n. 3, 132, 136–137, 170
Samaritan Project, 129, 136
Same-sex marriage, 129, 134–135
Sanders, R., 182
Sandstrom, S., 10
Santa Fe Independent School District v. Doe, 133
Sara Lee, 11
Sassen, S., 36
Schemo, D. J., 94–95 n. 14
Schlafly, Phyllis, 93–94 n. 3, 134
Scholastic Administrator, 116
School choice
charter schools, 39, 45–49, 56–57, 66, 70–71, 81, 100, 105, 109–110, 131, 160–184
magnet schools, 45, 131
parent organizations, 46, 48–49
vouchers, 84, 88, 130–132
School Choice Advocate, 83–84
School District of Abington v. Schempp, 132–133

School Information Partnership, 73–74
School reform, 2
    eugenic ideology in, 144–146, 153–156
    failing schools and, 107–108, 155–156,
        169–171, 181
    nature of, 80–82
    venture philanthropy and, 69–73
Schoolworks, 71–72
Scientific management, 190
Scientific pedagogy, 151–152
Scientific racism, 6
Scott, Janelle T., 48, 77 n. 2, 131, 170
Selden, S., 148, 150–151, 154–155
Sentell, W., 177, 180
Shabazz, Betty, 48–49
Shakespeare, W., 127
Shanker, Albert, 116
Shannon, P., 82
Sharpton, Al, 112
Shirley, Caroline Roemer, 162
Shorrocks, A., 10
Shupe, A., 125
SIECUS/Planned Parenthood, 134
Sikkink, D., 125
Simon, D., 174
Site-based decision making (SBDM), 114
Skinner, James A., 11
Small Schools (Scott & Klonsky), 77 n. 2
Smith, BetsAnn, 60, 64
Smith, C., 125
Smith, D. A., 39, 41
Smith, J. L., 33–34, 37, 39, 41, 43
Smith, Neil, 36, 42
Smith, R. N., 43
Social Darwinism, xii, 28, 143–144, 148–151
Social engineering, 24
Social promotion, 91–92
Soler, Mark, 94 n. 11
Sostre, L., 131
Souther, J. M., 167
Southern Education Foundation, 179
Southwest Airlines, 65, 66
Soviet Union/Eastern Block, 18, 189
Spanish-American War (1898), 16
Spatial fix (Harvey), 36–37
Spellings, Margaret, 72, 98
Spencer, H., 28

Spiro, J. P., 146, 150
Spring, J., 29
Springer, M., 105
SPS (School Performance Score), 181
Stacey, W. A., 125
Stack, M., 20
Standard Oil, 149
Standard & Poor's, 73–76
Standards movement, 5, 28, 91–92, 104
Stanford University, 105–107
Star Wars system, 17
Stecher, B., 105
Sternberg, J., 138 n. 1
Stiglitz, Joseph, 62, 101
Structural racism, 38
Students at the Center, 162
Sublette, N., 167
Sung, Y.-K., xiii, 131
Survivor (TV program), 72
Sweeney, S., 43, 44
Sykes-Picot Agreement (1916), 16
Sylvan Learning Systems, 87
Symbolic violence (Bourdieu), xiii

Takaki, R., 28–29
Tax increment financing (TIF), 37, 51 n. 2–3
Taylor, E., 165
Taylor, R., 125
Teachers
    alternative sources, 61, 71, 106–107, 111,
        176–180, 182
    attack on veteran, 176–180
    firing low-performing, 105–107
    important role of, xiii
    merit pay and, 105, 110, 116, 117
    unions of, xii, 5, 113–122, 169, 176, 177,
        179
Teachers College Press, xiii
Teach for America, 71, 106–107, 111, 178,
    182
teachNOLA, 177, 178, 182
Tea Party activists, 157
Technofix (Ordover), 157
Techno-globalization, 10–14
    economic prosperity and, 22–23
    wealth gap in, 10–12
Tennessee, 119

Terman, L., 152–153
Testing
  abuse and manipulation of, 180–183
  accountability and, 82–87, 100, 104, 109–110, 145, 151–153, 190
Texas, 88, 91–92
Thatcher, Margaret, 14, 154
Theodore, N., 35, 46
Thomas, Clarence, 22–23
Thomas, K., 165, 169
Thomas B. Fordham Foundation, 56, 59, 88
Thorndike, Edward L., 28, 147, 151–152
Thornton, M., 125
Thurgood Marshall Middle School (New Orleans), 182
Tickell, A., 35–36
TINA (There Is No Alternative to the Market) thesis, 58
Tisch, Meryl, 83
Tisserand, M., 176–177
Title I schools, 87
Tomlin, Lily, 80
Tomlinson, R., 76
Tough Choices or Tough Times (NCEE), 26–27
Troops to Teachers, 61
Trump, Donald, 62
Turner, B., 34, 40–41

Underclass theory (Wilson), 44
Undeserving poor (Katz), 44
Unemployment, 11, 20
Unions, xiii, 5, 113–122, 169, 176, 177, 179
United Federation of Teachers (UFT), 115
United Healthcare, 11
United Nations, 10, 89, 191
United Nations University–World Institute for Development Economics Research of the United Nations University (UNU-WIDER), 10
United States
  drive for political domination, 12–13
  as global superpower, 15
  transition from agricultural to industrial economy, 9, 26
  wealth gap in, 10–12, 20–24
U.S. Constitution, 8

Establishment Clause, 132–133
separation of church and state, 130, 132–133
U.S. Department of Education (DOE), 2, 73–74, 77 n. 4, 85, 87–88, 112, 119, 137–138
U.S. Department of Energy, 17
U.S. Department of Housing and Urban Development (HUD), 36
U.S. House Committee on Armed Services, 17
U.S. Protestant right. *See* Protestant Right
U.S. Steel Corporation, 149
U.S. Supreme Court, 132–133, 153–154, 156
United Teachers of New Orleans (UTNO), 169, 176, 177, 179
United Truth and Change Church (Chicago), 135
Universal Declaration of Human Rights, 191
University of California, 121
University of California Berkeley Haas School of Business, 65
University of Chicago, 37–38, 40, 136–137
University of Houston, 91
University of Illinois-Chicago, 37–38
University Village (Chicago), 37–38
UNU-WIDER (United Nations University–World Institute for Development Economics Research of the United Nations University), 10
Urban Institute, 70
Urbanski, Adam, 115, 116
Urban Superintendents' Academy, 66, 111, 115, 117

Valenzuela, A., xi
Vallas, Paul, 6, 162, 170, 171, 174–177, 180–182
Vander Ark, Tom, 113
Vanderbilt University, 105
Van Roekel, Dennis, 118–120
Varady, D. P., 41, 43, 44
Venkatesh, S. A., 34, 40–41
Venture philanthropy, 4–5, 55–77
  Broad Foundation for Education, 25–26, 55, 57, 58–77, 109–111, 116, 117, 119, 170

Venture philanthropy (*continued*)
  in Chicago, 57
  educational reform agenda of, 69–73
  Gates Foundation, 2, 10, 25–26, 46, 55, 57,
    59, 70–71, 76, 77 n. 2, 109–110, 113,
    117–118, 170
  impact of, 109–110
  leadership agenda in, 60–66
  military leadership in, 61–62
  nature of, 55–57
  neoliberalism of, 58–59, 62–69
  in New Orleans, 70–71
  in New York City, 57
  scholarship agenda in, 69–73
  sharing views about knowledge in, 66–69
  TINA (There Is No Alternative to the
    Market) thesis, 58
  Walton Family Foundation, 10, 26, 55, 57,
    59, 70–71, 76, 109–110, 170
Vergari, S., 127
Virginia, 136
Viteritti, J., 130
Volcker, Paul, 99–101
Vouchers, 84, 88, 130–132

Wacquant, L., 38
Wagner, Jane, 93 n. 1
Waiting for Superman (movie), 105–106, 106
Wallace v. Jaffree, 132–133
Wallis, C., 85
Wall Street Journal, 84, 87, 92
Wal-Mart, 8
Walsh, M., 133
Walton Family Foundation, 10, 26, 55, 57, 59,
  70–71, 76, 109–110, 170
Ward, Randolph, 111
War on Terror, 8, 18
War Resisters League, 16–17
Washington, Booker T., 22
Washington, D.C., 89, 117
Washington, Harold, 49–50, 51 n. 6
Watkins, William H., 1–6, 7–32, 20, 144, 164,
  189–192
Wealth gap, 1
  CEO salaries, 11
  expanding, 19–20
  racial, 10–12, 20–21
  in techno-globalization, 10–12

Weaver, Reg, 118–120
Weber, Rachel, 45
Weingarten, Randi, 115, 117–118
Welch, Jack, 62
Welfare reform, 80
Wells, A. S., 48, 131
White, Miles D., 11
White Evangelical tradition, 128–129,
  134–137
Whites
  chauvinism and racism of, 24
  living in poverty, 11
  wealth gap and, 10–12, 20–21
  White supremacist discourse, 45, 147–148
Whitty, G., 131
Wilcox, C., 125, 128
Wilen, W. P., 34, 40–41
Wiley, D. C., 134
Williams, R., xi
Williams Multiplex (Chicago), 46
Willinsky, John, 75
Wilson, D., 40, 50, 51 n. 5
Wilson, S., 181
Wilson, Thomas J., 11
Wilson, William Julius, 44
Winfield, Ann G., 6, 143–159, 148, 154–155
With the Best of Intentions (Hess), 77 n. 2
Woertz, Patricia A., 11
Wolff, E. N., 11
Wolfowitz, Paul, 14
Woods, G., 143
Working class, xiii, 19, 20, 40, 42
World Bank, 14
World Distribution of Household Wealth, The
  (United Nations), 10
World War I, 150–151, 190
World War II, 16–17, 22, 38, 150–151,
  153–154
Wouters, J., 50
Wright, P. A., 33–34, 39, 43, 44

Xerox Foundation, 26

Youdell, D., xi
Youth Law Center, 94 n. 11

Zimmerman, J., 127
Zinn, H., 149–150